NEW ORLEANS CITY PARK

The helicopter at the far left carried Pres. George W. Bush, surveying the extent of the flooding after Hurricane Katrina. Photographer David Grunfeld took this picture over City Park from an accompanying helicopter. (Photograph by David Grunfeld, courtesy of the New Orleans Times-Picayune)

NEW ORLEANS CITY PARK
From Tragedy to Triumph

BOB BECKER

PELICAN PUBLISHING

NEW ORLEANS

Library of Congress Cataloging-in-Publication Data

Names: Becker, Bob (Robert W.), author.
Title: New Orleans City Park : from tragedy to triumph / Bob Becker.
Description: New Orleans : Pelican Publishing, [2023] | Includes bibliographical references and index. | Summary: "The recently retired CEO of New Orleans City Park shares here all the major events that impacted the park in the last twenty years, from Hurricane Katrina to COVID-19. Located in the center of New Orleans, the park and its post-Katrina recovery were essential to the recovery of the entire city. This striking book with color images recounts the experiences, both funny and heartbreaking, of the board, staff, and visitors to the park at a time of great upheaval. Bob Becker was a highly visible member of the community during his tenure as park CEO, and his behind-the-scenes stories will be of interest to fans of the park as well as professional city planners, park managers, disaster recovery experts, and universities worldwide"— Provided by publisher.
Identifiers: LCCN 2022038976 | ISBN 9781455627417 (hardcover) | ISBN 9781455627424 (ebook)
Subjects: LCSH: Parks—Louisiana—New Orleans. | City Park (New Orleans, La.)—History. | New Orleans (La.)—Social life and customs—21st century.
Classification: LCC F379.N57 C5725 2023 | DDC 363.6/80976335—dc23/eng/20220826
LC record available at https://lccn.loc.gov/2022038976

All images courtesy of New Orleans City Park unless otherwise indicated
Endpaper photograph by Kathleen K. Parker/Shutterstock.com

Printed in China

Published by Pelican Publishing
New Orleans, LA
www.pelicanpub.com

Contents

Introduction

In 2000, local authors Bill and Sally Reeves, under contract with the Friends of City Park, produced a publication on the history of the park. That account is full of details about the founding of the park, its early development, and the changes that took place up until the twenty-first century. It is fact oriented and covers various aspects of the park such as tennis, golf, amusements, buildings, and landscaping. This account is not that.

While a certain amount of historical context is important and is included in this effort, in telling the story of my arrival at the park, the devastation it experienced in Hurricane Katrina, its recovery, and finally the impact of the worldwide pandemic known as COVID-19 on the park, I wanted to write a more personal story and one that allows the reader to see the stories behind the facts. This account certainly contains many details. It is, after all, a record of one of the two great watershed events in the history of the park: the Great Depression and Hurricane Katrina. (It is very possible that COVID-19 will be considered a third!) However, it also shares the experiences, both funny and heartbreaking, of the board, staff, and visitors to City Park at a time of great upheaval.

Many people helped in the preparation of this manuscript—those who shared their memories of the past and those who helped create the foundation for the future. You will meet many of them. While this story only covers a twenty-year period, it honestly seems like a lifetime.

I would like to thank the individuals who took the time to read full drafts of the manuscript and give me their thoughts, including Errol Laborde, Michelle Miller, Lucie Laurian, Jackie Sullivan, and David Gladstone, as well as many who read and commented on specific chapters.

I want to thank the hundreds who have served on the board of City Park and the ten presidents I have served under. Thanks also to the park for permission to use images from its photo collection. Thanks are due as well to of our dedicated staff, who, at times, worked under harsh conditions, when they didn't know from week to week if they had a job but who always believed we had a future.

Most of all I would like to thank my family, wife Pat and our four children, Jennifer, Kelly, Amanda, and Ryan, for being so supportive through the good times, of which there were many, and the bad times, which, when they were bad, were really, really bad!

When I came to New Orleans in 1971, I did not understand the importance of City Park or the connection that virtually every New Orleanian has to it. I am proud to have been a part of its incredible history and that I was able to be of service in its hours of sadness and joy.

NEW ORLEANS CITY PARK

CHAPTER 1

Where Is Louisiana?

When you come to a fork in the road, take it!
—Yogi Berra

My personal journey to City Park began in Buffalo, New York, where I was born and spent my first twenty-one years. My mother was a homemaker and, in her later years, ran a cafeteria at my elementary school. My dad worked at a company called American Optical and polished bombsite lenses during World War II. Neither went to college, but my mother, in particular, always made it clear that I was going to college.

In 1965, I entered the University of Buffalo.[1] I majored in history, and as I neared the end of my undergraduate career, I began to do some research on various occupations. I took the test as a codebreaker for the National Security Agency and quickly discovered that was not my forte. I was in the Air Force ROTC and wanted to be a pilot, but bad eyes ended that dream. I began to look at careers in city planning and city management, since, as a student of history, I had always been interested in urban development.

I applied to various graduate schools, was accepted at a few, and decided to go to the University of Iowa, principally because they offered me a graduate assistantship to help defray the cost of tuition. Going to Iowa seemed a little illogical to my friends, as some of them did not know the state even had any cities. But the program was only five years old when I enrolled in 1969, everyone was full of energy, and the faculty was terrific. So I flew to Iowa City and became a Hawkeye!

The program at Iowa had two distinguishing features that are now important in many graduate planning programs—a required internship and thesis. The head of our program, James Harris, arranged my internship, and I spent the summer of 1970 working with the City of Baltimore Planning Department, in the neighborhood planning division. It was a great experience, as I worked on neighborhood plans and capital budgets and learned how to review preliminary design drawings. I also found my thesis topic, which was on the charrette technique of community planning and engagement. When I went back to Iowa, I was one of the few students who had a topic, and I completed my thesis during the two-year program.

In 1968, at school in Buffalo, I met my wife-to-be, Pat. We married after college, and she moved to Iowa with me.

Near the end of my time at Iowa, I began to look for job opportunities. I sent out over three hundred resumes and letters inquiring about potential openings for a graduating planner. In April of 1971, Pat and I and several classmates traveled to the American Society of Planning Officials conference in New Orleans to interview and explore job opportunities. Frankly, I hardly knew where New Orleans was, let alone Louisiana. All I knew about both was that Mardi Gras was held there, and native son Louis Armstrong had popularized jazz as an American music form. So, even though Pat and I were running out of money, we decided to go to New Orleans in the hopes of both of us finding jobs.

It was fortuitous that when I arrived, the City of New Orleans Planning Commission was looking for entry-level planners. Harold Katner, who was the planning director, had developed a close relationship with the mayor, Moon Landrieu, and with that relationship came new funding, allowing the planning commission to recruit for four new positions. I interviewed with the commission's principal planner, Bobbie Abernathy. Bobbie was a planner's planner. A graduate of MIT, he was knowledgeable in just about every area of planning and had a knack for problem solving.[2]

I thought the interview went well, but receiving no offer, we returned to Iowa. By the end of April, I was getting desperate—school was ending, and I was getting my degree but had no job. The prospect of returning to Buffalo and living with my mother was not inviting. Then, suddenly, a couple of offers came. One was from Minneapolis, Minnesota, and another was from Leavenworth, Kansas. Neither appealed to me much (apologies to both cities). I had grown up in cold and snow, and the prospect of going even farther north to Minneapolis did not excite me. Neither did going to Kansas, particularly to a city known mainly for its federal penitentiary.

Then, as Pat and I were exercising to a Jack LaLanne record, Bobbie Abernathy called and offered me a job! I borrowed some money from my mother, and in June of 1971, we made our way to New Orleans. I told Pat that city planners move frequently, and we would probably only be there a few years. Who knew that we would still be in New Orleans through high points, such as the 1984 World's Fair, and plenty of low points, including a variety of floods, Hurricane Katrina, the BP Oil Spill, and COVID-19?

The City Planning Commission

The addition of four city planners represented the biggest expansion of the Planning Commission's staff in years. We were each assigned to one division: census and land-use analysis, transportation planning, zoning and subdivision work, or the capital budget. Jim Lewin, in the census division, has remained a friend since that time. My assignment to the capital budget division was extremely fortuitous, in that it gave me a crash course in the city's infrastructure and also introduced me to a great variety of public officials. Each year all of the public entities requesting capital funds from the city would submit their requests and then appear before the planning staff to justify them. I learned about the status of roads and bridges and the needs of our prison system, fire stations, and health department.

I also met two important groups of people who would become central to my career in New Orleans. One group represented Audubon Park and Zoo, and they were in the process of passing a dedicated millage to improve the zoo. Ron Forman, who had worked in the city's chief administrative office, became the assistant director of the Audubon Park Commission and later director of the Audubon Zoo and then the Audubon Nature Institute.

The second group represented City Park. Ellis Laborde, the longtime and much beloved general manager of the Park Commission, represented the park along with various members of his board.[3] I also met Beau Bassich, who held the title of executive director on the Board of Commissioners and was always involved in their capital budget requests. Through the years, Ellis often came with board members to the Planning Commission to reinforce their requests. I also learned that City Park was not a city agency. It was a quasi-state agency but had requested and received city capital funds for some time in recognition of its prominent role in providing recreation services to our citizens. Although I became familiar with specific requests, I did not fully appreciate the vastness of the park or how it was managed.

While I was serving as a planner and then chief of the capital budget division, the city was beginning to develop a new plan for the Central Business District (CBD). Harold Katner brought me onto his team for the effort. In this role, I learned about major project development, zoning issues in the business district, and capital projects supporting the new plan. I also met David Wallace and Dick Huffman, of the planning and architectural firm of Wallace, McHarg, Roberts, and Todd from Philadelphia, who were the lead consultants developing the downtown plan entitled the Central Area New Orleans Growth Management Program. The Growth Management Program was essentially a joint venture between the business community, represented by the Chamber of Commerce's Central Area Committee, and the city, represented by the Mayor's Office and the Planning Commission. I served on the Steering Committee for the study. The plan was completed in 1975 and resulted in many innovations in CBD planning, including a new zoning ordinance for the central area, the creation of historic districts in the downtown, and the creation of the Downtown Development District—one of the first Central Business District improvement districts in the nation.

The Planning Commission's assistant director was Bill Rapp, who had worked his way up from chief planner to second-in-command. Bill directly supervised me in the capital budget division and, as such, came to know many of the City Park board members. When Ellis Laborde retired in 1978, the board offered Bill the job of general manager. He left the Planning Commission, and I was appointed assistant director. When Harold Katner departed to become the director of the Sewerage and Water Board in 1982, I became the sixth planning director since the position was created in 1948.

I was involved in many projects and plans during my tenure, but certainly a highlight was the 1984 World's Fair. I was involved in all aspects of planning and permitting of the fair, and I met many individuals who later became central to my work at City Park, especially the architect Allen Eskew and landscape architect Carlos Cashio. While the fair proved to be a financial failure, the land in and around the fairgrounds was completely transformed, from mostly industrial and warehouse use to housing and entertainment, which the Growth Management Program had called for in 1975. It took an enormous event such as the World's Fair to speed up the land-use transition. I continued to supervise the preparation of the capital budget and became heavily involved in the location

of the Aquarium of the Americas at the foot of Canal Street. Ron Forman, who had led the renaissance of the zoo, was the chief proponent of the aquarium, and I got to know him well through the years of planning and eventually building the aquarium.

By 1987, circumstances at City Hall caused me to reevaluate my career. In the early 1980s, and particularly up through the opening of the fair, the city's finances were generally in good shape, which allowed me to greatly expand the planning staff and recruit very bright and energetic planners. But by the late 1980s, that situation had changed, and a dramatic tightening of the budget forced me to lay off much of the talent I had employed. In addition, pay raises for city workers ground to a halt. By this time, I had a growing family to consider, and my future prospects looked grim.

In 1988, Ron Forman approached me about joining his team at the Audubon Institute. He had tremendous plans to expand their offering of museums dedicated to wildlife and the natural world, and he wanted me to be a part of them. It was very exciting, and on January 1, 1989, I joined the Audubon team.

The Audubon Nature Institute

My position at Audubon began as a senior vice president for planning and park operations. The 400-acre Audubon Park, situated in the university area of the city, contained a golf course, some playing fields, a small tennis facility, a small equestrian facility, a long walking path, and a major zoo. (Interestingly, Audubon Park was the site of the first world's fair held in New Orleans, the 1884 Cotton Centennial Exposition.) The zoo, which had been described in the early 1970s as one of the worst in America, had been transformed into a modern zoological garden exhibiting more than sixteen hundred animals on approximately 50 acres in the park.

I knew little about the functions of a modern zoo but soon became involved in everything from building an animal healthcare facility to working with zoo designers and engineers. A modern zoo not only contains exhibits that, to the extent possible in a confined space, duplicate a particular animal's natural environment but also a commissary, animal hospital, offices for the animal staff, as well as animal holding facilities. I like to call this the religious part of a zoo, because the animal staff are passionate about the care and enrichment of the animals. They care deeply about their charges and work hard to ensure the animals are not only physically and mentally healthy but also can promote the educational mission of the zoo by teaching the public about the animals and their disappearing natural environment. It was always inspirational working with these dedicated people.

A modern zoo also has what I call a secular part: food and beverage, admissions, ticketing, first-responder responsibilities, grounds and facility maintenance, promotion and advertising, information systems, donor culti-

vation and fundraising, special events, and a host of other specific tasks and professions that provide the platform upon which the stars of the show, the animals, can thrive. It was all new to me, and while I enjoyed working with the entire Audubon team, I particularly enjoyed working with the curators and other animal staff.

Out of the approximately sixteen hundred animals that Audubon holds, I would estimate that around one hundred would be considered dangerous to the public should they find a way to escape. A general curator told me once that while these animals are usually the ones most fascinating to the public, they are also the ones that require constant vigilance because "they spend twenty-four hours a day trying to find a way out of their enclosures." Thus, zoo designers continually try to balance a design that allows the public the maximum view of the animal with being sure the exhibit is safe and secure. During my time at the zoo, a tiger got out of its main holding cell into the corridor, which is used by the keeper staff. A warthog broke out of its back-of-the-house containment, and an orangutan grabbed the hair of a keeper. More recently, two jaguars escaped and killed a variety of hoof stock before the zoo opened to the public that day. The staff trains constantly on safety procedures, and I joined the shooting team, which is the last resort should a large animal escape. It was and is a fascinating place, and I learned a lot not only about animals but also the secular part of the operation. It stood me in good stead when I got to City Park.

The planning part of my job revolved around developing new or renovated zoo exhibits with the zoo designer and the rest of the Audubon team. We also planned for a major new Institute initiative, which was the development of a Species Survival Center and Research Laboratory. While the zoo was involved in breeding programs with other zoos around the world, Forman felt they needed an offsite facility with substantial acreage to participate in other animal breeding programs. He had convinced the president of the Freeport-McMoRan Corporation to donate a substantial sum to get the project started. I helped negotiate a lease with the U.S. Coast Guard for nearly one thousand acres of their land in the lower coast of Algiers, on the Westbank of the Mississippi River in New Orleans, to house the survival center. Carlos Cashio was the lead designer on the project, and I worked with him, the zoo's animal staff, and senior Audubon staff to develop the plan and build the first phase. I also was significantly involved in the construction of a research laboratory on the site, which was devoted to finding ways to improve breeding. It was very interesting work.

However, my main job was managing the operation of Audubon Park. This was my first experience in park management, and in my twelve years at Audubon, I learned a great deal. Once again, I was exposed to a wide variety of operational issues, including responding to park users and solving problems inherent in a large park. The following are examples of some of the situations we dealt with.

- Some park users did not like the way we striped the walking path to separate the walkers from the bicyclists and skateboarders. Even though we engaged an expert in the allocation of space on walking paths, someone always thought we gave more space to bicycles or vice versa.
- I helped emergency responders pull a man out of one of our lagoons who had died after a late-night swim.
- One day, a distraught woman came to see me in my office concerning the disappearance of her German shepherd dog. She told me she was walking her dog in the park (off-leash, of course) during a heavy rain, and the dog had been washed down an open culvert. She demanded that we pay for her lost dog and claimed severe mental anguish. I paid for the dog. About a month later, the same woman came to my office and showed me a picture of what appeared to be a German shepherd, very badly beaten up and malnourished. She told me it was the same dog that had been sucked down the drain and somehow survived. After a long month, the dog had made its way back to the woman's house! She demanded that we pay for psychological counseling for both her and her dog. I settled with the dog owner.
- I placed wooden bollards along the park roadways to prevent cars from

being driven into the grass and onto the roots of our oak trees. I became famous for those bollards, which I also brought to City Park.

- One year, we decided to do a special exhibit at the zoo to increase attendance. Dinamation was a company that made and leased out robotic dinosaurs. With the Institute's designer, I built "sets" for the dinosaurs. We operated the special exhibit for six months and generated considerable income for Audubon.

- In order to better prepare myself for zoo management, I attended "zoo school" in Ogilvie Park, West Virginia. Zoo school holds a variety of training sessions, and I attended the one on zoo biology for non-biologists to learn more about the animals we hosted and their care and treatment. I attended the school in the winter, and one day after classes, I decided to walk down to a lake at the foot of a large hill where the conference center was located. I was in a business suit with dress shoes, and the weather was chilly, but I thought I would walk down to the lake and then back up to the conference center and the hotel. I walked down, and it was idyllic. It began to snow, and there were deer at the bottom of the hill. As I lost track of time, I began to realize I was getting colder.

The snow had turned into a blizzard, completely obscuring the top of the hill and covering the already frozen ground. I tried to walk back up the hill but could not find the path under the snow. I attempted to make my own path up the hill, but in my dress shoes I kept sliding back to the base. After several tries, I thought I might freeze to death at the bottom of the hill during zoo school. Finally, I took off my shoes and crawled back up the hill on my hands and knees. When I got to the top, the knees of my pants were torn, and I looked like a homeless person who had been given an old suit. Needless to say, I was the talk of the school and probably did not present the best image of Audubon!

- I parked cars for the zoo's many special events and helped volunteers and other staff set up for its largest fundraiser, the Zoo-to-Do.

- The Audubon golf course is in the front of the park between St. Charles Avenue and Magazine Street. It is a historic course, and when I arrived at Audubon, it was a par 68, standard for the time. However, with the development of golf technology, and the continued improvement of the players, the course became too cramped for the park. Golfers continually hit shots onto and over the walking path, endangering other park users. The course also had deteriorated, so we decided on a complete renovation that would shorten the course, increase play, and provide a safer experience for everyone. I interviewed various golf-course designers and recommended Denis Griffiths for the job. Forman found the funds, and we began construction. Some golfers adamantly objected to shortening the course to a par 62 with many more par 3s, calling it a "Mickey Mouse" executive course that would never get any play from "real" golfers. Also, a small group of neighbors thought the course should not be renovated but removed and, unfortunately, proceeded to picket. When we set up barricades to separate the protestors from the contractor, they attempted to scale the barricades, whereupon my park police and I had to push them back over! This experience prepared me for a much more dramatic golf conflict at City Park.

- A cult once contacted me, desiring to set up a fire circle in the front of the park during Halloween so they could practice their "religion." At the risk of denying someone their religious rights, I told them they could not set the park on fire.
- The park had a historic swimming pool, which operated until desegrega-

tion and had so deteriorated that it had become a hazard, and an anomaly because of its size. To secure city permission to cave the sides of the pool in and cover it with dirt, we had to save an end wall of the pool in recognition of its history. That wall, without anything around it, stands today.

All in all, I had a wonderful experience operating the zoo and park. I learned a significant amount about a type of work that the typical city planner never experiences.[4] I was promoted to managing director of Audubon Zoo after several years.

Joining City Park

In early spring of 2001, Ron Forman came into my office and said he had been contacted by Dr. Everett Williams, the former New Orleans schools superintendent and now a member of the board of the City Park Improvement Association. He inquired whether Ron had anyone on his staff who might be interested in the general manager position at City Park. Ron asked me, and knowing a little bit about City Park from my time at the Planning Commission, I said I would be pleased to learn more about the opening.

Soon after that, Roy Perrin contacted me. I came to find out he had been brought in as the interim general manager, after the board determined that their current general manager was not doing the job and relieved him of his duties. Perrin indicated that he and Minette Bruce, a CPA and the interim chief financial officer, were tasked with looking into the fiscal situation at the park and wanted to brief me about it.

We met at a local coffeehouse, and they gave me a rundown of the situation they had inherited. It was not good. They said the park lacked leadership, and in fact, due to the organizational structure in place, there was confusion among the staff as to who was in charge.[5] The staff was demoralized from years of no pay increases and lack of resources to do their jobs. Perrin and Bruce went over the latest financial information about the park with me. Although I had a limited understanding of the situation, after the briefing I did see that they lacked money and were overly dependent on a few park "businesses" for most of their operating revenue. Still, I was interested in the position and arranged to meet with the park's search committee in June.

The committee was composed of board members Cheryl Cabes, Ed Harold, Jim Hunter, Mike Moffitt, Everett Williams, Bob Brown, Rick Butler, Arlene Nesser, Suzanne Mestayer, and Ed Mathes. During a wide-ranging interview, they confirmed what Perrin and Bruce had told me about the park's condition and the confusion arising from the organizational structure. The committee and I agreed that if I was to join the park, there could only be one leader, and I would be the "face" of the park. I had looked at the organizational chart I was provided and prepared a new one. I also indicated that instead of being named general manager, I would want the title of chief executive officer, and my senior leadership team would also have title changes. While I did not have a thorough understanding of the financial condition, it was clear to me that more aggressive fundraising and business practices had to be brought to bear to improve the park's standing. I also conveyed my surprise that the budget contained no public operating funds and that that would have to be addressed. (Typically, public parks are predominantly funded from public tax sources, with self-generated revenue making up only a small proportion of the total finances. Learning that City Park had no public operating funding was, therefore, completely surprising.)

After the meeting, I received an offer. At a special meeting of the Board of Commissioners on July 12, 2001, I was appointed to the position of chief executive officer. The board hosted a small cocktail party afterward so I could meet all the members, and I formally joined City Park on July 31, 2001.

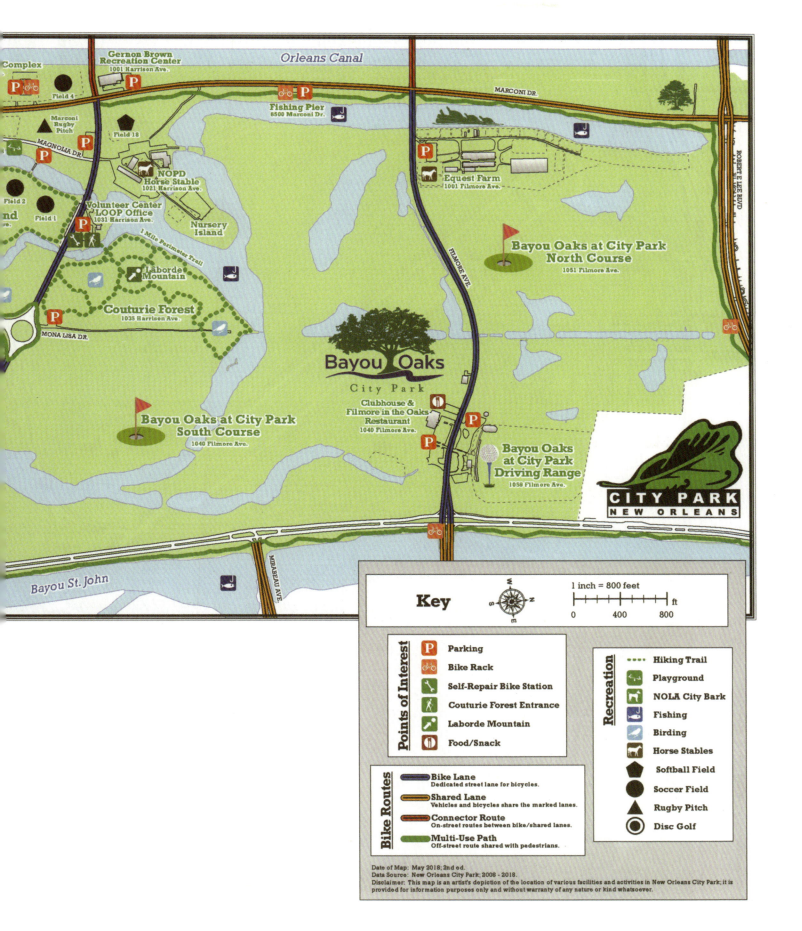

Complex

Gernon Brown
Recreation Center
1001 Harrison Ave.

Orleans Canal

MARCONI DR.

Field 4

Fishing Pier
6500 Marconi Dr.

Marconi
Rugby
Pitch

Field 18

MAGNOLIA DR.

Equest Farm
1001 Filmore Ave.

NOPD
Horse Stable
1021 Harrison Ave.

Field 2

Volunteer Center
LOOP Office
1031 Harrison Ave.

Field 1

Nursery
Island

1 Mile Perimeter Trail

Laborde
Mountain

Bayou Oaks at City Park
North Course
1051 Filmore Ave.

ROBERT E LEE BLVD

Couturie Forest
1035 Harrison Ave.

FILMORE AVE.

MONA LISA DR.

Bayou Oaks

City Park

Bayou Oaks at City Park
South Course
1040 Filmore Ave.

Clubhouse &
Filmore in the Oaks
Restaurant
1040 Filmore Ave.

Bayou Oaks
at City Park
Driving Range
1059 Filmore Ave.

CITY PARK
NEW ORLEANS

MIRABEAU AVE.

Bayou St. John

Key

1 inch = 800 feet

0	400	800	ft

Points of Interest

- 🅿 **Parking**
- 🚲 **Bike Rack**
- **Self-Repair Bike Station**
- **Couturie Forest Entrance**
- **Laborde Mountain**
- **Food/Snack**

Recreation

- ┈┈ **Hiking Trail**
- **Playground**
- **NOLA City Bark**
- **Fishing**
- **Birding**
- **Horse Stables**
- **Softball Field**
- **Soccer Field**
- **Rugby Pitch**
- **Disc Golf**

Bike Routes

- **Bike Lane**
  Dedicated street lane for bicycles.
- **Shared Lane**
  Vehicles and bicycles share the marked lanes.
- **Connector Route**
  On-street routes between bike/shared lanes.
- **Multi-Use Path**
  Off-street route shared with pedestrians.

Date of Map: May 2018; 2nd ed.
Data Source: New Orleans City Park; 2008 - 2018.
Disclaimer: This map is an artist's depiction of the location of various facilities and activities in New Orleans City Park; it is
provided for information purposes only and without warranty of any nature or kind whatsoever.

CHAPTER 2

The Cliffs Notes History of City Park[1]

Acquiring the Park

The first land that eventually became City Park was owned by colonist François Hery soon after Bienville founded the city in 1718. Hery was a contractor and planter who probably planted indigo as a crop and raised cattle on the property. He surrendered the property to Jacques Lorreins, who died in the 1780s, passing the land to his daughter and eventually to her husband, Jean Louis Allard. The park property eventually took his name, with early maps referring to the land as the Allard Plantation. While it was used primarily as a dairy farm, the plantation also raised corn and sugarcane.

Louis Allard inherited the land along with his two siblings and promptly mortgaged the property in 1829 to the Consolidated Association of the Planters of Louisiana. However, Allard fell on hard times, subsequently defaulting on the loan and eventually losing the land in a sheriff's sale in 1845. At the time, the plantation included nineteen enslaved people,

10 horses and mules, and 140 head of cattle. John McDonogh acquired the property that year. Allard was allowed to live on the land, but he died shortly thereafter.

McDonogh died in 1850. His will bequeathed in equal, undivided shares the land to the cities of Baltimore and New Orleans. Soon, the New Orleans newspaper, the *Daily Picayune*, and others began to advocate that the property be used for a public park. By 1852, the New Orleans Common Council, responding to growing demands, declared its intention to lay out a park on the Allard Plantation tract. This idea ran into an immediate problem. McDonogh's estate was still open, and the City of Baltimore had a half-interest in the property. The City of New Orleans filed suit to expropriate the land from the McDonogh estate. The Fourth District Court appointed three independent commissioners to appraise the property and resolve the question of outstanding taxes that had accrued. Finally, in 1854, the Fourth District Court approved the expropriation and declared the land a public park. It was not until April 4, 1859, that New Orleans and Baltimore finally reached an amicable settlement, and New Orleans obtained clear title to the property. While the City of New Orleans sold much of McDonogh's estate in 1859, it kept the 213 acres of land declared to be a public park.

This tract stretched from Metairie Road (now City Park Avenue) north toward what is now Friedrichs Avenue, west to what is now Marconi Drive, and east to a point just before the New Orleans Museum of Art.[2] Over the next eighty-plus years, at least seventeen separate property acquisitions, the last occurring in 1943, assembled the park's current 1,300 acres.

Early Park History and the Creation of the City Park Improvement Association

Once the park finally had a legal definition, visitors began coming to look for some respite from the oppressive heat of the city. Around 1859, a fence was built along Metairie Road (renamed City Park Avenue in 1902) and a few benches were installed, along with a small cottage for someone to work the grounds. The Civil War stymied further development, although the New Orleans City Railroad opened a line from the foot of Esplanade Avenue all the way to Bayou St. John. In 1867, a park-keeper was hired to cut grass, although he apparently supplemented his

income by illegally selling hay and chopping down trees to sell the wood.

By the early 1870s, even the minimal improvements deteriorated, and locals began to pasture cattle in the park. In 1872, the *Daily Picayune* reported:

> Nothing more was heard of the park. People forgot where it was. Once in a while a stealthy suicide crept out to its coverts and nourished the roots of its great oaks with his blood. Then the weeds grew higher. . . . Apart from the world, like a pariah in the very haunts of men, the City Park stood abandoned, desolate and mysterious.[3]

In one of the major scandals of Reconstruction, the Louisiana Legislature passed laws allowing the state to seize control of New Orleans' parks. (Prior to the creation of the city's Home Rule Charter in 1954, the state legislature had to grant the city specific authority to undertake most activities. When the legislature was unhappy with the city, it passed laws revoking certain powers.) The legislature established a commission that was granted exclusive management of the parks, stripping the City Council of its authority. While the Park Commission survived until the end of Reconstruction, its record of achievement was dismal. It spent all the tax that had been passed to fund the commission's expenses and mortgaged the property to pay for improvements that never materialized. In 1877, the state abolished the commission for squandering city funds.

In one of its few efforts to improve City

Park, in 1872 the Park Commission hired the New York City landscape architectural and engineering firm of Bogart and Cutler to develop the park's first master plan. At the time, the firm was highly thought of, having supervised the construction of Central Park using the plan developed by Frederick Law Olmsted. A local civil engineer, George H. Grandjean, was selected to implement the plan, but because of budget constraints, it was never finalized.

For most of the 1880s, City Park was in a period of almost total neglect, and no city or state law identified the park or created a management structure to develop it. In contrast, Audubon Park was the center of attention, particularly after it hosted the World's Industrial and Cotton Centennial Exposition from 1884 to 1885.

As the park's collapse entered its darkest hours, interest from residents in the nearby Esplanade and Bayou St. John neighborhoods and local businessmen began to emerge. Chief among these was Victor J. Anseman, a florist who had lived on Metairie Road as a child. Anseman began to advocate for action and attention to the almost forgotten City Park, and he assembled a group of civic leaders in June of 1891 to discuss the possibility of creating an organization that could take develop and manage it. Felix Dreyfous, a notary and the most influential of the civic leaders, drafted the Articles of Incorporation, and on August 13 of 1891, the City Park Improvement Association (CPIA)), a private, nonprofit organization, came into being.

The City Council, grateful to have an organization interested in the park, passed Ordinance 5547 on August 29, 1891,[4] giving the CPIA control over it: "The said association shall have the full and exclusive power to govern, manage, and direct the said park and ordinances for the government thereof, not inconsistent with the law of the city ordinances, to elect or appoint such officers and committees as they may deem proper, to prescribe and define their respective duties and authority, to fix the amount of compensation of their employees, provided that neither the city nor said park be liable therefor, and generally to do all things in regard to said park tending to the ornamentation and beautifying of the same for the health, pleasure, instruction and enjoyment of the people."[5, 6]

Victor Anseman, the florist who initiated interest in the park, became the first "keeper" appointed by the CPIA.

In 1896, the Louisiana Legislature followed suit and placed New Orleans City Park under the control and management of the CPIA through Act 130. This act also placed Audubon Park under the care of the Audubon Park Association. The act further defined the role of City Park: "City Park shall be used only for park purposes and for educational or cultural uses. For purposes of this Section, park purposes shall include rest, recreation, exercise, pleasure, amusement, and enjoyment for the public, and ornament of the City."[7]

The actions of the New Orleans City Council and Louisiana Legislature specified the four basic missions of the park—ornamentation or beautification, recreation, education, and cultural enrichment.

It should also be pointed out that Section 4 of the 1896 law contained a mandate from the State of Louisiana: "Be it further enacted, etc., That for purposes of the preservation, improvement, and beautifying of the said parks, and providing for the expenses incidental thereto, there shall in each year, be set aside by the Common Council of New Orleans, as a first item in its Budget, out of the Reserve Fund, a sum of at least thirty thousand dollars, one-half of which to go to the New Orleans City Park Improvement Association, and the other half to the Audubon Park Association, and shall be payable to said Associations, in the same proportions, whenever available, upon the receipt of the respective President and Treasurer of said Associations."

This requirement that the city support City Park annually out of its operating funds has almost never been met.

Early Developments

After the CPIA took control, it initiated a series of actions, including installing a fence along City Park Avenue, placing more benches, filling low areas, planting a variety of fruit trees, and holding a number of entertainment celebrations as fundraisers. Board member George H. Grandjean drew up plans for projects including excavating and enlarging Bayou Metairie and adding various islands, inlets, and peninsulas. The board also hired the surveying firm of Daney and Waddill in 1898 to draw up the first park master plan. It called for a large lake in the shape of Lake Pontchartrain to be located near what is now the New Orleans Museum of Art and a smaller lake in the shape of Lake Maurepas behind the museum. The two lakes, filled with water from Bayou St. John, added more water features to those designed by Grandjean and still define the front of the park today.[8]

The board also began efforts to acquire land to expand the park. In 1896, it purchased several tracts that gave the park water frontage along Bayou St. John and extended its boundaries to Esplanade Avenue. These acquisitions provided the land that later became Lelong Drive, now one of the main entrances to the park. The board continued to acquire land throughout the first half of the twentieth century, with the smallest tract of less than 1 acre purchased in 1900, the last acquisition in 1943 (the McFadden property), and the largest in 1926 when the park acquired 900 acres of property from the New Orleans Land Company, extending its boundaries to what is now Allen Toussaint Boulevard.[9]

In the coming years, the Board of Commissioners of the City Park Improvement Association made a series of other improvements, including paving some roadways; constructing one of the nation's first golf courses, the South Course in 1902; installing a racetrack and grandstand where Tad Gormley Stadium sits today; and dedicating the Peristyle in 1907, an elegantly designed open-air venue for dances and entertainment events. Some of the other enhancements that rapidly followed included:

- Construction of the Owen Memorial Fountain and Pizzati Gate in 1910
- Construction of the Isaac Delgado Museum of Art in 1911 (renamed the New Orleans Museum of Art in 1971)
- Construction of the "Casino Building" in 1912 (now also home to a location of Café Du Monde)
- Completion of the Monteleone Gate at the front of the park in 1914
- Construction of Popp Bandstand in 1917
- Expansion of the tennis courts in 1922
- Construction of the Irby swimming pool and bathhouse in 1924
- Expansion of the South Golf Course to nine holes in 1921 and construction of a clubhouse and caddie quarters in 1926

In addition to the physical improvements undertaken in this period of rapid growth, tree and landscape plantings had been under way since the early 1870s. That planting consistently followed a "gardenesque" landscape-design philosophy. A 2007 report by the state said, "Gardenesque landscape design was promoted by John Claudius Loudon, a horticulturist who rejected the prevailing idea that landscaping had to take either a formal, geometric form or assume a rambling, picturesque aspect. Instead, he argued for a blending of the two in what he termed Gardenesque. The curvilinear roads and lagoons in City Park are done in the Picturesque style, while the Rose Garden and linear plantings of non-native trees reflect the formal aspects of traditional gardens. The older portion of the park, especially south of Interstate 610, retains much of the original Gardenesque design advocated in early master plans."[10]

By the end of the 1920s, the board decided that with the park's growth, a long-range update to the Daney and Waddill master plan was necessary. Potential consultants were narrowed down to the Olmsted Brothers of Brookline, Massachusetts and the firm of Bennett, Parsons and Frost from Chicago. In 1929, the Bennett firm was selected to produce the plan.

The Bennett, Parsons and Frost Plan and the WPA

The Bennett plan had many key principles.

1. Extend the existing irregular flow of

walks, roads, and lagoons, honoring the board's desire to utilize the natural land contours rather than forcing a classical rigidity and regularity.

2. Add two new golf courses to contribute operating revenue to the park.

3. Keep the golf course expansion and construction on the eastern or Bayou St. John side of the park.

4. Keep pedestrian activities near the front of the park, with a proposed City Park Stadium farther back and on the Marconi side.

5. Continue the mall effect created by the construction of Lelong Drive on the other side of the museum, to connect to Marconi. This City Park Mall was later renamed Roosevelt Mall.

6. Create new lagoons with several islands, today called Scout, Goat, and Nursery islands.

The new plan was approved, although the park did not have any funds to implement the ambitious agenda. (Some proposed elements, such as an open-air theatre and a yacht harbor fronting on Bayou St. John, had no chance of being built.)

However, fate intervened in the form of the Great Depression. Often called the first great watershed event in the park's history, the Great Depression, while bringing an unprecedented level of poverty to the country, had an unforeseen benefit of giving rise to the national relief programs of the 1930s. These programs, aimed at putting vast numbers of people back to work, had a profound impact on City Park.

Funds came from a variety of relief agencies, including:

- The Federal Reconstruction Finance Corporation
- The Public Works Administration
- The Works Progress Administration (WPA)
- The Civil Works Administration
- The Federal Emergency Relief Administration

The most important of these agencies to the future of City Park was the WPA, which Franklin Roosevelt created by executive order in 1935.

Beginning in 1931 and continuing through 1939, these entities funneled millions of dollars and thousands of workers into the park. (Some estimates put the federal assistance at over twelve million in 1930 dollars and over twenty thousand laborers.) The park received this huge infusion of capital and labor because first, it had a specific master plan, which was a requirement of the relief agencies; and second, the relief agencies favored landscape projects since they employed many workers.

The list of improvements is enormous, and they jump-started the development of the park and the utilization of land that had been acquired but not improved, in a way the park itself could never have afforded.

Improvements included the installation of gas, water, drainage, and sewer lines in the center of the park; eight new bridges and three refurbished bridges; the construction of Roosevelt Mall; and the paving of large portions of Marconi Drive and major avenues within the park. WPA workers built a golf club and caddie house, as well as a complex of storage buildings, shops, hothouses, and shelter houses. Art Deco-style concrete benches were installed throughout the park, and numerous concrete sidewalks were laid. One of the largest projects of the WPA was the construction of City Park Stadium (now called Tad Gormley Stadium). The 26,000-seat venue, completed in 1937, hosted high-school football games. In addition, extensive landscape projects were carried out, including planting thousands of trees and creating the Rose Garden, the forerunner to today's Botanical Garden. The WPA arts program also employed Mexican artist Enrique Alférez to create sculptures throughout the park, including decorative gates and bas-relief work on numerous bridges depicting the nobility of man working with his hands.

When the master plan of Bennett, Parsons and Frost was created, the park did not know how it was going to raise the funds to carry out its ambitious program. Yet in less than a decade, the plan was largely implemented. The very fact that the Board of Commissioners had a plan in place when the disaster of the Great Depression hit made the federal funding possible. Seventy-five years later, the foresight of the board and staff was rewarded once more when Hurricane Katrina struck!

1940s Through 2000

The years following the tremendous development by the workers of the WPA and other agencies included a variety of other improvements and notable events. More tennis courts were added, and Storyland (a children's playground themed around popular nursery rhymes) opened in 1956.

City Park, like so many facilities in the South, served only White citizens until the efforts of the National Association for the Advancement of Colored People (NAACP) and other groups finally led the Supreme Court to strike down the "separate but equal" doctrine in 1954. While the Board of Commissioners was slow to implement the court's ruling, in 1958, the park's general superintendent was instructed to integrate all facilities, ending the shameful practice of segregation.

Tad Gormley Stadium held many war-bond drives during the Second World War, as well as a Beatles concert in 1964 and the US Olympic Track and Field Trials in 1992. The Rose Garden was enclosed with a fence, a garden director was hired, and work began to make the Rose Garden into a full-fledged Botanical Garden, including the Pavilion of the Two Sisters, which opened in 1994. The park's annual Celebration in the Oaks began in 1987 and evolved into the premier holiday event in the region.

In 1943, the city acquired the only remaining "out" parcel in the park from William McFadden, a Texas oilman. The four-acre property contained his mansion, three other houses, and a greenhouse. Over the years, the property has been leased to the US Department of Agriculture, to Samuel Barthe for a private school, and eventually to Christian Brothers for the same use.

The Friends of City Park was organized in 1979 as the park's principal support group and has raised millions of dollars for capital improvements.

Although the federal government, in 1969, effectively ended the practice of constructing interstates through major public facilities such as parks, planning for a highway spur through City Park was far enough along that in 1971, despite much opposition, construction began on one of the last interstate highways (I-610) through the center of the park parallel to the railroad tracks. Although the park was paid for the right of way and used the money to further improve the golf courses, the interstate created another barrier separating the north part of the park from the southern portion. Together with the railroad tracks, the interstate presents a serious physical and psychological obstacle to a unified park. Besides drastically limiting the ability of park users to move north and south, the noise from the highway has a major negative impact. Highway departments have installed sound barriers along sections of interstates, but mitigating the noise impacts of highways in public parks is not a high priority for state or federal highway funding.

The EDAW Plan

Despite the numerous improvements, the underlying problem of revenue generation had never been comprehensively addressed. In 1980, the board engaged Revenue Consultants, Incorporated of Fort Lauderdale, Florida to examine this issue. In May of that year, they released their report, "Evaluation of Revenue Producing Facilities in New Orleans City Park." They examined all of the park's revenue-generating operations, including the facilities the park operated (golf courses, tennis courts, shelter rentals, ballfield rentals, and stadium rentals) and those operated under some sort of concession contract (food and beverage, bicycle rentals, tennis pro shop, boat rentals, fishing, and amusement rides). They made a variety of recommendations to improve the park's image and, therefore, the likelihood of people coming to the park and engaging in paid activities. They also advised that the park consider additional revenue-development facilities. Specifically, they recommended:

- Miniature Golf
- Aquatic Center
- Recreational Vehicle Park
- Electronic Game Room

- Baseball Batting Machine
- Souvenir Stands
- Petting Zoo
- Garden Center
- Stadium Use
- Overnight Accommodations
- Ski Nautique
- Baseball Field Quadruplex
- Bumper Boats
- Radio-Controlled Boats

Through the years, the park did implement several of these recommendations, including the baseball quadruplex and batting cage in the late 1980s and miniature golf after Hurricane Katrina. Other uses have been explored in some manner, specifically the Aquatic Center. While the Electronic Game Room in the 1980s referred to games such as foosball and pinball, today, game rooms featuring modern video and digital games have been investigated by a number of parks.

These revenue-producing ideas led directly to the park's hiring in 1981 of the design and architectural firm EDAW Inc. to create a new master plan. Their original recommendations contained three alternatives, each with a different impact on potential revenue.

Alternative A included building a water park, a theme park, a family recreation center, and a recreational vehicle camping facility. Other recommendations included a private picnic area, removal of the South Golf Course, improvements to the Rose Garden, an outdoor performing arts center, and additional parking.

Alternative B contained fewer major active recreation revenue generators but still included a water park, an amusement/family recreation park, a recreational vehicle camping facility, and the closure of the South Golf Course. It also included an expansion of the New Orleans Museum of Art.

Alternative C was very similar to B, with a different physical arrangement.

Of major interest was a recommendation contained in Alternative B:

> Of additional note, is the inclusion of some 14 acres of land along Robert E. Lee Boulevard that is proposed as a parcel to be leased to a private developer for residential development. The most compatible land use probable for a land lease option would be residential of a single family or townhouse density. Too narrow for active recreation uses, the parcel is currently underused and its development for residential land use would have minimal negative impact on the surrounding park land and on adjacent neighborhoods. This study does not presume to be a marketing analysis for any land use other than recreational, thus further study would be necessary to identify the costs and benefits of such a land use proposal.[11]

The consultants estimated the residential development would yield $900,000 per year in rent at ten units per acre.

This recommendation set off a firestorm of opposition among the park's neighbors and some elected officials.[12] The idea of leasing out park land (which some equated to, in effect, selling the land, if the leases were to run ninety-nine years) was horrifying to green-space advocates and the communities surrounding the park. It indicated, however, how desperate the board was to generate enough revenue to keep the park from deteriorating. Again, the fact that the park was not supported by any dedicated public tax source caused consideration of this extreme alternative.

The commissioners sent the consultants back to the drawing board to develop new recommendations that did not rely so heavily on possible new revenue-generating uses, even though the board recognized that the park faced "very serious financial problems." In February of 1983, a revised proposal by EDAW was widely distributed, then incorporated into a final approved master plan and adopted on March 27, 1984. The major physical recommendations of that plan were:

1. Convert part of the South Golf Course to public green space (the area directly around Big Lake).

2. Convert the eighteen-hole South Golf Course into a nine-hole course (the area behind Christian Brothers School).

3. Close the park's administrative offices over the Casino Building and build a visitor center and restaurant in the Casino.

4. Expand the Botanical Garden and restore Storyland.

5. Convert the area between Palm Drive and Roosevelt Mall into a jogging course with exercise stations and water fountains.

6. Locate the Louisiana Children's Museum on a site at the end of Roosevelt Mall.

7. Build a baseball quadruplex north of I-610 by closing two holes of the East Golf Course.

8. Build a new soccer field in the area across from what is now the NOLA City Bark dog park.

9. Improve the West Golf Course into a PGA-caliber course.

Because the new plan eliminated many of the revenue-generating ideas of the original draft, the board also proposed a city property tax of two mills to support the park. To properly operate and maintain the park's grounds and buildings, the lack of public tax support would have to change.

Board president Robert A. Peyroux said that failure to pass the tax would have serious consequences: "If the voters say no, and the [state and local] governments say no, the park will slowly deteriorate. We could close part of it and maintain the part we leave open, or we could let it all go downhill."[13]

The park's general manager, city planner Bill Rapp, said the two-mill tax would give the park only about half the money it needs to operate and invest in capital facilities. "We're at a point where we do not maintain in a first-class condition all of the things we offer to the public. Unless we get additional funds to maintain all the nice things we have, the landscaping, picnic shelters, we're going to have to start making some choices."

In May of 1983, the park engaged the Joe E. Walker Research firm to estimate the number of annual visits to the park and to gauge the public's receptiveness to a property-tax increase to support the park. Walker concluded that the park receives nine and a half million visits annually and that, under the right circumstances, a one-mill property tax dedicated to the park would have at least an even chance of passing.

Major components of the plan were eventually implemented, including closing the entire South Golf Course and building the baseball quadruplex and children's museum. But the property tax was never put before the voters. It appears that the park could not generate the political support from the city to place a tax measure on the ballot.

Revenue Master Plan and Management Study[14]

In 1990, the board again sought recommendations to address its dismal financial situation. They engaged the American Institute for Leisure Resources in Wheeling, West Virginia to study the park's revenue and management structure and propose improvements. They came to some important conclusions.

1. The park had to find alternate sources of revenue.
2. A director of development must be hired and a Development Division established to pursue grants and other private and governmental support.
3. An expanded and aggressive marketing

program had to be established for increased promotion and publicity.
4. The park should create a trust instrument (now the endowment fund) to attract a variety of contributions from the private sector.

On the management front, the report suggested that the board craft a more efficient governing structure by establishing a smaller Executive Council to set policy, and commissioners not serving on that council should have assigned committee responsibilities reporting to the council. It also suggested that a general manager be employed to operate under policies established by the governing authority. (The park had a general manager, but apparently that position did not have the customary authority, and/or it reflected the confusion of having both an executive director and a general manager.)

Unfortunately, funds did not permit the hiring of a full-time professional development director, so Beau Bassich, the board's executive director, assumed that responsibility but without any staff support. While the board had a committee structure historically, these recommendations caused a more formal structure to be put in place.

Once again, the park's inadequate funding platform was recognized and the need for alternate revenue sources emphasized. The chicken-and-egg dilemma continued, with the board knowing the steps necessary to generate additional funds, such as securing public backing and expanding its public and private development efforts, but the funds not being available to take those steps.

That was the situation when I joined the park on July 31, 2001. Six weeks later, on September 11, the United States was attacked. My staff and I watched it unfold on the television in the boardroom—uncertain of what the future might bring.

CHAPTER 3

The Pre-Katrina Years

You only find out who is swimming naked when the tide goes out.
—Warren Buffett

I had only been in my office a few days in August of 2001 when one of our maintenance workers wanted to see me. I was eager to meet the park staff, since I had only met the board and a few of the managers, so I asked my secretary to send him in. I invited him to sit down and tell me why he wanted to see me. He asked me whether we had enough money to get everyone paid at the next pay period! I was stunned. That the park was in tough financial shape was not in question, but to have a member of the staff wonder whether we would have enough money to make the next payroll was a wake-up call. I assured him that we were fine (although I didn't know for certain) and that he should not worry about being paid.

I immediately went to see Minette Bruce, the interim chief financial officer, to get an update on the finances. When she and Roy Perrin briefed me during the interview process, they described the financial situation, so I thought I had some understanding of where we were. I was wrong. Minette, in her usual straightforward manner, said the situation was bad. She took me over to the office of the past CFO, pulled out a drawer, and showed me many checks that the park had written to vendors but were never sent because we had no money to cover the costs. Clearly, things were much worse than I thought. (I never could tell my wife that reliance on my paycheck was day to day!)

The more I learned, the more apparent the depth of the problem became. The park had little cash, almost no reserve funds, old equipment, a demoralized staff, virtually no endowment, and no plan for how to get better. Some employees were buying supplies with their personal credit cards because the park could not get credit. A look at the park's financial audits for fiscal years ending in September 2001 and 2002 tells the story.[1]

On September 30, 2001, the bank balance of cash and certificates of deposit was $308,892! Considering that the park's payroll plus benefits for the year was $5,387,000, or $448,917 a month, no wonder my employee was concerned. The park's reserves are held in a government investment pool titled Louisiana Asset Management Pool (LAMP), and in 2001 those reserves totaled $232,326. The net operating loss was listed at $1,041,057, which the park made up by drawing down on its already meager reserves, not making insurance payments, not paying city sales taxes, and putting off paying various vendors and creditors. The retained earnings had dropped from $700,000 in 2000 to $164,000 in 2001.

In their notes, the auditors attempted to strike a hopeful tone while recognizing the seriousness of the problem: "The Park has incurred substantial operating losses for the years ending September 30, 1998 through 2001. In addition, certain capital improvements have been funded, at least partially, through operations. . . . The Board and management of the Park are implementing a plan to improve the Park's financial position through increased revenues from additional programs and general price increases for services currently provided, targeted expense reductions, a moratorium on unfunded capital expenditures, and negotiations with creditors to extend the terms of amounts due."

On the management front, there were similar issues. We were spending money we did not have, particularly on overtime. Our website and technology were old and our equipment, especially for grass cutting, was worn out. There was an unworkable arrangement in the golf operations where the director of golf and senior golf managers were employed under contract with KemperSports Management, but the staff were civil-service park employees, which made accountability and discipline extremely difficult. There were no regular staff meetings, and communication vertically and latterly among the park's operating units was erratic, to say the least. The board was trying to provide too much guidance to staff, in recognition of the fact that there was no leadership from the park's top managers. Worst of all, there was no clear path forward and no clear consensus on what needed to be done to show operational and physical improvements.

Strategic Planning

By early summer of 2002, it was apparent that we needed a planning effort to pull the board together and set a direction for the future. We decided to hold a strategic planning retreat away from the park. Ron Forman graciously let us have the Audubon Center for Research of Endangered Species boardroom at the Species Survival Center on the Westbank.

I secured the help of several consultants and public-interest organizations for various parts of the retreat. Jane Brooks, a professor at the University of New Orleans (UNO), put together a slide presentation of images of great parks throughout the world. Allen Eskew, a local architect and the architect of the 1984 World's Fair, helped to organize the retreat and created graphics to describe where we were on a journey to "great park" status. Dr. Timothy Ryan, also a professor at UNO, undertook a study of the economic impact of the park. Katherine Rowe, of the Trust for Public Land, did a presentation comparing City Park to other parks of our size, utilizing a variety of metrics. Jude Olinger presented a recently completed visitor satisfaction survey, and Beau Bassich gave a history of the park.

Important findings at the retreat included:

- In 2002, the park had over 900,000 individual visitors making a total of 11 million visits. The park was widely utilized by visitors from throughout the metropolitan area and was generally well thought of—except for maintenance and cleanliness.
- The park experienced net operating losses from 1997 to 2001; 2002 began to reverse that trend.
- The park's dependence on good weather was highlighted by the impact of Hurricane Georges and Tropical Storm Allison in 1998 and 2001 respectively, which cost the park over $400,000 in lost revenue from just the month of September. (Later in 2002, Tropical Storm Isidore and Hurricane Lili again cost the park lost revenue from flooding.)
- The park's endowment was miniscule.
- The park lacked operating reserves and was totally reliant on self-gener-

ated revenue (an old story).
- The park faced a growing backlog of deferred maintenance and a lack of funding for capital improvements.
- The park's expenditures on an operating and capital basis were substantially behind those of the other major parks studied.
- A five-dollar property tax among residents of New Orleans appeared to be the most likely form of elective taxation.
- While the park received no local or state tax funding, its operations generated nearly ten million dollars in tax revenue for state and local governments.
- The park had no master plan to guide its development in the future.

A three-year strategic business plan was developed based on the findings. It was broken down into five functional areas: revenue, expenses, organization, visitor experience, and constituency development.

1. Revenue
   - Seek funding for capital improvements from city and state
   - Pursue new revenue opportunities, such as concerts, festivals, new uses, and contracting out the golf operations
   - Grow current revenue from Lark in the Park, Celebration in the Oaks, and a new event in the stables

- Build the endowment to $400,000
- Create a Development Department
- Grow reserves in LAMP) to 10 percent of operating budget
- Seek long-term public tax funding of between three and five million dollars a year

2. Expenses/Operations
   - Control expenses through cost-saving measures such as limiting overtime and contracting out certain services (tree care, for example)
   - Streamline contracts and improve risk-management functions
   - Create a Central Purchasing Department
   - Develop partnerships with organizations to grow volunteer hours
   - Limit the addition of full-time employees
   - Upgrade employee compensation by 10 percent
   - Utilize performance reviews as basis for promotions, salary adjustments, etc.

3. Organizational Structure
   - Restructure board committees, schedules, etc.
   - Examine longer-range organizational strategies, including the role of the Friends, Garden Foundation, and Park Employment and Procurement Corporation
   - Reorganize staff
   - Improve coordination of fundraising activities and planning among park support organizations
   - Examine steps necessary to receive a tax

4. Visitor Experience
   - Fund technology upgrades, including phone and Internet
   - Implement new sales system to improve reservation system
   - Move reservation functions to Internet
   - Provide in-depth customer service training, and create uniforms and ID tags for all employees
   - Develop two new programs to address user needs and increase revenue
   - Reexamine physical master plan for the park

5. Constituency Development
   - Begin public education program to raise awareness of the park's funding status
   - Educate elected officials on park's funding status
   - Continue development of a government relations program
   - Continue development of a neighborhood outreach program

The participants concluded that if this strategic plan were carried out, the park could advance from essentially being in intensive care to becoming a park of regional or even national significance.

Management and Capital Funding Initiatives

Over the next couple of years, we began

to make management and physical plant improvements envisioned in the strategic plan. Minette was made our permanent chief financial officer. I promoted Robert DeViney from director of special events to a newly created position, chief operating officer. I hired Melissa Ogden as the park's first-ever director of development. I brought on Tony Biagas as our director of athletic services, and I added director of park horticulture to Paul Soniat's portfolio as the director of the Botanical Garden. George Parker as director of recreational services, Pat O'Shaughnessy as director of sales, catering, and concessions (and chef extraordinaire), Christine Casey as director of human resources, Billy Bayle as police chief, Ernest Greve as director of maintenance, Merlin Haydel as risk management director, and Beth McFarland as director of public relations rounded out our management team. Dottie Ziegler became my executive assistant.

We reduced the amount of overtime we were paying from general operating funds and obtained a grant for overtime from a local businessman on the board. We also reduced our full-time employment, relying more on part-time workers. We hired a volunteer coordinator to increase the basic maintenance work that could be done by volunteers. We secured limited funds from the city to improve our radio communication system, so we could be in contact with our employees across the 1,300 acres, and used some reserves to obtain a few new pieces of grass-cutting equipment.

We froze hiring so we could generate additional reserve funds (which increased to $503,000 by 2002) and secured funding for some capital initiatives. To increase visitation to the Botanical Garden, we secured funding from the Joe W. and Dorothy Dorsett Brown Foundation in 2004 for a new exhibit focusing on model trains and reproductions of some of the city's historic architecture made from plant materials.

With funds from the Friends of City Park, we bought a new scoreboard for Tad Gormley Stadium, since the existing one had completely broken, threatening our income from stadium rentals. A local philanthropist I had met through my work at Audubon, Nancy Marsiglia, provided funding for a new sports field at Harrison and Marconi, increasing our revenue from that source. We opened a Conservatory in the Botanical Garden, which had been in the works before I arrived, and the New Orleans Museum of Art opened their Sculpture Garden in an area adjacent to the museum that the park had leased to them.

We also began an aggressive program to place protective wooden bollards on various roadways to keep cars from driving off the road and damaging the trees and grounds.

We developed a new tagline and put it on all of the park uniforms: *Every Great City Needs a Great Park.*

We instituted new events. For instance, in 2002, we brought the purple dinosaur character, Barney, to Tad Gormley Stadium for a children's concert, supported by a grant from a local television station. With funds from the Friends' biggest fundraiser, Lark in the Park, we installed lights around the practice track, which had been built for the Olympic Trials and is now utilized by joggers and athletic trainees.

Before I arrived, the park had dismissed its golf director and brought in a sports management company, KemperSports Management. In the early 2000s, the golf complex included four courses and a driving range. (In 2001, golf accounted for about a third of the park's $10,000,000 operating revenue.) The arrangement of an independent contractor managing a staff of civil-service employees was unworkable. Morale was bad, disciplinary actions went unresolved, and I felt it was damaging not only to the employees but to the revenue that golf was expected to make.

To address the issue, I went to the Civil Service Commission and requested that I be allowed to terminate all of the golf employees from park service and permit KemperSports to rehire them as private employees. This was one of the first actions designed to bring in private management of some of the park's assets, in order to reduce operating costs and improve day-to-day operations. I negotiated with Kemper for some salary increases for the employees (which the park paid for) as an incentive for them to move from public to private employment. Most agreed, and since there was little opposition at the Civil Service Commission meeting, Kemper took complete charge of the operation of the golf complex.

In 1995, the widow of a wealthy ball-bearing magnate named Henry Timken had a discussion with her attorney, Charles Snyder, about a piece of property she owned between Lake Salvador and Lake Cataouatche. Mr. Timken had acquired almost four thousand acres of marsh to use as a hunting camp when he visited Louisiana. His widow was no longer interested in the property, and she inquired of Snyder whether she could donate it and to whom. Snyder, who was a member of the park board, suggested giving the land to the City Park Improvement Association, so that the park could benefit from potential oil and gas leases. In December 1995, the property, called Couba Island, was donated to the association. The association immediately signed a long-term lease with the Louisiana Wildlife and Fisheries Commission to manage the island for one dollar a year. In the early 2000s, the park received several checks from oil and gas drillers for exploratory wells, each check being around $250,000. These payments were extremely helpful during that time as they built up some cash reserves to buy equipment. They stopped when the companies decided that the price of oil and gas were not high enough to justify further exploration and eventual extraction. Since then, the island has continued to erode, as has much of Louisiana's coastline, and by 2020, it had been reduced to around twenty-eight hundred acres. As the island constitutes a major buffer reducing the impact of storm surge during hurricanes, its continued erosion is of major concern. Several efforts have been made to convince the state to purchase the property from the association so it could be stabilized. While not yet successful, it remains a major priority for the park.

As previously mentioned, we managed to cobble together enough money to hire the park's first development director, Melissa Ogden, implementing a recommendation first made in 1990. While we did not have funds to outfit a complete development department, I did convince the Friends of City Park to hire a lobbyist who could help secure various types of funding from the state. Later that year, acting upon a recommendation from board member Sally Perry, the Friends engaged Darrell Hunt, a well-respected lobbyist in the halls of state government.

We also began reaching out to city, state, and federal sources for capital funding. In October of 2002, we invited Mayor Ray Nagin to lunch with our Executive Committee at the park. Members of the board and I made a presentation on the park's financing, how other great urban parks were funded, and the park's current status. The mayor spent two hours with us and expressed his strong interest in getting the park more resources.

Mayor Nagin made good on his commitment in the summer of 2003 when he issued a challenge to match up to $1 million of park-raised funds with $1 million of city funds. We accepted immediately and, using funds raised by Lark in the Park, met the challenge. We used the funds for several infrastructure projects, including sidewalk improvements along City Park Avenue, renovations in the Amusement Park, replacement of the air-conditioning in the Tad Gormley Stadium press box, and renovations to the ball machine in the Quadruplex. The city also funded several other capital projects, including renovations to Pan American Stadium at $1.5 million and revamps of various sports fields.

We also doubled down our efforts at the state level. We secured an initial appropriation of $550,000 for various tennis center improvements, which after Hurricane Katrina was increased to $3,565,000[2] to move the courts from the front of the park to a new location near Marconi and Harrison, in line with the new master plan.

We also secured $400,000 in planning funds for renovations to the East Golf Course. However, when we asked to be assigned a golf course architect for the project, we were told that, unlike most other states, Louisiana did not recognize golf course architecture as a profession. We would have to hire a landscape architect as the professional of record, and that firm would engage the golf course architect. This was accomplished when the state hired Torre Design Consortium as the landscape architect and Bobby Weed as a subcontractor to Torre as the golf course architect. An additional $6.6 million in construction funding was also approved. (Post-Katrina, this was increased to a total of $9.9 million.)

We also turned to the federal government

through Sen. Mary Landrieu. As it turns out, it took Katrina to free up federal funds.

The Slot Tax

In my initial discussions with Darrell Hunt, I emphasized the need for some level of public tax support. During the strategic planning session, the Trust for Public Land emphasized how our funding formula of 100 percent self-generating revenue was so at odds with the funding of other great parks. Most parks receive 75 percent or more from public tax sources and then raise the remaining from activities in the park. City Park was the opposite, and this was the principal reason why it did not have adequate funds for any part of its operation. This was not a new observation, as it had been mentioned throughout the park's history as a major problem that impacted everything else. (The reasons why City Park had never had a dedicated source of public tax support stemmed in part from the historic separation of the park from the city's Audubon Park, its subsequent identification as a "state responsibility," and a desire of past park boards to maintain its independence from political interference.)

Darrell and I discussed what sources of revenue we could possibly secure from the state. He emphasized that we had to look for new sources that had not been previously dedicated, since it was almost impossible to take revenue from some other recipient and divert it to the park. He mentioned that the only new source of revenue being discussed by the governor and legislature was allowing racetracks to add slot machines in a casino-like atmosphere. The horseracing industry was facing declining revenue, and they viewed slot machines as the only way they could afford substantial purses to keep the sport alive. Since the state would place a tax on the revenue the racetracks generate, there could be an opportunity to get a part of that tax.

As this discussion was occurring, we were behind on our insurance payments to the state. Louisiana is self-insured with a disaster balloon policy with private insurers. Each state agency is allocated funds in its budget to pay its share of the total insurance bill based upon claims that are that agency's responsibility. City Park, because we were not in the state's general fund, did not receive any appropriation and had to pay the insurance bill out of earned revenue—something the park had not been able to do for several years.

Darrell thought there was an opportunity to include City Park in the racetrack slot-machine legislation by arguing that we would use those funds to help pay our insurance bill, in effect recycling the money. This would be new money, so our only problem would be to get included in the bill. Thanks to the work of Hunt and our legislative delegation, $200,000 was credited to the Pari-Mutuel Live Racing Facility Economic Redevelopment and Gaming Control Act to the Beautification and Improvement of the New Orleans City Park Fund. This was the first state or city money that was ever dedicated to the park, and although the funding was not large, it was an enormous step in the right direction. It was even more remarkable because the tax was generated by all the racetracks in the state, which meant that communities outside of New Orleans were, in effect, supporting City Park.

In 2005, another opportunity arose to get operating funds from the state. The Fair Grounds Race Course in New Orleans had been purchased by Churchill Downs, and they were deep into negotiations with the Bayou St. John Neighborhood Association over whether the latter would support the zoning change necessary to permit a slot-machine casino to open at the track. Once again, the racing industry argued that without the supplemental revenue of slot machines, they could not offer enough prize money to keep racing alive. The neighborhood countered that they would be impacted by the operation, and the negotiations raged over topics such as additional security patrols, sanitation, and cleanup efforts outside the track and contributions to the association for other types of programs. We felt that if City Park could be one of the recipients of the state tax on slots, it would be an added benefit that the neighborhood would appreciate.

The state legislature voted to allocate 30 percent of the state tax, not to exceed $1.3 million, to the Beautification and Improvement of the New Orleans City Park Fund![3] The law was sponsored by Representatives Emile Bruneau, John Alario, Charles Lancaster, and Steve Scalise and Senators Ed Murray and Ken Hollis, all supporters of the park. In August of 2005, the New Orleans City Council approved a zoning change authorizing the casino.

This was a huge step forward in bringing the long-hoped-for public tax support to fruition. Finally, a significant amount of tax support (albeit from people who went and gambled at the Fair Grounds) was being dedicated to the park.

Over the previous several years, we had made a lot of progress implementing the recommendations of the strategic plan, and it was time to turn our attention to developing a true master plan to guide the physical development of the park.

CHAPTER 4

The Plan[1]

Plans are useless, but planning is essential. Plans are nothing; planning is everything.
—Dwight Eisenhower

One of the most important findings that came out of the strategic planning process was the need to update the park's master plan. In 2004, from a physical perspective, the results of the park's previous master planning were apparent. The last master plan was adopted in 1984 and was what we might call a restrained plan as a result of the public uproar over the proposal to lease land for residential development and other money-making initiatives proposed in 1981. If we were to move the park into the twenty-first century, we needed a more ambitious and comprehensive plan.

Such a plan was going to be expensive, so we set about raising the necessary funds to hire a nationally recognized planning team. We had to show that we had "skin in the game" before we could ask others for help, so we pledged $50,000 and then initiated a private fundraising effort. Foundations such as the Freeport-McMoRan Foundation, the Brown Foundation, and the Greater New Orleans Foundation put up $166,000 to round out the funding.

While there were several fine park master-planning consultants, I was familiar with Wallace Roberts & Todd of Philadelphia through my work with them at the Planning Commission. Dave Wallace had an outstanding reputation, and I contacted him to see if they would be interested in helping prepare our plan. I also knew that we would need an economic consultant to provide guidance about uses that would support the park's operations and help satisfy unmet community needs. Economic Research Associates was selected. Finally, we needed a local planning firm that was familiar with the park and could be counted on to implement the recommendations. Once again, my work at both the Planning Commission and the Audubon Institute was instrumental in helping us select the local firm Cashio Cochran LLC for that role.

We settled on 2018 as the aspirational goal year when all the recommendations would be implemented, only fourteen years away. It would be the 300th birthday of the city and was a perfect target for the completion of the plan.

Summary of Market Factors by ERA

Economic Research Associates for the 2005 master plan essentially played the same role as Revenue Consultants Inc. played in the abortive 1981 plan. That is, they examined market factors in the New Orleans metropolitan area that could influence the type and location of land uses to be considered and recommended uses that addressed market deficiencies, community needs, and revenue generation. One of the goals in developing the plan given to the consultants was financial self-sufficiency. After extensive research, ERA summarized the difficulty of achieving this goal.

- The park has no dedicated source of capital or operational funding.
- Most facilities and activities are seasonal and weather dependent.
- The park has virtually no reserve to cushion bad months/years.
- The park provides community services and facilities, such as the stadiums, that require high levels of subsidization.
- The park's extensive area of lawns and gardens adds to operations and maintenance requirements.

While none of these were particularly new findings, they did support previous studies of the park's financial condition and were valuable for informing a new generation of park advocates.

After considering many variables, including market orientation and competition, location, park image, and management expertise, ERA came up with recommendations for three different types of uses: revenue, community, and cultural.[2]

Revenue Uses

ERA considered a wide variety of potential revenue uses, including paintball, an amphitheater, and a conference-center hotel at the golf complex. They settled on recommending the following five uses:

- *Splash Park*—The emphasis of this facility would be on "wet" rather than "immersion." The consultants felt that it could generate between $150,000 and $200,000 in net income a year.
- *Skateboard Park*—This could meet a need in the city while generating roughly $20,000 to $35,000 in net income. (While many cities provide free skateboard areas, ERA felt that the park could charge for its use.)
- *RV campground*—This use was previously recommended in 1981,

and ERA thought it could take advantage of the growth in a new lifestyle activity. Net income could range between $175,000 and $225,000.

- *Permanent festival area*—Another recommendation from the past, ERA felt that this was an extension of our current special-events offerings, and if an area had supporting infrastructure, such as electricity and restrooms, it could generate net income between $100,000 and $200,000.
- *Restaurant*—ERA thought that this was a good opportunity, and one such as the Tavern on the Green in Central Park could generate between $50,000 and $100,000 of net income.

Community Uses

ERA also indicated two community needs not currently being addressed but that would not generate enough income to cover their operating costs. Those needs were:

- *Additional sports fields*—Their research demonstrated that there was a considerable gap between the demand for sports fields and their supply, particularly with the growth in adult leagues and in sports participation by girls/women.

- *Community center*—ERA felt that there was a great need for venues offering basketball courts and meeting rooms. This type of facility would also be insulated from the weather and generate some income.

Cultural Uses

The consultants felt strongly that a characteristic of other great urban parks was the existence of cultural facilities, of which City Park's offerings were limited. They did not believe that the park should build and run cultural facilities but that various cultural institutions should be encouraged to find suitable locations in the future. (The park had offered the Children's Museum a site in the 1984 plan, but it was not until thirty-five years later that a new Louisiana Children's Museum opened.)

Under the revenue component of ERA's recommendations, the reader might recognize the Splash Park and RV campground from the 1981 EDAW plan. The park has hoped to have a water-recreation component since the mid-1950s, when the Irby Pool was closed during desegregation, and for several years during Carnival, Tad Gormley Stadium served as an RV campground.

Other Plan Research

In addition to ERA's market study, we initiated some research to provide input to the plan. The Cashio firm provided an acreage analysis of the park's current land uses and studied alternative uses. They examined prior land-use and revenue studies to make recommendations. The firm conducted a regional telephone survey and an online survey through a master-plan website to ascertain what uses the general public thought appropriate.

In addition, the consultants examined other great public parks such as Hermann Park in Houston, Central Park and Bryant Park in New York, Golden Gate Park in San Francisco, Balboa Park in San Diego, and Forest Park in St. Louis as well as several parks in Europe for emerging trends in large urban parks.

This research, along with the assessment, surveys, and other community feedback, contributed the following input to the plan.

- Add museums/cultural facilities to those the park already offered.
- Create more concert and festival areas.
- Increase the amount of undeveloped open space available to the public.
- Develop programs for all ages.
- Build a children's water play area and Skateboard Park.

- Develop a dog park/animal agility center.
- Improve the lagoons' water quality for better fishing.
- Create a comprehensive forestry program.
- Build walking/jogging and bicycle paths.
- Renovate the golf complex.
- Renovate the park's aging infrastructure and better maintain the buildings and grounds.

Utilizing these background studies, the consultant team, in concert with the park board and management, began to develop the key goals and strategies of the plan.

Mission/Goal/Vision

The City Park Improvement Association constructed the park's *Mission Statement* after examining their incorporation documents and the legislation that tasked the group with the purposes of the park they were authorized to maintain: "Preserve and improve City Park spaces for recreational, educational, cultural and beautification purposes." These four purposes are weighted equally, with no one purpose superseding another.

The *Goal of the Plan* was to "make City Park the premier urban park in the nation." The park board and the staff were united in the belief that the goal of the plan must be aspirational and challenging if we were going to rally the community behind the effort. The rest of the goal was contained in the following sentences: "Through 2018, existing park facilities and infrastructure will be repaired and renovated with new facilities and uses introduced. The park will be financially self-sufficient, properly maintained and will offer an extensive array of programs and cultural educational experiences to the public to commemorate the 300th anniversary of the founding of the City of New Orleans."

The plan also contained an extensive *Vision,* which is summarized as follows:[3]

In 2018, we envision:

Expanded recreation opportunities where . . .

- Healthy living is encouraged for all ages and abilities with places to play, compete, and enjoy fresh air and nature.
- New facilities and activities meet the needs of the community.
- Public transit links the park with neighborhoods throughout the city.

Strong sense of community where . . .
- Lifelong learning opportunities are encouraged.
- Families enjoy the park's variety of activities at every stage.
- Neighbors meet through park programs and build long-term relationships.

- Public health is encouraged and celebrated.
- Environmental opportunities in fields such as environmental sciences, business, and recreational management are developed.
- Local businesses are complemented by improvements in the park.
- Citizens are engaged in their community.

Integrated natural and functional systems where . . .
- Native Louisiana plants and animals thrive.
- Stewardship is a popular and re-warding recreational activity.
- Water quality is high and routinely maintained.
- Trails and roads are safe and enjoyable.
- The urban forest contributes to the park's character and quality.

Distinctive identity where . . .
- City Park's distinct heritage is preserved and celebrated.
- A vibrant horticultural palette displays seasonal color of plant communities from New Orleans, the South, and exotic locations around the world.
- The surrounding neighborhoods enjoy and benefit from the park's year-round activities.

- Citizens take pride in their park.
- City Park is nationally recognized.
- Tourists find the park fun, safe, and well maintained.

Financial self-sufficiency where . . .
- Park management and governance are responsive to ever-changing conditions.
- Funding of park improvements and operation is abundant and widely supported.
- Public/private partnerships are mutually beneficial and grow with the park.
- Ongoing evaluation directs improvements at all levels.

Later, we shall see how many of these specific vision objectives were actually implemented!

Overarching Strategies of the Plan

Based on all of the research, community input, and direction established by the mission, goal, and vision, the following major strategies were incorporated into the plan.

1. *Closing the South Golf Course.* During my time at the park, two trends were evident. First, there was not a demand for the four golf courses the park operated in 2005. While golf had been a major revenue generator since the opening of the first nine-hole course in 1902, the number of rounds had steadily declined in the 1990s and early 2000s to the point where it did not make economic sense to operate such a large complex. Second, there was great public demand for more general open space and space to address other critical needs of the mission, such as walking paths, festival gathering space, and additional cultural facilities. The research we undertook for the plan confirmed these needs. In 2005, golf uses took up almost 40 percent, or over five hundred acres, of the park's land.

By closing one of the golf courses, we could reduce our golf maintenance costs as well as free up park land for these other uses. Since the park had built a golf clubhouse on Filmore (taking the place of the original clubhouse, which had been cut in half by the construction of I-610 in the 1960s), it made sense to close the course farthest away from the clubhouse. It would also be the course closest to the largest concentration of park users. So, we decided to close the South Course and repurpose its approximately one hundred acres for other uses.

2. *Emphasizing amusement and entertainment activities in the front of the park.* This area, particularly between Victory and Dreyfous, already contained the amusement park, the Botanical Garden, the New Orleans Museum of Art, the Sydney and Walda Besthoff Sculpture Garden, as well as the historic Casino Building, where we operated

a food and beverage facility with a reception room on its second floor. The odd man out, so to speak, was our tennis complex. Tennis had been in this location since the 1920s, which at one time contained one of the largest collection of courts in the South. However, through the years, as is typical of many sports, its fortunes had risen and fallen with the popularity of this pastime. In recognition of this, in the 1990s, the park had reduced the number of courts in order to have space to build parking for tennis players and users of the front of the park. (At one point, the park considered building a garage under the tennis courts to supply parking without reducing the number of courts.) The complex contained both hard-surface and clay courts separated by a parking lot. A new tennis headquarters had been built on Victory, replacing the historic building nearer the Casino Building, which had been turned into a headquarters for the park police. Like many facilities in the park, maintenance had been substandard, and we felt that active sports facilities were not in keeping with the other uses in the area. By moving the entire tennis complex to a new location, we would also free up space to support nonrecreation uses.

Therefore, the plan proposed moving the tennis courts and clubhouse to a new site on Marconi Drive, where a multipurpose picnic facility was located. There we would build a new clubhouse and twenty-six courts, including both hard and soft surfaces. In the place of the tennis complex, we would create a more vibrant focus for the historic core of the park by establishing a more diverse family activity center. We called this new center Tri-Centennial Place and proposed a series of improvements, including miniature golf, a public fountain, a café and restaurant, an outdoor marketplace, a performance stage, improved parking, and a Great Lawn that could be used for concerts, plays, and other types of outdoor gatherings. Later amendments to the plan added a Splash Park.

3. *Creating a service corridor adjacent to the railroad tracks and I-610.* All large parks have "back of the house" areas. The plan proposed to consolidate those places along a service corridor adjacent to the railroad tracks that cut the park in half. The tracks would shield views of the south from the north, and landscaping could soften the views of the north from the southern part of the park. This area already housed a 1930s maintenance complex, and the plan was to abandon that wretched facility and build a new maintenance complex in the corridor. In addition, we hoped to construct a new catering complex to replace the current kitchen and storage area, which was in the old driving-range building along Marconi Drive. The plan also envisioned expanding our greenhouse, the propagation facility for the horticultural initiatives in the park, which was located in the proposed service corridor.

4. *Making major investments in the remaining golf courses.* While we were closing the South Golf Course, we also saw the

need to rehabilitate the other courses, golf clubhouse, and driving range. We hoped these improvements would increase our revenue on the reduced golf footprint.

5. *Creating a series of bicycle and jogging paths.* In 2005, there were no bicycle paths or even sidewalks in the northern two-thirds of City Park. Many of the existing sidewalks in the southern part of the park were in disrepair, despite the improvements we made along City Park Avenue with city funds. A comprehensive system was proposed, which featured protected bicycle paths along Wisner Boulevard, Robert E. Lee Boulevard (now Allen Toussaint Boulevard), and Marconi Drive. These would connect to shared-use paths along Harrison, Filmore, and Zachary Taylor. Also, a walking and bike path system would be built around Big Lake near the museum and on the Festival Grounds proposed for the major space vacated by golf.

The Projects

These strategies were to be implemented by a comprehensive capital improvement program totaling $115 million. The projects included the following:

- Infrastructure improvements, including renovations to the sewer, water, and drainage systems, much of which were more than seventy-five years old.
- Renovation of the North, West, and East golf courses and construction of a new golf clubhouse.
- Tri-Centennial Place improvements.
- Building the Festival Grounds.
- Building a multipurpose facility and gym.
- Renovating the amusement park and sports stadiums.
- Constructing an RV campground.
- Building a new tennis complex.
- Building a children's Splash Park.
- Building a new catering and maintenance complex.
- Renovating sports fields and constructing a Skateboard Park.
- Constructing an environmental education center and renovating and expanding the Botanical Garden.
- Investing in the lagoon system and renovating Storyland.

Other projects included extending the streetcar into the park to provide better access to the interior, where the major attractions were located, and the construction of a sound wall to mitigate the noise coming from I-610. (Had this plan been in place when the state negotiated a right of way through the center of the property, a sound wall would have been required in addition to the payment.)

Land Use

The single best change that the plan caused

in the park's land use was the reduction of acreage devoted to active recreation and the increase of passive open space. Approximately 50 percent of the park, or around 660 acres, was dedicated to recreation uses, including golf courses, stadiums, and sports fields. This percentage was reduced to 44 percent primarily through the conversion of the South Golf Course to passive leisure, cultural, and education uses. Undeveloped open space increased from 23 percent of the park's property to 27 percent. Other land-use categories included lagoon areas; park support space for warehousing, horticulture, maintenance, and catering; vehicle parking; and roads and paths. A proposed map depicted these reallocations using sixteen different land-use categories.

In addition, the master plan contained renderings of impacted areas of the park, such as the different uses in Tri-Centennial Place and pictures of similar uses in other cities, all designed to give citizens a more complete understanding of the proposal.

The Financing Plan

The financing plan had to conceptualize how to raise two sources of funds: the $115 million capital investment, and a significant increase in basic operating funds, the lack of which had plagued the park almost from its inception. It had to be a partnership among the city, the state, and the park, with the inclusion of federal partnerships for specific initiatives.

The Capital Plan 2005-18

City Park	$17,500,000	Self-generated revenue and fundraising
City of New Orleans	$13,000,000	City bond issues
Dedicated Tax	$45,500,000	A portion of a three-mill property tax
State	$26,000,000	State's construction budget
Federal	$13,000,000	Through earmarks and other federal programs
Total Cost	$115,000,000	

The Operating Plan 2005-18

	Current	Proposed
City Park	$10,600,000	$11,600,000
City of New Orleans	$0	$0
Dedicated Tax	$0	$2,500,000 (A portion of a three-mill property tax)
State	$200,000	$2,000,000 (Tax on slot-machine revenue)
Federal	$0	$0
Total Cost	$10,800,000	$16,100,000

Since the plan was to be implemented in phases and over thirteen years, the amount of capital funding projected from the city, state, and federal government seemed achievable. But the lynchpins of the funding plan were a city property tax and an expansion of the funding the park had received in 2004 from a tax on slot machines at racetracks. The plan envisioned changing the park's operating model from nearly 100 percent self-generated revenue to one in which the state and the city would contribute public tax dollars of $4.5 million annually, or nearly 30 percent of the operating budget. This would finally produce a financial model that, while still requiring the park to raise 70 percent of its operating revenue through activities (and the opposite of most great parks' models), would provide public tax funding for the first time and in a sufficient amount to greatly improve park maintenance and operations.

Public Reaction

The plan was covered extensively by the media. In January of 2005, Martha Carr of the *New Orleans Times-Picayune* wrote an in-depth piece about the plan with comments from Lt. Gov. Mitch Landrieu and Mayor Ray Nagin. I was quoted several times in the article trying to explain why the plan needed to be bold and what could happen if it were not implemented: "The plan is to make City Park the premier urban park in the nation. And that's what we ought to strive for . . . we ought to want to be the best. There is no reason we shouldn't be able to do this for our citizens. We are a heartbeat away from disaster here, and we are doing what no one else in the country does, which is live without any substantial public funds to operate . . . we can't stay where we are, because we're falling down. We're going backwards."

We presented the proposed plan to the public at a hearing on February 22, 2005. The board's president, Rick Butler, called the hearing to order, and I showed a brief PowerPoint presentation on the major aspects of the plan. Approximately 250 people attended the hearing to provide their input, and many people subsequently sent in comments by email or letter. Most comments supported the plan or only had issues with portions of the proposal.[4] Some responses came from organizations such as the Audubon Society and the Girl Scouts, but most comments and suggestions came from individual members of the public. The major comments concerned the following:

- Several golfers objected to the closing of the South Golf Course, and some recommended it be converted to an executive course. Other speakers supported devoting that land to other uses. We noted that the number of rounds at the South Course had declined from 30,000 four years before to only 12,000 estimated for 2005. This lack of use and the desire to provide land for other uses made the recommendation to close the course obvious.

- Some speakers objected to only the citizens of New Orleans having to pay a property tax when the park was a regional facility, and they suggested that a regional tax would be fairer. While we agreed that such a tax would better represent the users of the park, we felt that there was no momentum for it, and the park could not wait for this concept to develop. We also felt that with the slot tax approved, the state was beginning to

step up and was, in effect, standing in the shoes of the surrounding parishes to support the park.

- Some speakers noted that the park board should be more accountable to the people. While not a direct comment on the plan, it reflected the fact that some people still did not like the composition of the board

- A large group of birders testified that the plan should go further in promoting birdwatching as a popular form of recreation.

- Some people favored extending the streetcar line into the park, and some opposed it.

- We received a few comments about locating the Festival Grounds on the eastern side of the park, as opposed to the western side where most events were held.

After making some minor adjustments to the plan as a result of the comments, the Board of Commissioners of the City Park Improvement Association adopted the first master plan for the park in more than twenty years on March 29, 2005. Over the Fourth of July weekend, we began implementing the plan by closing the South Golf Course. Five months after the adoption of the plan, Hurricane Katrina struck the city.

CHAPTER 5

Katrina

When interviewed by a reporter about another boxer's plan to defeat the heavyweight champion in an upcoming fight, Mike Tyson said, "Everyone has a plan until they get punched in the mouth."

My staff and I had been keeping an eye on a tropical depression that formed southeast of the Bahamas on Tuesday, August 23, 2005. Then, on Thursday, the storm crossed over Florida into the Gulf of Mexico as a Category 1 hurricane named Katrina.[1] Most Louisianans begin paying attention to storms once they enter the Gulf. Katrina was originally projected to curve back up toward Florida. Then all the hurricane prediction models showed it heading in the direction of New Orleans.

Getting Out of Town

By Thursday, it was clear that the city would feel some impact from Katrina, even though the projected location of landfall was still not certain. I instructed our department heads to begin preparations in their area of responsibility. This included removing and storing anything that could become a projectile in high winds, relocating computers away from windows, making sure all the park's vehicles were full of gas, and securing equipment such as chainsaws that might be needed after the storm.

On Friday morning, it was still not clear that the hurricane would directly impact the city, but by that evening, the governor, Kathleen Blanco, had issued a state-of-emergency declaration.

Saturday was a beautiful day, not unlike what is often experienced before and after a major storm event. I told all the managers we would be closed Sunday and Monday, so they should complete their preparations and then evacuate if possible. The storm had been picking up strength, and by the weekend, it was a Category 3 hurricane, which would yield significant wind and water damage. I told my wife and son that we would evacuate early Sunday morning unless the storm suddenly changed direction. (We had gone grocery shopping Saturday morning, as we felt that even if we did leave, it would only be for a few days and then we would be back. Our refrigerator was full—bad decision!) By 4:00 P.M., the State Police implemented the contraflow plan, which turned over all lanes on interstate highways to outgoing traffic, including I-10 westbound toward Baton Rouge.

By Saturday evening, government authorities announced a voluntary evacuation north of Plaquemines Parish. Most of my employees had already decided to leave. Rob DeViney went to Lafayette that afternoon, while Minette Bruce went to Florida, Paul Soniat to North Louisiana, and Don Watson, our controller, to his wife's sister's house in Houston. Pat O'Shaughnessy also took his family to Houston Sunday afternoon. Mike Mariani, our maintenance director, and Billy Bayle, our police chief, had decided to stay, Mike in the Administration Building and Billy in his apartment at the Park Esplanade, just across the bayou from the park.

Pat O'Shaughnessy is the park's director of sales and catering and, as such, is responsible for holding weddings and special events in our facilities. He and his staff cater most of those activities. During the weekend of Katrina, we had three weddings scheduled for Friday, Saturday, and Sunday in the Botanical Garden's Pavilion of the Two Sisters. This is how Pat described the weekend:

"Based on the projections of the storm, we went ahead with the Friday and Saturday evening functions. Sunday's wedding was in question. I had been in touch with the bride's mother throughout the week, and the plan was to go ahead with the wedding. She was pretty set on having it since a lot of her guests were from out of town, and they were already in town. As of my last communication with her on Saturday afternoon, we were moving ahead with the wedding. I told her that I would touch base with her Sunday morning. The wedding cake and flowers for Sunday were delivered on Saturday to the Pavilion. We had completed the food prep on Friday. My only concern was having enough staff to pull it off. When the Saturday wedding was complete, I had the staff completely reset the room so that we could be ready for the uncertainties of the next day. I also told the staff that we were going ahead with Sunday's wedding, so make sure they were here. Sunday morning, I headed in about 6:30. At that time, it looked like the storm had grown in intensity, and the course had moved to more of a direct path toward New Orleans. I decided that the wedding could not happen. I called the bride's mother and informed her that it was best for all concerned that we cancel the wedding. I could tell from her reaction that she was relieved that I had made the call to cancel the wedding. I proceeded to contact my employees and inform them of the cancelation."[2]

There are several organizations that are tenants in the park. A few of them provided their stories about that weekend.

Joey Scaffidi, headmaster of Christian Brothers School located in the McFadden Mansion, said, "The homework assignments on the classroom boards were dated August 26, 2005, with a due date of Monday, August 29. When the teachers and students left the City Park campus that fateful weekend, it was with the full intention of returning there for school and work on Monday. That, of course, never happened. Even as late as Saturday morning, the tackle football team was engaged in a scrimmage before the news came [on Sunday] that an evacuation of the city was in order for the approaching Hurricane Katrina."[3]

Leslie Kramer, owner of Equest Farm, the equestrian facility located on Filmore, said, "The Saturday before Katrina, we were in Oxford, Mississippi, for the opening weekend of volleyball. I received a call from one of my horse transport drivers at 6 A.M. asking me what I wanted to do. I had no idea Katrina was heading straight to New Orleans. I enacted my hurricane plan, which had been in place since 2000. The plan was simple. If there was a Category 3 or better in the Gulf, I had to decide whether to leave or stay. We had evacuated twice before this over the years, only to have a three-day vacation for the horses. Luckily, I decided to evacuate. The vans started arriving at the barn at 8 A.M., and the horses were loaded and sent to two places, the Lamar-Dixon Expo Center in Gonzales, which had generators, and my sister's farm in Hammond. We sent enough feed and hay to last for two weeks and evacuated eighty horses in six hours. All were safe and survived. Unfortunately, when New Orleans was flooded, Lamar-Dixon became a center for dislocated people and their animals. We moved the customer horses to a facility in Dallas and kept the school horses in Hammond. All the customer horses were returned to their owners and distributed to other barns around the country, and all but seven school horses were sold. Equest was finished, or so I thought."[4]

On Friday, August 26, Jacqueline Sullivan, deputy director of the New Orleans Museum of Art, began to implement the facility's emergency plan. This meant moving all the art off the floor and away from windows and skylights, filling up emergency generators, and securing outside sculptures. She allowed various staff members to shelter with their families at the museum. They brought clothes, food, books, guns, and ammunition, and some even brought urns filled with their loved one's ashes. On Sunday morning, Jacqueline went to the museum to be sure final preparations had been made and to speak with the staff.

She later recounted, "I left the museum after 1 P.M. on Sunday and went home to take care of getting myself out of Jefferson Parish, along with James and two dogs, Jack and Elle. My best effort was to get packed and on the road by 3 P.M. We were going as far as Gonzales, La. and staying at the St. Theresa of Avila Convent, which was connected to the grade school where my brother, Jay, had been the principal for 25 years. . . . We did not pull up into the schoolyard until after 8 P.M. in the rain. . . . The convent had a small emergency generator my brother, Jay, had purchased for just these types of events, and the men in the house set it up outside a window and ran an extension cord to the T.V. and the refrigerator. We continued to watch the horror of the day, including flooding, looting, fires, gas explosions, people stranded in distress, and total destruction of one of the most beautiful cities in the world."[5]

In addition to our staff and our tenants, several of our board members evacuated. Rick Butler, our president, went to Houston and Paul Masinter, head of our Legal Committee and soon-to-be president, went to Baton Rouge, where he bought a house for a temporary residence.

At four o'clock Sunday morning, August 28, I packed up with my wife, son, and our dogs, entered the contraflow lanes of I-10 at Clearview Parkway (driving westbound in the eastbound lanes), and headed to Dallas, where one of my daughters had a house.

At 10:00 A.M., while I was driving, the National Weather Service issued a warning, which predicted the impact of Katrina.[6]

DEVASTATING DAMAGE EXPECTED . . . HURRICANE KATRINA . . . A MOST POWERFUL HURRICANE WITH UNPRECEDENTED STRENGTH . . . RIVALING THE INTENSITY OF HURRICANE CAMILLE OF 1969. MOST OF THE AREA WILL BE UNINHABITABLE FOR WEEKS . . . PERHAPS LONGER. AT LEAST ONE HALF OF WELL CONSTRUCTED HOMES WILL HAVE ROOF AND WALL FAILURE. . . . POWER OUTAGES WILL LAST FOR WEEKS. . . . WATER SHORTAGES WILL MAKE HUMAN SUFFERING INCREDIBLE BY MODERN STANDARDS. THE VAST MAJORITY OF NATIVE TREES WILL BE SNAPPED OR UPROOTED. ONLY THE HEARTIEST WILL REMAIN STANDING. . . . LIVESTOCK LEFT EXPOSED TO THE WINDS WILL BE KILLED.

Shortly after the warning was issued, Mayor Ray Nagin, on Sunday morning, ordered a mandatory evacuation.

By the time we arrived at my daughter's house, the first rains began to fall on New Orleans. I reached Chief Billy Bayle, who told me he and Mike Mariani were holed up in his apartment, and the wind and rain were strong, so they could not get out to check on the park.

The Levees Break

Sunday evening, the news media reported that the storm had taken a slight eastward track, which was good news for New Orleans. On Monday morning, all my efforts to reach staff were futile. No 504 area codes worked, so it was impossible to locate any of our employees. Still, early Monday morning on August 29, the situation seemed manageable, and I felt confident that when we returned to clean up the debris, we would find we had dodged "the big one." In the early afternoon,

I was shocked to get a call on my cell phone from Mike Mariani, from the second floor of our Administration Building. He told me there were about six inches of water in the building and that it was rising fast. Somehow, despite the deteriorating conditions, Mike had left Billy Bayle's apartment and ventured into the park, ending up in the Administration Building. I told him to be careful and try to get to the high ground of the railroad tracks before the water got too deep. He said he was afraid to leave, as he believed he saw an alligator swimming outside the building. Mike told me he had heard that the wall along the Seventeenth Street Canal had broken, and water was coming into the city. (The wall had been breached Monday morning, allowing storm surge from Lake Pontchartrain to pour into New Orleans. The flooding soon reached City Park. Water also entered from the Orleans Canal near the pumping station at the edge of the park. By the end of Monday, all four of the main drainage canals had been compromised, flooding 80 percent of the city.)

Rob DeViney lost contact with Mariani and Bayle and did not reconnect for several days. When he did reach Mariani, he said that he and Bayle had made their way to the meadow beside the museum, where they were airlifted to the Causeway exit at I-10. There, they got a ride to Lafayette to his son's apartment.

By midday on Monday, the extent of the disaster was becoming clear. While damage from wind and rain had been significant, the failure of the federal flood-protection

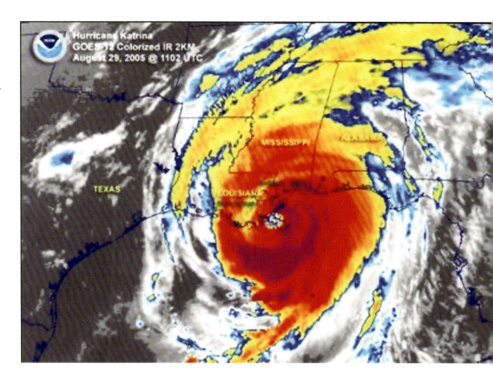

levees was the real cause of the catastrophic damage. We tried to find our house on Google Earth to see if it flooded, but images were not clear, so, like many others, we lived with anxiety about the extent of damage to our home until we were able to get back to the city and inspect.

The First Days

By Tuesday, the full magnitude of the disaster became apparent. News videos showed the park under water, like so much of the city. All you could do was watch television hour after hour while the situation worsened. I reached Minette Bruce in Destin, Florida, and we decided to ask one of the banks we did business with to write payroll checks, if we could find our staff. Christine Casey, our human resources director, was in Shreveport, and I had her contact Minette to recreate an employee database.

On Wednesday, August 31, I got in touch with more of my far-flung staff. Merlin Haydel, our risk manager, was in Monroe, Louisiana and John Hopper, our development director, was, strangely enough, only a few miles from my daughter's house in McKinney, Texas. John had gotten ahold of Dell Technologies and arranged for a few laptops. Dottie Ziegler, my secretary, texted me from a hotel in Baton Rouge; George Parker, our amusements director, was in Baton Rouge; and Tony Biagas, our recreation director, and Pat O'Shaughnessy were in Houston. Pat had arrived there on Sunday after canceling the wedding.

The U.S. Army Corps of Engineers was having trouble plugging the breaches in the canal walls, which was essential before they could start draining the city. On television, looting seemed widespread, and large crowds were gathering at the Convention Center, as they had been told to make their way there for evacuation. Mayor Nagin estimated deaths in the thousands, although apparently no one had seen him in days. It was almost impossible to reach state government in Baton Rouge for help.

On Friday, September 2, I connected with Jim Hahn, who was the regional director for KemperSports, which managed our golf courses under contract. He told me that they could pay their employees for several weeks before furloughing them and that he would request a donation of equipment from golf companies they did business with, since he assumed (correctly) all of ours was destroyed.

On Friday, I also got ahold of Princeton University, where my son was a sophomore. I told Hilary Herbold, the associate dean of undergraduate students, that I was going to send my son back to school, but he had only the clothes he evacuated with. I also did not know if we could pay tuition, as it was unclear if my wife (a teacher) or I would have a job when we returned to New Orleans. Dean Herbold told me to get Ryan to Princeton, not to worry about the tuition, and they would give him a Princeton credit card so he could charge anything he needed. She was truly a lifesaver I have never forgotten!

Minette Bruce and I had talked several times over the preceding days about our financial situation and what we needed to do with our employees. It was abundantly clear that the park was heavily damaged, and most if not all of the facilities that accounted for the majority of our revenue (amusements, golf, stadiums, etc.) were under water. Minette felt that out of more than two hundred full- and part-time employees, we could keep twelve people on staff with the funds we had on hand. Twelve! We began to identify who those twelve would be. How do you decide who is essential to help you begin a recovery? Our CFO and controller were essential to keep financial records and to process what payroll we were going to have. The plumber and maintenance director seemed essential to get some buildings into shape so that we had a place to organize the recovery besides our cars. Several of the department heads could assess damage, organize volunteers, and reach out to their contacts for financial help. Our chief development officer could organize our fundraising and outreach efforts. Determining whom we could support and whom we must let go was one of the worst jobs I have ever had. I ended up talking with many employees or their spouses and trying to explain why they did not have a job. Many were inconsolable, others resigned to their fate. I swore I would never lay off anyone again. Minette and I decided to reduce our own salaries in order to save cash.

To get payroll checks to employees who had evacuated, Minette, who was now staying in Baton Rouge, and Rob, who was in Lafayette, met halfway at the Grand Bayou Casino Truck Stop in Grosse Tete. There, they both signed the checks that Don Watson had produced, and Minette took them back to the State Library's offices to mail them to our staff.

A week later, I spoke to a representative of the Azby Fund, a local philanthropic organization with an interest in the Botanical Garden. The fund had previously made a commitment of $1 million toward the expansion of the Conservatory in the garden. We discussed how that pledge could be repurposed considering the disaster. We agreed that some of the commitment would

support ten of the garden staff for several months, with the remainder going to repair the Pavilion of the Two Sisters, which was our primary wedding venue and an essential facility for generating catering revenue. So, with the addition of those ten, we were going to rebuild the park with twenty-two people! Christine, Minette, and I fielded many inquiries from our employees about their last check or when they could get back to work. We had to tell nearly two hundred people that there was no job to come back to.[7]

On September 6, Rob, Christine, Herb Summerall (our Civil Service consultant), and George Parker got to see Stuart Johnson, the head of state parks in Baton Rouge. He offered to have a temporary office set up at the Office of State Parks, which we later moved to the State Library, so we had a place to sit and receive mail since we were out of the city. I tracked down Darrell Hunt, the Friends' lobbyist, and asked him to get with members of our delegation to secure an emergency operating appropriation, since we did not know how long we could keep on even the twenty-two people we had identified.

On Tuesday, September 13, I traveled with John Hopper to Baton Rouge, where we stayed at Minette's sister's house and reunited with DeViney, Casey, Parker, Summerall, and Hunt. The National Guard and other military units had effectively quarantined the city and were only allowing in essential people who had entry passes. After several days of trying, I had managed to have Sen. Mary Landrieu's office send a pass to my son-in-law's office in Dallas, so we could enter the city through the checkpoints.[8]

Armed with an entry pass, on September 14, DeViney, Parker, Hopper, and I made our way from Baton Rouge to the park in my Tahoe. We passed through several checkpoints coming in on Airline Highway, as the interstate was closed. Even though all of us had seen pictures of the devastation on television, we were shocked at the destruction. Trees were down everywhere, and there was almost complete silence, as if the life of the city had been sucked out. Everything was gray or brown. All the major roads entering the park were either blocked by downed trees or barbed wire placed to discourage looters.

We first made our way toward the Botanical Garden on Victory Avenue and were trying to figure out how we could get in to assess the damage. Almost immediately, we heard a helicopter hovering overhead and what sounded like gun turrets rotating. We realized we could be shot as looters. Then, a National Guard jeep came around the corner, and several fully armed Guardsmen demanded to know what we were doing there. Since you generally don't loot a botanical garden, we persuaded them that we were with the park, and they allowed us to get inside. We went to the Pavilion of the Two Sisters, where we saw the remains of the cake from the canceled Sunday wedding more than two weeks before! Pat O'Shaughnessy and his son made their way to the pavilion about a week later, and this is his memory of the condition:

We made our way to the pavilion. We entered from the back. Upon entering the main room, it was an eerie picture. The room was still set up for a wedding, with everything still in place except for a few table linens that had been blown off the tables lying on the floor in puddles of water. Numerous French doors had been blown open, with a couple of the doors broken loose from the doorframes. The floral arrangements were still in place on the buffet tables but had long lost their color. The wedding cake which we stored in the cloakroom was covered [in] mold. My son and I began to load my truck with any equipment we could salvage. We concentrated on small items like chafers, serving trays, and linens.

Pat and his son made several more trips in the following weeks, salvaging more equipment and files.

DeViney, Hopper, Parker, and I made our way over to the Administration Building, which had flooded on the ground floor and been broken into. Mold was everywhere, along with overturned desks, file cabinets, and chairs. We took accounting records and servers out of the building. We made our way to the room on the first floor that held the park's archives, including books that contained the minutes from every City Park Improvement Association board meeting since 1891! The Archives Room had been built to survive a fire but, unfortunately, not a flood. Yet in an incredible stroke of good luck, all the minute books were up on shelves, above the floodwaters. We wanted to get the books out of the building before mold set in, but I did not have enough room in my car to hold them. Just as we were wondering what we were going to do, John Benton, the owner

A National Guard jeep in front of the museum (Photograph by David Grunfeld, courtesy of the *New Orleans Times-Picayune*)

of Bayou Tree Service and a strong supporter of the park, showed up in a large truck. We were able to load the books into his truck, and he kept them at his office for years!

We next went over to the art museum and talked with Sullivan, who gave us Meals Ready to Eat. The basement had taken on about four inches of water. There were 42,000 works of art stored there, but as they were on elevated steel racks, they were not damaged.

After our delicious lunch (which really was good, considering there was nowhere else

The National Guard camp at City Park (Photograph by David Grunfeld, courtesy of the *New Orleans Times-Picayune*)

to get food), we made our way up Wisner, weaving left and right to avoid fallen trees and high water, to Robert E. Lee Boulevard (now Allen Toussaint Boulevard) and then to my house in the Lake Vista subdivision. We carefully drove up an adjacent street, parked, and then hiked to my house, since the entrance to my street was flooded. I was relieved to find that only a third of the house was flooded, with a huge tree down in my front yard that had just missed my roof. We cleaned a few things out of the flooded den,

Mold in the Administration Building, two weeks after the hurricane

then traveled down Carrollton to Hopper's house near the zoo.

The trip up to the north end of the park allowed us to really see the extent of the damage. Most of the interior of the park was flooded, and Wisner still had patches of water on the roadway so, in some parts, you could not tell where Bayou St. John began. The worst flooding was at the northern end, where it reached eight feet high. As you went south, the water was about three feet high at the Botanical Garden, with little flooding

Damage to a maintenance building

from Dreyfous to City Park Avenue. Overall, around 90 percent of the park flooded to some degree. Because the Army Corps of Engineers was unable to close the breaches in the canal walls for almost a week and needed an even longer time to pump out the city, most of the buildings and grounds sat in brackish water for up to a month. This obviously compounded the damage, since no remediation work could begin until the water was gone. Flooding in Tad Gormley Stadium reached the crossbars of the goalposts, and all the amusement rides were damaged or destroyed. The same was true of every park building. We also saw that all the equipment was under water or extensively damaged, including tractors, lawnmowers, bucket trucks, golf carts, vehicles, and bush hogs. In addition to the buildings and equipment loss, brackish water from Lake Pontchartrain had turned the park brown and killed all the grass and vegetation. We later assessed that 1,000 trees were killed outright, and at least 1,000 more died from the water within six months.

Lawnmowers were extensively damaged

This flooded bucket truck shows a water line

On our way in from Baton Rouge, John had asked if we could stop at a convenience store that was open on Airline Highway. He went in and returned with ten gallons of water. The rest of us thought that odd because we were planning to drive back to Baton Rouge the same day, but then there were a lot of odd things going on, so we chalked it up to being prepared.

On the way to Hopper's house, we passed the zoo, which had become an army campground and was not flooded because it was near the river on high ground. When we got to

Botanical Garden following the flooding (Photograph by David Grunfeld, courtesy of the *New Orleans Times-Picayune*)

Hopper's house, he took the water bottles and went inside. Later, we discovered that he got the water for his houseplants! After he was through with his watering, he wanted to check on his sister's house close by. We got there, and while he went into the house, the rest of us got out of the car and decided to take a short walk to observe the damage. Rob and I went in one direction and George in another. A few minutes later, we saw George

Tad Gormley Stadium after Hurricane Katrina (Photograph by David Grunfeld, courtesy of the *New Orleans Times-Picayune*)

rushing back up the street, waving for us to get into the car. A few minutes after that came heavily armed National Guard troops, who told us to leave immediately, which we did and drove back to Baton Rouge. Everyone returned to their evacuation location.

On Friday September 16, we went in search of the Federal Emergency Management Agency (FEMA). We went to the Governor's Office of Homeland Security and Emergency Preparedness in Baton Rouge and were told that FEMA had moved to an old Godchaux department store on Main Street. When we arrived, we stood outside like a group

The golf clubhouse following the flood (Photograph by David Grunfeld, courtesy of the *New Orleans Times-Picayune*)

of homeless people. No one would admit us without an appointment, and of course, we had no appointment because we knew no one at FEMA. That's why we were there, to see someone! Finally, we stopped a young man with a FEMA badge coming out of the building. Bruce Lelong was a structural engineer with the URS Corporation, which had been retained to conduct damage surveys. He got us into the building, where we made our first FEMA contact, Bob Grieve, who we believed oversaw public infrastructure repair. We talked with him about making the park a priority in cleanup operations. He told us we would have to fend for ourselves for a while because of the extent of the devastation but did say that emergency cleanup was a Category A activity, which would be 100 percent reimbursable. So, we could spend our own funds and then be reimbursed. However, we had no money to front this activity. He told us to stay in touch, which was also a problem because of the limited cell service available. John Benton called to see how we were doing, and I asked him if he could clear downed trees off of Victory and Dreyfous streets in the park at least to a point where we could get to the garden. We would have to pay him later.

On Monday, September 19, my wife and I left our daughter's house in Dallas and made our way to Jane and Walter Brooks' house in Jefferson Parish, a suburb of New Orleans. Their house had taken on about nine inches of water, but they were able to tear out the damaged sheetrock, and we stayed with them until the middle of October while I worked on our house and the park. Pat's school had informed all the teachers that they had to be back and teaching by October or they would lose their job. So we appreciated being able to stay with Walter and Jane, particularly since our house had no power and, typical of the aftermath of most hurricanes, it was godawful hot.

By the middle of September, Don Watson, who had evacuated to Houston, returned to his Kenner home to inspect it for damage. He then made his way to our temporary office at the State Library and, with the help of some information specialists at the Department of Culture, Recreation and Tourism, managed to process the payroll with the accounting server we had rescued from our building and a backup tape he had taken with him when he evacuated. He stayed in Baton Rouge for about a week and then traveled back to Houston, where his wife was staying, only to learn that Hurricane Rita was taking aim at Houston. So, they returned to Kenner and commuted back and forth to Baton Rouge for several weeks.

Everyone was affected differently. Minette Bruce had sold her house just weeks before the hurricane. Rob DeViney's house had four and a half feet of water. Paul Soniat, who had a house uptown, had some roof damage but no flooding. Pat O'Shaughnessy's house north of the lake had no damage. I eventually tore off the flooded part of my house, which we never rebuilt. Each time we ventured back into the park, it was surreal: complete darkness, no sounds, everything brown and broken.

By the end of September, the reality of the most extensive damage ever done to a major urban park was sinking in. Every building in the park had been damaged or destroyed. All our equipment was gone. We had no supplies or even the smallest hand tools. We had no money and only a handful of employees to recover 1,300 acres. The city was in ruins, and the state, particularly after Hurricane Rita had struck the western portion of Louisiana, seemed in no position to help. I remember thinking it would be twenty-five years before we could recover.

CHAPTER 6

Digging In

It's not what happens to you, but how you react to it that matters.
—Epictetus

In the middle of October, Pat and I were still at the Brookses' house. Every day Pat would go to school, and I would go work in the park and then, on weekends, work on our home. (One really bad decision we had made was to fill up our refrigerator before evacuating, thinking we would only be gone a couple of days. When I was able to spend time at the house, I had to haul out our refrigerator, which contained rotting food and was the worst smell I had ever experienced. A neighbor who helped me drag it out told me he would never do it again!)

One Saturday, I was cutting up the large tree limb that had fallen on the lane side of the house when I saw a lone man walking down the path in my direction. Few neighbors were back, so I was pretty much on my own, but I had a chainsaw in hand for protection! It turns out the man was from the electric company, and he was walking the lanes with electric meters hanging from his belt. He stopped by the tree and asked if I would like my electricity restored. I thought it was a sign from God! This was a time when the city

was requiring that a licensed electrician sign off on restoring power to individual homes, and who knew how long that would take? I said yes immediately, he installed the meter, and the lights and then the air conditioner came on. I returned to the Brookses' house and told my wife that we had power and air conditioning. We thankfully said goodbye to Walter and Jane and went home! (Of course, the air conditioner only lasted a couple of months, and we had no hot water as the water heater was damaged, but nevertheless, we were home.)[1]

Pat and I decided to celebrate the return to our house by trying to find someplace where we could buy food, even if it was just takeout. New Orleans was out of the question, since nothing was open. We went to neighboring Jefferson Parish and drove down Clearview Parkway, looking for any signs of an open restaurant. We finally found a fast-food chicken establishment and joined a line of cars for the drive-up window. When we got to the window, we saw a sign that said: *We have a box that has two pieces of chicken and a biscuit.* Frankly, we were thrilled to find anything open, but when we got to the window, Pat decided that she might like some other side orders. So, I said, "We will take two boxes of the chicken and a side of baked beans and another side of coleslaw." There was a moment of silence, and then a voice said, "We have a box of chicken with two pieces and a biscuit." I said that I understood that, but we would also like two side orders. Again, silence, until the voice in the box came on and said in the loudest tone possible: "WE HAVE A BOX OF CHICKEN WITH TWO PIECES AND A BISCUIT. PERIOD!" We got the message and took our two boxes of chicken, grateful that we were able to score any food, and went back to our dark neighborhood!

With our few park employees, we set up our administrative office in the Tennis Center on Victory across from the garden and Storyland. Minette and Don established our fiscal operations and salvaged some furniture from the second floor of the Administration Building. Our police chief, Billy Bayle, had taken the police jeep with him to the parking lot of his apartment complex, and it was the only park vehicle to survive the flooding. The positive-voltage cable from the battery had eroded off, but Don and Billy were able to reattach the cable using a hose clamp. Don told Billy that if the engine caught on fire from the repair, he should jump out of the jeep immediately!

We cleaned out the Garden Study Center building in the Botanical Garden and used that as our base of field operations. We scrounged all the tools that we could find, or that were donated to us, and kept them in the Study Center. O'Shaughnessy and Val Taylor frequently grilled a hot lunch to serve employees and volunteers who were cleaning up the garden and other parts of the park. Minette and Don tried to contact vendors to cancel contracts and ask them to get their equipment. Mike Mariani repaired a few pieces of lawn-cutting equipment, and all staff began to rotate on the machines. This was easier in the early days, as most of the grass was dead and not yet recovering.

Pat operated our sales office out of his house for a few months, as the park had virtually no ability to communicate with anyone. None of the cellphones and computers were functioning. Most of his communications were with families who had planned events in the park. As he described it, "I had the unenviable task of contacting all of the upcoming brides to either cancel their weddings or try to convince them that we were going to reopen and it was safe to continue the planning process for their wedding at the park. I do have to say that once we got past the initial tears, the majority of the brides were very understanding. One thing that I would do differently is not to give every bride my home number." As we had little money, Pat had to also try to make brides understand why they could not get a refund check immediately.

In late October or early November, George

The former Wisner tennis court became part of our temporary offices for five years

WISNER TENNIS CENTER
N.O. CITY PARK
IMPROVEMENT ASSN.
INCORPORATED 1891

Parker secured an office trailer for us, and it was installed on the east side of the Tennis Center. Our plumber connected the facilities with a pipe that ran across the front of the building. George, Hopper, Pat O'Shaughnessy, and his assistant, April Laughlin, were in the trailer while Minette, Rob, Don, and eventually Julie LaCour, Denise Joubert, Cathy Hoffman, and David Carpenter were housed in the Tennis Center. Eventually, another trailer was placed on the west side of the center, where the actual tennis staff were housed. The garden staff were working in the garden while the Azby Fund renovated their administrative offices.

In late October, I attended a meeting of the Bring New Orleans Back Commission—Land Use Sub-Committee. This group was formed to study how the storm altered land uses and to develop recommendations on how to reshape the future. Larry Schmidt with the Trust for Public Land and Walter Brooks,

Trailers served as temporary offices

head of the Regional Planning Commission, chaired the committee. After the meeting, I drove with Pat to Dallas to pick up our dogs, which we had left with my daughter when we returned to New Orleans. In Dallas, I got a call from someone who said that he was from the General Services Administration and that he would be negotiating with me to place trailer housing in the park!

In November, through some heroic work by Minette Bruce to pull together a variety of documents, we submitted a Community Disaster Loan application. We were later told we did not fit the eligibility criteria. (Fifteen years later, the question of eligibility came up again when the park applied for a disaster loan related to the COVID-19 pandemic!)

Weird and Poignant Moments

We have come to discover that in the wake of a major disaster, weird things happen. Things that would never occur in normal times seem

The cleanup effort included the removal of thousands of trees killed outright by the storm or later by standing water (Photograph by David Grunfeld, courtesy of the *New Orleans Times-Picayune*)

almost routine. Here are a few of those strange and sometimes poignant happenings.

In November, I believe, Chief Bayle came to me and told me that a group of Apache Indians had arrived and set up shop on Scout Island, teepees and all. They had arrived in the middle of the night in a rainstorm. They had been recruited by a contractor to come to New Orleans and provide labor for the cleanup effort, but when they arrived, the contractor was nowhere to be found. Someone directed them to us. We told them we had no facilities and urged them to seek assistance from some other agency, but they told us they were staying. Other contractors had begun illegally camping in the park, and we had no means to evict anyone. In early December, the ACLU visited us at the Tennis Center and told us we had to provide decent sanitary facilities, electricity, showers, and recreation amenities for the Apaches. We politely explained that we had no showers or decent facilities and certainly no recreation facilities for anyone, especially people occupying the park temporarily. They threatened to sue. We said fine, go ahead. About two weeks later, when we went to check on the Apaches, they were gone. Apparently, a medicine man from their tribe had arrived from Arizona and persuaded them to leave!

One day in early October, Tony Biagas, who was in charge of our stadiums, came to me and said large tents, trailers, and equipment were being moved into the parking lot in front of Tad Gormley Stadium. We went to the stadium and encountered Rev. Jerry Davis of the Christian World Embassy, who informed us he was setting up a relief station at Gormley. I told him we did not give permission for this operation, and he replied that he went to the City Council and they authorized it. He, of course, could not have known that the City Council had no jurisdiction over the park, so he thought he had permission and set up his relief operation. And quite an operation it was. Large tents held kitchens and tables where food was distributed, and semi-trucks arrived every few days with supplies. He obviously was providing a needed service, so we agreed on some "rules of the road" for his operation. He stayed until early 2006. According to Reverend Davis, the Tad Gormley operation fielded some 17,000 volunteers, served 500,000 meals, brought in 700 semis with supplies, and eventually distributed $75 million worth of goods and services.

Pat O'Shaughnessy catered more than fifty weddings from a barbecue grill behind the Pavilion of the Two Sisters.

Almost as soon as Katrina's winds and rain subsided, contractors from everywhere began showing up to clean up the city. Since no hotels were open, they came with trailers, RVs, and tents and staked out ground in the park. Before we knew it, we had hundreds of campgrounds. It was the Wild West. There were no lights, so at sunset every day, the few of us still working left while the lights of campfires began to glow throughout the park. At this time, there was no police presence in the park because they were needed elsewhere in the city. So, it was scary. If you got into trouble, the cavalry was not coming to save you—even if we could have communicated with the cavalry!

I got the idea that we should be collecting rent from the temporary housing going on. I instructed Merlin Haydel, our risk manager, to go from tent to tent and RV to RV and ask for $300 in monthly rent to remain in the park. Merlin soon informed me that he needed someone with a weapon to accompany him,

After the storm, contractors cleaning up the debris citywide camped in the park

as most of the settlers thought we had to be kidding. Chief Bayle joined Haydel as they tried to collect rent. The news media interviewed me on national television, asking why I was charging rent from people who were trying to clean up the city. I told them that there were no volunteers in the park—everyone here was being paid to provide cleanup services—so they would have had to pay for housing if they were someplace else. It seemed fair to charge to stay in the park. In fact, almost all the settlers agreed to pay once they understood that the funds were going to help the park. In November, we contracted with a company called Storm Force to help establish rules for what had now become the City Park Campground and with rent collection. By the end of December, Storm Force had collected a little over $53,000 in rent. We estimated that over three hundred pieces of equipment were being stored in the park, so we began charging for that. Storm Force also experimented with providing showers and laundry services, as no one knew how long the contractors would be in the park. Collecting rent was apparently stressful, because Merlin left the park in December. While it is just an estimate, I believe that at one time we had over 500 trailers, tents, and RVs on the grounds. They gradually decreased over time, but in January of 2006, we still had 158 trailers and 40 tents.

As if it wasn't hard enough trying to control hundreds of contractors camping in the park and trying to collect badly needed rent, in February 2006, I was contacted by the Office of State Parks. They told me that because City Park had received monies in the past from the federal Land and Water Conservation Fund, I had to receive approval from the National Park Service for the rental-fee structure we had put in place and turn over a list of the amenities we were providing! Apparently, Baton Rouge did not know there had been a hurricane in New Orleans. I don't believe I ever responded to that request.

In October, a New Orleans Police Department captain showed up and wanted to know if it would be okay to locate the Third District police station in the park, since their facility had been damaged and was not operable. They proposed to set up three or four travel trailers, along with parking for a variety of police vehicles. Since we had virtually no law-enforcement presence in the park, we thought this was a wonderful idea. Marked police cars and uniformed officers coming and going would give people a sense of security. We gave them a place next to our old tennis clubhouse and across from our main playground. One day, when I looked out my office window in the trailer directly across the parking lot from the police compound, I was startled to see the police marching prisoners in handcuffs in single file across the parking area in direct view of children playing on the playground. Later, I came to find out that the police had moved the narcotics squad into the compound, and they would make frequent arrests, holding prisoners in the buildings until they could be transported to a more secure facility. So, far from having a friendly police presence, we were the epicenter of drug arrests in plain view!

Sometime in late November, April Laughlin, who was pulling double duty as a salesperson for our catering operation and a receptionist at our trailer, told me that there was a woman at the front of the trailer who wanted to pay for a birthday party for her daughter. A birthday party! April tried to explain to her that we had no venues for such an event, and the woman began to cry, so April came to get me. I went to the front of the trailer and repeated that we did not have any birthday-party venues that were available or suitable. The woman tearfully told me that her house had been flooded and gutted, and she could not have a birthday party for her little girl in a gutted house, and I had to help her. It was heart wrenching. I told her we would fix up something. Rob DeViney managed to get a pressure washer and clean off the Peristyle and secure some port-o-lets, and that little girl had her birthday party in the park. Tears all around.

In October, we heard that Qatar was considering a major gift to Xavier University. A Saudi Arabia delegation had visited New Orleans during the years before Katrina, and several of the park's supporters thought there could be an opportunity to solicit support from the kingdom. So, in late October, I wrote to the Royal Embassy, conveyed the extent of the damage from the hurricane, and, without a hint of trepidation, asked for $53,475,000 to fully fund the restoration of the park and $10 million for operating revenue! Desperate times called for aggressive action, and I felt there was no sense in requesting a few million from the oil-rich kingdom. We did not hear back from the embassy and naturally assumed they were not interested. Then in June, the Saudi ambassador, His Royal Highness Prince Turki Al-Faisal, and his entourage visited the park. They were interested in our equestrian facility, since the prince was a horse enthusiast. Leslie Kramer of Equest Farm gave them a tour, but unfortunately, nothing more was heard from the Saudis. An interesting side note, however, is that one member of the prince's entourage was Jamal Ahmad Khashoggi, who twelve years later was assassinated by the Saudis as he sought a marriage license in Turkey!

In early 2006, I was contacted by SGI (Soka Gakkai International), a Buddhist group that promotes peace and cultural understanding through personal transformation, who said they wanted to plant some trees in the park. It seemed typical of the kind of interest and donations we were receiving, so I quickly expressed my appreciation of the gift. They said they would come out to Lelong Drive on a Saturday to make the donation. When I arrived on the designated Saturday, I was surprised to find a stage and sound equipment set up and even more surprised when busload after busload of Buddhists began arriving. Other dignitaries also arrived, such as Renée Gill Pratt, the city councilwoman for District B. I was invited to the stage, and gracious remarks were made all around. When I went to the microphone to express my appreciation for their gift, the head of the Buddhist delegation slipped an enormous medal around my neck and pronounced me a member of SGI. The medal was "in honor of your dedicated efforts for Liberty and Peace." I was not sure what I had done to promote liberty and peace, but he told the assembled crowd that with the conveyance of the medal, I had become "one with nature!" All the Buddhists clapped at this very high honor, and I have kept the weighty medal ever since. Whenever I had a disagreement with my staff over some issue, I reminded them that I am "one with nature!"

In 2006, the city told the park they wanted to have a place where they could create a "recovery village," with prototype buildings that could be replicated in various neighborhoods. Why not? The city moved two shotgun-style residential buildings into the park on Harrison Avenue, next to one of our picnic shelters. Apparently, the implementation of the concept was slow and did not fulfill the city's goals. In 2008, we asked the city to remove the structures, as we were renovating the shelter and could open it to the public. They agreed to take out one of the structures and then donated the remaining building to the park, which we utilized as a volunteer headquarters. Today, a shotgun house sits in the middle of City Park!

It was a very strange time indeed!

CHAPTER 7

Silver Handcuffs and
Other Adventures with FEMA

Considering the dire circumstances that we have in New Orleans—virtually a city that has been destroyed— . . . things are going relatively well.
—FEMA Director Michael Brown, September 1, 2005

We had our first post-Katrina City Park Improvement Association board meeting on October 25 in the boardroom of the New Orleans Museum of Art. From there, we could look out on the devastation in the park and plot our recovery strategy. It was wonderful to see everyone and hear about their experiences either evacuating or staying. I met with David Doss of Sen. David Vitter's staff the next day and briefed him on the situation. On Monday, November 7, we had our first face-to-face meeting with Ray Stout, who was the FEMA PAC (public assistance coordinator) assigned to our agency.

How FEMA Operates

Since this was our first disaster, we knew little about how FEMA operates. The first thing we came to understand was that FEMA has relatively few employees. They staff up when a disaster is expected, hiring all sorts of temporary administrators, architects, en-

gineers, recovery specialists and many other professions. Even the temporary employees are replaced after a few months. This constantly revolving door of people you communicate with makes continuity extraordinarily difficult, as the PAC you had yesterday may not be the one you have tomorrow.[1]

We also came to understand that FEMA is guided by the rules and regulations of the Stafford Act, which is America's principal disaster legislation. The Stafford Act divides up different levels of assistance into categories, with different rules for each category. For instance, Category A and B work involves cleanup and actions necessary to mitigate further damage, such as tearing out sheetrock from an area of a building that flooded. Categories C through E specify renovation or new construction, depending on the particular condition of a building.

At the November 7, 2005, "kickoff" meeting, our PAC advised us that in order for the federal government to pay 100 percent of the cost of any Category A or B work, we had two weeks to complete all the mitigation and repair work on 120 park buildings! We thought this was pretty ridiculous. Rob DeViney had quotes from two remediation companies who both bid on a time and material basis, something that is generally not allowed in the federal procurement code. Stout wanted us to get more quotes, which promised to be difficult with limited communication available in the park. A national company called Belfor had submitted the low "bid," and Stout told us to go ahead and award them the work since time was running out. Our staff monitored the work, and basic repairs and remediation were nearly completed by the end of December. Years later, auditors from FEMA questioned awarding the contract based on time and material rates, even after FEMA obligated them for payment. We learned another important lesson about dealing with FEMA: their internal auditors or auditors from their Inspector General's Office will return and question how you awarded work, despite FEMA's project managers signing off on the expenditures.

While FEMA has people on the ground for disaster recovery, they often supplement their staff (because, remember, they have relatively few people) with third-party contractors. We dealt with several, particularly those who worked for James Lee Witt Associates. Witt was a former FEMA director who saw an opening in the market and filled it.

Probably the best thing FEMA ever did for City Park was to recognize early on that there was no way we could ever have cleaned up all the debris across 1,300 acres. Thus, they tasked the U.S. Army Corps of Engineers with the job. The Corps, for its part, preapproves various disaster-recovery firms so that they can select one or more of them to immediately enter the scene and begin cleanup and debris-removal efforts. One day in late September, I was cleaning out the part of my house that had flooded, and a large, jeep-like vehicle came up the street. Two men got out and asked if I was Bob Becker. They were W. T. "Teddy" Phillips, Jr., and Ken Graham with the disaster-recovery company Phillips & Jordan. They told me the Corps had tasked them with cleaning the park, and they wanted to meet me and discuss how they would go about that effort! Truthfully, they did not need much direction from me. Within days they had hundreds of people going from one end of the park to the other picking up limbs, hauling out debris that had floated in, raking up leaves, and cleaning off sidewalks and roads. It was a herculean effort that took about a month and really made our recovery possible.

On November 9, we met with another representative from FEMA, recruited from a Saccharin plant in Alabama, named Tom Dziubakowski. We met upstairs in our tennis building with Rob, Minette, and Alan Heintzen, a board member and our treasurer. Tom was there to outline the rules and procedures for us to eventually file claims for building, equipment, furniture, and supply damage. Early on, we had estimated our total building damage at $43 million. At that time, the cost-sharing provisions of the Stafford Act were still in place, and Tom informed us we would have to come up with $4.3 million in matching funds.[2]

He told us that we had to secure competitive bids for all work in writing. We explained how that would be hard to do, since we had no phone service, no Internet service, no fax machines, and no copy machines. How were we to advertise the work to find contractors for bids? More importantly, how were we supposed to come up with 10 percent of the estimated cost to match the government's 90 percent when we had no money and no revenue?

Then Tom told us that we had to follow the rules or the government would come and put us in "silver handcuffs." Silver handcuffs! Here we were sitting on the second floor of the tennis clubhouse, which had received three feet of water, with a total of twenty-two employees, virtually no money and no equipment, and he was informing us that our government, which was supposed to be here to help us, would put us in handcuffs if we messed up on the rules! It was almost more than we could take. To this day, Rob, Minette, Alan, and I laugh about the meeting. (As late as September 2006, FEMA threatened penalties against the park for what they termed misleading information related to various damage claims. In one instance, they disputed that we had lost hand tools, driving-range mats, and even boats to the rising water, insisting that those items must have been stolen. They even accused us of trying to fund the park's master plan with hurricane relief funding.)

Project Worksheets

Claiming damage under the provisions of the Stafford Act can be a daunting and frustrating process. You cannot just make one claim for overall damage and request a single payment. As previously mentioned, claims for cleanup and mitigation activities comprise separate categories from renovation or new construction activity. For those actions, each building must be identified separately and have an independent claim. You must document when the building was built, what it was made of, and whether it was a historic structure, in addition to estimating its repair or replacement cost. Furnishings in a particular building also have a claim separate from the structure. While you can lump together requests for equipment, you must identify each piece and state when it was purchased, how long it had been in operation, and what it was used for. FEMA requires these details because they only pay for actual eligible damage, not what they refer to as deferred maintenance costs.

The Stafford Act also does not allow all damage to be eligible for funding. Landscaping is not eligible, nor is "decorative planting." Tree removal is only eligible for reimbursement from where the tree broke off from its base but not the stump that is left.

This process can get to the point of ridiculousness. When we went to develop a claim for damages to the irrigation systems on our golf courses, we were required to find every sprinkler head, photograph the head, and document the damage. Of course, most of the sprinkler heads were buried in the ground, having been under floodwater and migrating soil. We had no maps of where all the sprinkler heads were, so we had to bring a previous golf-course superintendent into town to locate and document each head and its damage!

Another golf-damage claim further demonstrates how ridiculous the process can become. In assessing damages to the West and North Golf courses, FEMA decided that mowing and herbicide treatment of the courses, which were recommended in preliminary damage assessments, were ineligible work items because they were "deferred maintenance." Thus, they disallowed over $850,000 in claims, funds we desperately needed to repair and restore the courses. FEMA relied on a report by the United States Golf Association's director of the Mid-Continent Region that "the remnants of the flood are really not the issue on the golf courses from a turf standpoint, but rather simply an overgrown or abandoned condition." Of course, the reason the courses were abandoned and overgrown was because *they were flooded,* and it made normal maintenance impossible! FEMA did not approve any money to replace our grass-cutting equipment until August 2006, and

by then, the courses were overgrown and infested with invasive species. We urged the state in 2008 to appeal this decision, as they were the applicant for the claims, which they did and eventually were successful in having the funds restored.

We also put in a claim for all the plant material in our Botanical Garden, which was initially denied as decorative planting. We had to appeal that decision, arguing that the plants were the essence of the "business" of the Botanical Garden, that there would be no Botanical Garden without the plants, and they were not decorative but integral "living" inventory. We finally prevailed.

We claimed damage to the turf field in Tad Gormley Stadium. The turf had been flooded and died, and we wanted funds to replace it so we could play football on the field again. The claim was denied under the argument that the field was landscaping! We pointed out that football fields are not considered landscaping but are integral to the ability of a sports stadium to fulfill its mission. After much debate, we prevailed on this one as well.

Damage versus deferred maintenance was a frequent sticking point. Let's say you have a building that was built twenty years ago. Let's also say you could not keep the building in perfect shape. Perhaps you hadn't repainted it, or some termite damage had not been addressed, or the roof had been patched rather than replaced. This could constitute deferred maintenance and is not eligible for repair dollars. The trick is to be able to estimate the cost to repair or replace the building and subtract from those funds some percentage for the deferred maintenance that had occurred. Unless the deferred maintenance is extremely obvious (which it was for several of our buildings), it is hard to determine in a building that had wind and water damage what was caused by the event and what existed before. We spent tremendous amounts of time and effort on each building trying to make these determinations.

The same issue applies to equipment. If you have a lawnmower that is destroyed by floodwaters, it's not as though it is worth the same as a new mower. Its value must be depreciated to reflect its actual age or wear. Again, it took countless hours of effort to make these determinations.

The result of this process is hundreds of Project Worksheets (PW) to keep track of every claim. Here is just a small example of how each park claim was catalogued, an estimate of damage was assigned, and the damage was summarized.

East Golf Course Shelter at Tee # 6	$2,315.98	Building Repair
Boat Equipment Storage House	$1,603.43	Repair windows, replace shingles
Wisner Tennis Center	$98,062.36	Mold Remediation/ contents removal
Gormley Stadium	$16,168	Replacement cost for food
Amusements Restroom	$6,181.50	Building Repair

These projects are grouped into categories such as "Category B—Emergency Protective Measures" and "Category E—Buildings and Equipment."

The process is slow and must be reviewed at various levels of the bureaucracy before FEMA will "obligate" the money identified in the PWs as being appropriate. Sometimes FEMA must bring in a variety of professionals who specialize in specific kinds of damage or rebuilding. Is it a historic structure or one of unusual design or constructed of unusual materials? This painstaking process slows the distribution of funds to the needy agency so that rebuilding can begin. City Park alone had more than one hundred PWs, and at the fifteenth anniversary of Hurricane Katrina, the park still had not resolved all of those claims!

In the six months since the hurricane struck in late August, City Park received just $6,500 from FEMA, for damages sustained to inventory at the tennis courts and the Softball Quadruplex!

In 2006, I wrote a letter to the editor of the *Times-Picayune* decrying the unnecessarily slow and tedious process adopted by FEMA. I felt that this was an outstanding example of the "perfect being the enemy of the good"! In an effort to make sure that the government only paid for actual damage and not deferred maintenance or unnecessary supplies and furnishings, they had adopted a process that seriously delayed getting funds to the entities who needed it most to begin the rebuilding process. I suggested that it would be far better to invest in technology, such as aerial photography and drone analysis, which could quickly assess the total damage being applied for and then allocate the funds to the damaged agency. Sure, it is possible that some damage could be overlooked or underestimated, just as it is possible that some damage could be overestimated. But the damaged agency could be offered a choice. Take an overall estimated damage claim immediately and have the funds to begin rebuilding, or decide to go the PW route and potentially get more money but prepare to wait years or even decades for the funds. Taking City Park as an example, if we would have been offered a choice of getting a $30 million lump-sum payment immediately or $35 million over a fifteen-year period, the choice would have been simple, and the rebuilding would have been accomplished much sooner. Although many changes have been made to the Stafford Act since Hurricane Katrina to facilitate a quicker response, the basic PW system has not had substantial changes.

Arbitration and the Inspector General

When the applicant for recovery dollars and FEMA's review personnel cannot agree on all or some of the eligibility of the claim, or more often, the estimated cost of damage repair, the process calls for "arbitration." In February of 2008, a FEMA team of engineers assessed damage to the park's roadways, walkways, and curbs. They determined that much of the damage the park reported was not disaster related, making it ineligible for Public Assistance funding.

The park and the state did not agree with the assessment, and follow-up inspections were conducted in March. FEMA then determined that the total eligible claim was $181,805. We urged the state (who was the actual applicant for these funds) to appeal this assessment and claim a total of $2,396,574 in eligible damages. The appeal was denied, and a second appeal was made in October. The park and state's claim was supported by an engineer's opinion that heavy traffic from debris-removal operations over roadways weakened by flooding had accelerated deterioration of the roads, making them eligible for funding. FEMA agreed to put the claim to arbitration for a total of $2,200,000.

In November of 2009, we were still not approved for funding when a FEMA geotechnical specialist reviewed soils and geologic data for City Park and concluded that the park had a history of flooding and soil subsidence that would have adversely impacted local pavement prior to the disaster and made it vulnerable to extensive damage by heavy equipment operations. After considering all the information, the Arbitration Panel concluded that $1,911,855 of the claim was eligible for Public Assistance funding, a decision the park and the state agreed to. The funding went from $181,805 to $1,911,855 because the park urged that the original determination be appealed and, when those appeals were lost, that it be moved to arbitration. Rob DeViney pursued this appeal with dogged determination and is largely responsible for securing an additional $1.7 million in federal funds for the repairs.

In May of 2010, the Department of Homeland Security's Office of Inspector General (OIG) audited forty-six park PWs totaling $18.3 million. They determined that $226,034 in federal funds were spent in violation of federal regulations and de-obligated the amount (meaning, they wanted the money back). The OIG found that these funds paid for a "cost plus a percentage of costs" contract generally prohibited by federal law. This project was the remediation contract signed with Belfor in the days immediately following the disaster in 2005. While FEMA agreed with the OIG, DeViney argued that our project officer in those early days agreed that the contract could be awarded based on similar approvals of work at Tulane University and other places.

The magnitude of the disaster, the inability to secure normal contract prices, and the urgency to protect buildings from mold and other deterioration were the determining factors.

Once again, we were forced into requesting an arbitration proceeding to resolve the finding, and once again, the park's position was upheld. The Civilian Board of Contract Appeals overruled the decision to claw back the $226,034 in May of 2011, almost six years after the hurricane.

In 2020, we were still pursuing resolution of disaster claims—fifteen years after Hurricane Katrina decimated the park! Other hurricane-designated disasters that impacted City Park have come and gone, and a new disaster in the COVID-19 virus struck, and the park is still dealing with Katrina claims. If there was ever clear evidence of the ridiculous nature of the FEMA damage-claim process, our experience was it. And I am sure we were not alone.

CHAPTER 8

The Travel Trailer Fiasco, Fall 2005

In any moment of decision, the best thing you can do is the right thing, the next best thing is the wrong thing, and the worst thing you can do is nothing.
—Theodore Roosevelt

Approximately 228,000 homes and apartments in New Orleans were flooded by Hurricane Katrina; 39 percent of all owner-occupied units and 56 percent of all renter-occupied units received some degree of water damage.[1] Hundreds of thousands of residents were displaced throughout the country, unable to return until they had a place to live. Almost immediately following the storm, Gov. Kathleen Blanco and Mayor Ray Nagin called for temporary travel trailers to provide emergency housing.

We understood that the federal government would lease sites for temporary housing, and since we knew we would run out of money to pay even our small staff in a few months, we made it known that the park was available. In this way, we thought we would be contributing to the recovery by providing people with a temporary place to live, and we could earn some desperately needed money.

Carlos Cashio, one of our consultants on the master plan, contacted me and said he had partnered with the Shaw Group and John Williams, a local architect, to identify potential sites and do designs for these trailer locations. The Shaw Group was a large construction company based in Baton Rouge and was working on a variety of site locations under contract with FEMA. We met in Baton Rouge on September 9 and identified potential sites in City Park.

In early October, the National Park Service reviewed trailer sites in New Orleans for compliance with the Historic Preservation Act and the Land and Water Conservation Fund Act. They said they would not take a hardline position in reviewing potential sites. They later retracted this position, but in the beginning, it seemed as though federal agencies would do everything possible to approve sites throughout the city.

In the middle of October, I attended two meetings on housing at the Emergency Operations Center in the Hyatt Regency Hotel. Basically, these meetings described how bad the situation was. Almost immediately, a scramble began to identify potential sites for the travel trailers.

On October 15, the Shaw Group submitted a proposal to FEMA for 1,840 units on 230 total acres of park land. Three days later, Minette and I attended a meeting on a boat at the riverfront of the French Quarter. When we were invited, we did not know the purpose of the meeting. We arrived to find government officials all around and a representative of Habitat for Humanity who announced that they intended to build a subdivision in the park. When the emergency was over, they planned to relocate the units throughout the city. They did not ask for permission—just announced it as though it were a fait accompli! This was just another example of the confusion that reigned supreme when different arms of the government were trying to implement reconstruction or mitigation actions, often ignorant about what others were doing. The Shaw Group and Carlos Cashio had no idea what Habitat for Humanity was talking about.

On October 27, I received a call from someone who said he was from the General Services Administration (GSA) and would be contacting me about sites for housing temporary trailers in the park. At the end of the month, Mayor Nagin issued an executive order suspending the Comprehensive Zoning Ordinance to allow for the placement of travel trailers throughout the city.

The Sites

In conjunction with the Shaw Group and Cashio Cochran LLC, we developed plans for three travel trailer sites. (A fourth site on the North Golf Course was also discussed, but we were told elected officials went to the governor to get any mention of that site deleted. They apparently felt that it was too close to the Lake Vista neighborhood, an upscale subdivision at the northern end of the park.) The plans were for considerably fewer trailers than the Shaw Group had originally proposed.

- One site was on ten acres in the location identified in the master plan as the area for our relocated tennis complex, on Marconi between Harrison and Zachary Taylor. It was currently vacant and seemed to be an ideal location. The design called for 184 travel trailer sites (12 with ADA accessibility) as well as places for such things as laundries, security and administrative trailers, maintenance facilities, guard shacks, and dumpsters. The design also proposed a roadway system with a single entrance and exit for security purposes.
- A second site was located just north of Zachary Taylor on approximately fifteen acres of land, which at the time was part of the destroyed East Golf Course. This site would have held 221 travel trailers. The plan called for using the old South Golf Course clubhouse, which is adjacent to Pan American Stadium, as a

laundry, security, and administration building. This design also included a single entry and exit on Zachary Taylor near the old clubhouse.

- The third site was located on approximately fifty acres of land north of Friedrichs Avenue on what is now the park's Festival Grounds and, at the time, was the recently retired South Golf Course. The plan contained three individual pods—200 travel trailer sites in Pod A, 248 in Pod B, and 142 in Pod C, for a total of 590. Each pod included laundry, mail, and dumpster sites, with security and maintenance buildings at an entrance off Henry Thomas Drive.

A grand total of just under a thousand units were proposed, on less than 10 percent of the park's land.

The Process Collapses

Initially, we were told that all the sites were designated exclusively for first responders and other emergency personnel necessary for the recovery. However, in early November, FEMA said it could only pay public entities for trailer locations if they were open to all displaced residents. We were not concerned about who resided on the land if the trailers were temporary and would be removed at the government's expense once the need

had ended. However, not everyone in the surrounding neighborhoods was happy that individuals residing in the park would not be emergency personnel or teachers but anyone from any neighborhood.

We learned an important lesson. At the beginning of the disaster, people did not care about such issues as who would be living in trailer sites because they were displaced or too busy fixing their own houses or businesses. However, as soon as three months after the storm, people began to be concerned about who would be living near them, even if it was temporary and even if it was in the park.

The GSA contacted me in early November to begin discussing financial terms for renting the park's land. These conversations continued for several months as the proposal wound its way through the federal bureaucracy. In early December, Mayor Nagin approved 1,300 units for the park, although we had developed plans for 1,000.

Between December of 2005 and March of 2006, residents surrounding the park began to oppose locating nonexclusive trailers in the park. In a bizarre move, the National Cancer Coalition objected to all travel trailers in the park. In January, the National Park Service caved to pressure and revised its October position, concluding that it could not waive its temporary-use policy. This meant it would not approve temporary use of park land for the trailers.

Of course, even in a national disaster, some rules and regulations could not be relaxed,

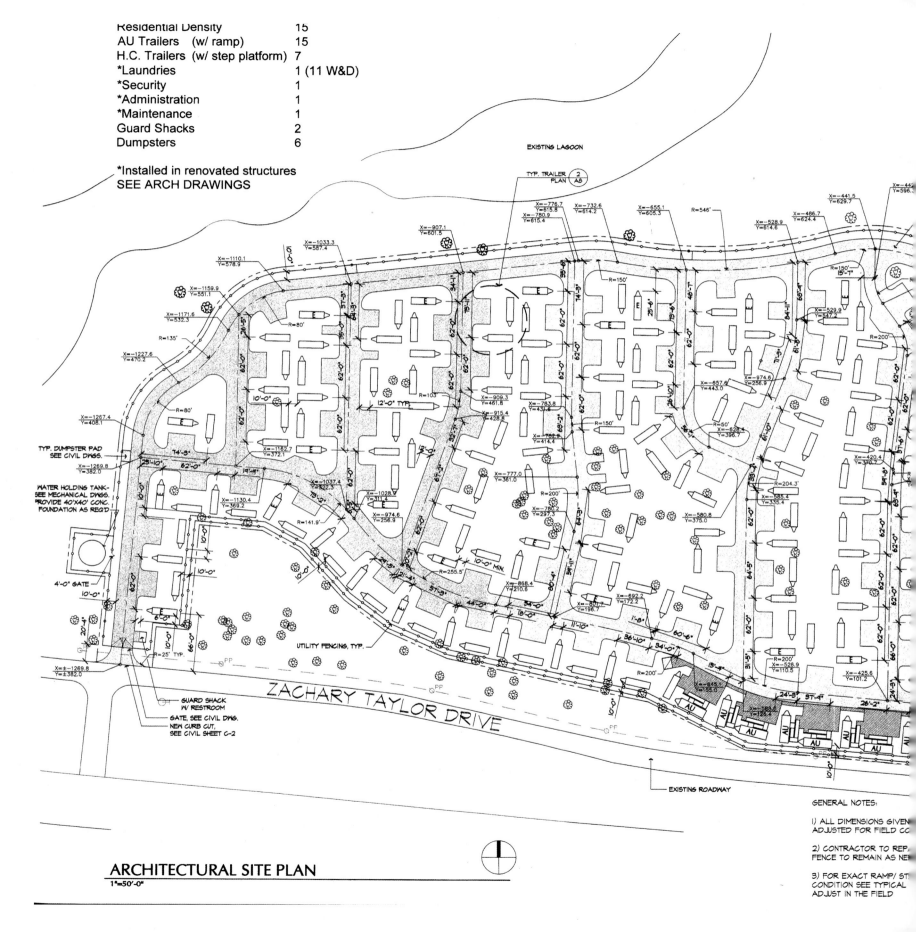

Residential Density 15
AU Trailers (w/ ramp) 15
H.C. Trailers (w/ step platform) 7
*Laundries 1 (11 W&D)
*Security 1
*Administration 1
*Maintenance 1
Guard Shacks 2
Dumpsters 6

*Installed in renovated structures
SEE ARCH DRAWINGS

EXISTING LAGOON

TYP. TRAILER 2
PLAN A8

TYP. DUMPSTER PAD
SEE CIVIL DWGS.

WATER HOLDING TANK-
SEE MECHANICAL DWGS.
PROVIDE 40'X40' CONC.
FOUNDATION AS REQ'D

4'-0" GATE

GUARD SHACK
W/ RESTROOM
GATE, SEE CIVIL DWG.
NEW CURB CUT,
SEE CIVIL SHEET C-2

UTILITY FENCING, TYP.

ZACHARY TAYLOR DRIVE

EXISTING ROADWAY

ARCHITECTURAL SITE PLAN
1"=50'-0"

GENERAL NOTES:

1) ALL DIMENSIONS GIVEN
ADJUSTED FOR FIELD CO

2) CONTRACTOR TO REP/
FENCE TO REMAIN AS NE

3) FOR EXACT RAMP/ ST
CONDITION SEE TYPICAL
ADJUST IN THE FIELD

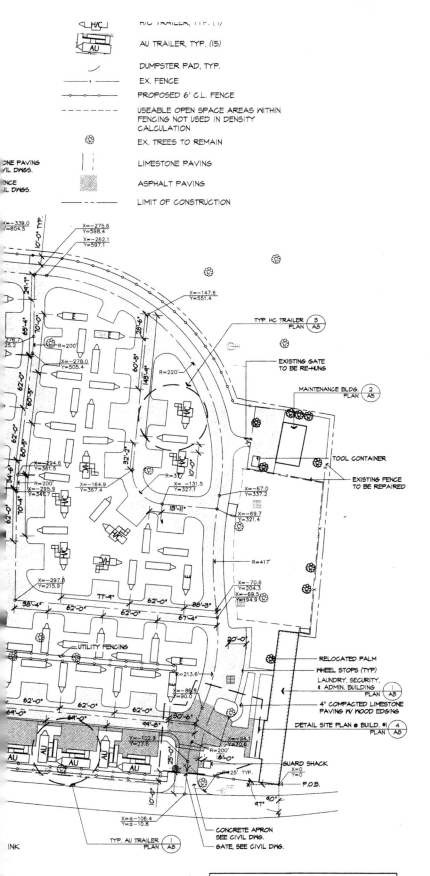

Legend

H/C	H/C TRAILER, TYP. (7)
AU	AU TRAILER, TYP. (15)
	DUMPSTER PAD, TYP.
—x—	EX. FENCE
—o—o—	PROPOSED 6' C.L. FENCE
– – –	USEABLE OPEN SPACE AREAS WITHIN FENCING NOT USED IN DENSITY CALCULATION
	EX. TREES TO REMAIN
	LIMESTONE PAVING
	ASPHALT PAVING
———	LIMIT OF CONSTRUCTION

ONE PAVING
/IL DWGS.

ENCE
IL DWGS.

TYP. HC TRAILER 3 PLAN A8

EXISTING GATE TO BE RE-HUNG

MAINTENANCE BLDG. 2 PLAN A5

TOOL CONTAINER

EXISTING FENCE TO BE REPAIRED

RELOCATED PALM

WHEEL STOPS (TYP)

LAUNDRY, SECURITY, & ADMIN. BUILDING 1 PLAN A5

4" COMPACTED LIMESTONE PAVING W/ WOOD EDGING

DETAIL SITE PLAN @ BUILD. #1 4 PLAN A8

GUARD SHACK

P.O.B.

CONCRETE APRON SEE CIVIL DWGS.

GATE, SEE CIVIL DWGS.

TYP. AU TRAILER 1 PLAN A8

UTILITY FENCING

INK

Plan for the Zachary Taylor site, containing 221 trailers, security, laundry, and administration buildings

100% SUBMISSION

SITE MAP

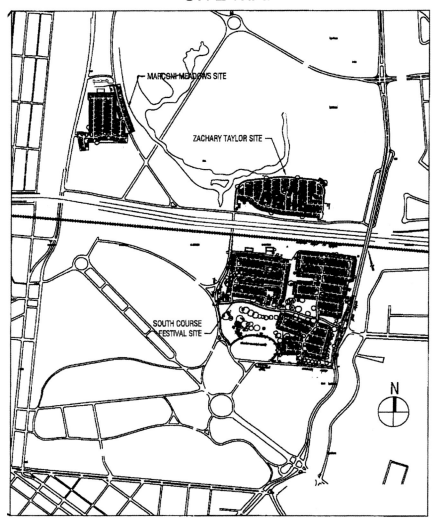

South Festival Park site, including the area south of I-610 and north of Friedrichs

The Festival Park site included space for nearly six hundred travel trailers. At the end of September 2005, FEMA proposed to lease a total of 250 acres of land from the park in order to accommodate approximately two thousand travel trailers. That number was later reduced to approximately one thousand units.

even for a use that was temporary. In February 2006, FEMA prepared their Environmental Impact Assessment on the sites and advertised for public comment. The evaluation included soil sampling by the Environmental Protection Agency (EPA), archaeological examination of the sites, research into endangered species living in the area, and the comments of Native American tribes. Five months had passed since the park was approached about providing land, and this was supposed to be a process to provide temporary emergency housing! We completed our negotiations with the GSA in the middle of February and submitted a signed lease for their signature. The lease would have paid the park $2,679,250 annually for the trailer sites. Those funds would have been hugely helpful in our recovery, but GSA never signed the lease.

In late March, the National Park Service concluded it couldn't approve temporary uses on land that had received grants from the Land and Water Conservation Fund for more than six months. The park had received several grants in previous years. The temporary uses would require new legislation and a separate Environmental Impact Assessment.

Finally, on April 5, 2006, Mayor Nagin, reacting to growing opposition to temporary housing sites throughout the city, signed another executive order suspending his previous one approving travel trailer sites in New Orleans. On April 26, 2006, after seven months of effort, City Park withdrew its offer to the GSA to lease land for the recovery.

The travel trailer saga is one of the more unhappy episodes in the park's attempt to recover from Katrina. The longer the process dragged on, the original reason for proposing sites in City Park, which was to temporarily house displaced citizens, became secondary to people's concerns about who would be living in the park. The confusion was compounded by the changing positions of a variety of federal agencies, including FEMA, the National Park Service, the EPA), and the GSA. One can only hope that if a tragedy of the magnitude of Katrina ever happens again, a much more expedited process will be in place to allow citizens to return to their city.

CHAPTER 9

Getting Organized

Dealing with travel trailers, Apache Indians, well-meaning but overwhelmed public officials, and contractor squatters took up an enormous amount of time but were not contributing to our long-term recovery. We needed to get organized around a series of actions that, when taken together, would form the path forward. After discussing ideas with my team, we developed a four-point plan.

- Clean up the park
- Open existing revenue-generating facilities
- Embark on an aggressive fundraising effort
- Utilize the recently adopted City Park master plan as a blueprint for recovery

Cleaning Up the Park

With few staff and virtually no equipment, we knew it was impossible for our team to clean up all the fallen trees, dead plants, destroyed and abandoned equipment, and debris that floated in and damaged buildings. As previously mentioned, one of the best actions FEMA took on our behalf was to task the Corps of Engineers with cleaning the park. The Corps, in turn, brought in debris-removal contractors. Considering there were more than one thousand trees down, it was a massive effort. (Since FEMA would not pay for stump removal, that part of the cleanup had to wait.)

After the basic cleanup, we could turn our attention to keeping the park clean. That effort was made somewhat easier by the fact that the floodwaters had killed most of the grass, so we could make it through the fall and winter before real grass cutting was necessary. Volunteers greatly aided our efforts to maintain the park. Residents from the surrounding neighborhoods and groups that came to the city to help in the recovery volunteered to clean flowerbeds, remove trash from drains, paint buildings, and cut grass.

A group of neighbors organized by a sixteen-year-old from the Bayou St. John neighborhood came into the park every weekend to clean and cut grass at the Lelong entrance. They called themselves the Mow-Rons, and they maintained the front of the park for months using their own equipment and fundraising to buy additional mowers, using the catchy slogan, "Weeding by example."

With donations from the Selley Foundation, we were able to purchase more grounds equipment, including mowers and attachments to a couple of our tractors that we repaired. Because we had so few people, we all took turns riding mowers and taking care of particular sections of the park. Many of us found great solace and calmness in riding the mowers, as we could see real results, and it took our minds off our troubles for a short period of time.

Because the park has so many facilities, it was tempting to try to work on many of them at once. But that was not a strategy for success, so we started in our Botanical Garden thinking that if we got that in shape, we could work our way outward. The Azby Fund, as previously discussed, provided funding to repair the Pavilion of the Two Sisters and the garden administration building. Reopening the pavilion was crucial to our strategy because, as the park's main reception facility, it could generate much-needed revenue from weddings and other events. The National Guard, volunteers, and our staff began work on the garden itself. Since most of the plant material and electrical and irrigation systems were destroyed, recovering the garden was a huge undertaking. Guardsmen removed old plants and brought in new soil. We repaired the electrical system and then the irrigation system. Once the garden was presentable, Pat O'Shaughnessy and his meager staff were able to cater weddings early in 2006, despite having only a small warming kitchen and barbecue grill to prepare food. In 2006, the garden staff opened a retail garden-supply operation to provide plants and soil to surrounding residents and to raise funds for the garden. After several months, we discovered why garden-supply businesses are generally run by large organizations, and we abandoned that effort!

In the days immediately after the storm, some residents strung ropes across a couple of tennis courts that had their nets blown away and began to play some form of tennis. We cleaned up a few of the courts and secured some netting, and spotty play resumed with tennis players thrilled to have someplace to pursue their favorite sport.

Opening Revenue-Generating Facilities

When Hurricane Katrina struck, the park had about $600,000 in the Louisiana Asset Management Pool (a kind of government savings bank) and $500,000 in operating cash. Although we had only twenty-two employees, there was tremendous demand on our funds, including many requests for us to pay back rental deposits that had been made for weddings and birthday parties. We had no idea if the state would be able to come to our aid, as the southern half of Louisiana's economy had been obliterated by Hurricanes Katrina and Rita. We needed to find ways to begin to generate our own revenue.

With the garden and pavilion in the process of being repaired, we felt that it might be possible to hold some version of Celebration in the Oaks—the park's popular Christmas light show. That event, begun by Paul Soniat and Beau Bassich in the late 1980s, was a major profit center for the park and had become one of the most attended holiday events in the state. It is held in the Amusement Park and Botanical Garden. Fortunately, some of our exhibits and displays had been stored in our warehouse and escaped major damage. Now that electricity was being restored in the garden, staging an light show was possible. What to do about an amusement park whose rides were all damaged and not close to being repaired? We decided to bring in some rented rides, put them on Victory Avenue, and surround them with a fence. Every one of our staff worked the event, from taking tickets to keeping the lights on to picking up trash. We managed to open for nineteen days (usually the event runs for more than a month) over Christmas in 2005. It was one of the first events to be held in an otherwise dark city, and it was wonderful for our staff to see the happy looks on children and adults alike as they had an opportunity to forget their

problems and enjoy the season. On a bitterly cold opening night, we hosted more than five thousand people starved for their city and City Park. People hugged each other and asked, "How did you make out?" or "Where are you living now?" City Park had the only lights for miles in all directions and glowed like a beacon in the night. We generated over a quarter of a million dollars in revenue, which helped propel us into 2006.

As we tried to figure out how else we could generate revenue to keep going, we looked to our golf driving range. The range on Filmore was a cash cow before the storm. It was one of only a few driving ranges in the region and could accommodate more than fifty golfers trying to improve their game. It was now in ruins. The building that supported the range by selling the balls, golf gloves, and hats took on eight feet of water. Most of the mats from which the balls were hit floated away, as had the baskets that held the practice balls. Of course, the machine that picked up the balls was under water as well. In addition, the company that had run our golf complex under contract, KemperSports, had left never to return, so there was no golf staff. Rob DeViney and I went out to the range and tried to figure out how to get it operating.

First, we had to collect golf balls, which we did by having our staff walk the range and pick balls out of the dirt and mud. Then we went in search of our mats and baskets, which had floated all over the northern part of the park and even across the bayou. The building had

The restored Botanical Garden

no electricity but did have water, so we cleaned off the mats, baskets, and balls we had collected. We scrounged up an eight-by-ten tent and put it beside the building. We had no golf clubs, but we figured people who wanted to play could bring their own. We decided we would charge a flat ten dollars for either a big or little bucket of balls. We put the sign out in front of the tent and waited.

Literally within minutes, cars pulled up with people asking if the range was open. When we said it was, they asked if we had clubs, and when we said no, they said they would go home and get their own. People started showing up, paying their ten dollars, and hitting golf balls. Frankly, we thought we were brilliant managers who had taken this ruined facility and turned it into a moneymaking operation! However, it was not long before we began to run out of golf balls with no machine to pick them up. Finally, in desperation, we ran out onto the open range and called for the current crop of golfers to stop hitting balls. We then told them that we had no way to pick up the golf balls they had just hit, and for others to enjoy the facility, we needed them to stop, walk out onto the range, and pick up balls! We did not know what to expect, but with hardly a complaint, they walked out and began picking up golf balls so the next group of users could enjoy the experience.

We were slowly able to bring the facility back to a semblance of operation. Our maintenance director fixed the ball-retrieving machine, and we ordered a trailer that took the place of the building while it was under repair. By February of 2006, the driving range had reopened for good.

Storyland was repaired and opened in March. By September, we also opened Tad Gormley Stadium on a very limited basis.

While, through herculean efforts, we were able to open some of our facilities and generate some revenue, we all knew there was no way we could begin a serious recovery without an infusion of operating capital. We were beginning to receive assistance from FEMA in repairing facilities, but they did not allocate funds to pay salaries and employ additional staff. We told the state's commissioner of administration[1] and legislative delegation that if we did not have help with our operating budget, we would have to abandon the park. In March 2006, I appeared before the Louisiana House Appropriations Committee and stated, "The bottom line for us is we're simply running out of money. We have done everything we can to raise money, to open our facilities, to get back up. If we don't get some sort of help, we will end up closing this park probably at the end of September."[2] I said the consequences of us abandoning 1,300 acres in the middle of New Orleans would be catastrophic in terms of the city's ability to recover.

With the help of the commissioner and our legislative delegation, we were able to persuade the legislature to appropriate $1.2 million in the state's general fund for the fiscal year beginning in July of 2006. This allocation enabled us to hire back more staff and speed up our recovery. The appropriation was the first ever for the park from the state's general fund—something the park board and management had tried for years to secure. It

Storyland before the repairs (Photograph by David Grunfeld, courtesy of the *New Orleans Times-Picayune*)

took Katrina to see that effort realized. The state kept us in the general fund operating budget for three additional years, which was crucial to our ability to recover. We received $2.275 million in FY 07-08, $3.559 million (which included more than $1 million for past insurance payments) in FY 08-09, and $1.3 million in FY 09-10. Beginning with the 2010-11 fiscal year, the state deemed us sufficiently capable of generating our own revenue, along with the increasing proceeds from our share of the state tax on slot machines at the Fair Grounds Race Course, to remove us from the state's general fund. For several years, particularly from 2007 through 2010, the park received funding from both the state's general fund and the slot tax. This enabled us to match a variety of public and private grants and make other investments in repairs and new projects. When the state removed the park from the general fund, it forced us to allocate 100 percent of the slot tax to the operating budget.

Mounting a Fundraising Effort

In the first months after the disaster, fundraising efforts of any significance were greatly hampered by the fact that we had virtually no communication with the outside world. There was no phone service, no fax, no Internet or computer linkages, and no mail delivery within the city. (Later on, we had our mail delivered to the State Library in Baton Rouge and then to a post office on St. Bernard Avenue until the postal service was able to start delivery again.) Contact was face to face.

By the year's end, we divided our fundraising efforts into two different strategies. The first focused on the private sector, i.e., individuals, philanthropic organizations, local and national foundations and trusts, planned giving, and corporate donations. The second strategy centered on appealing to the public sector—that is, raising funds for operating expenses and/or capital improvements from various levels of government.

Public Fundraising

While the state had put the park in the general fund operating budget, we knew this was not a permanent arrangement. It was made clear to us that once our operating budget had stabilized and we had reopened many of our revenue-generating venues, we would be phased out. And that is exactly what happened. While we had not yet realized the revenue from the slot tax at the Fair Grounds, we knew that eventually, the racetrack casino would open, and revenue would begin to flow. Our allocation in the 2005 authorizing legislation was 30 percent of the total tax collected, not to exceed $1.3 million. Most experts expected that the Fair Grounds slot revenue would exceed projections, and thus, the tax generated would as well. We went back to our delegation and succeeded in having our limit raised to $2 million, to take advantage of the increased revenue if it materialized. We were now able to receive a total of $2,200,000 in annual revenue from the state, which could be used for either capital or operating expenses! While it certainly was not traditional public tax revenue, such as a property or sales tax, nevertheless, it was tax revenue dedicated to us. As long as people kept going to the Fair Grounds and playing the slot machines, we would benefit.

Another example of the state's assistance with our operating budget came in the early spring of 2006 when I received a call from John Alario, who would become the president of the Louisiana State Senate. The park had lost over two thousand trees from the storm and had little funding to begin a reforesting program. This situation came to the attention of Alario, and although he did not represent New Orleans in his district, he called to ask if I needed assistance in funding a tree planting program. I was stunned to receive the call and told him we very much could use some state assistance. Senator Alario succeeded in putting $1 million in the state budget for reforestation in City Park. This action was typical of the senator, who was always a major supporter of the park and helped us get numerous projects included in the state's construction program.

The concept of tax increment financing (TIF) is a well-known financial tool to promote private development. It segregates a portion of taxes (usually property tax) that would be generated by a private development and pledges them to infrastructure improvements that were necessary to make the development possible in the first place. By freezing tax payments to the public body at the level they were at before the new development, the increase in tax payments made possible by the new development would go toward needed infrastructure, while the public body continued to receive what they had been receiving before the improvements. The tax payments are usually pledged for between ten and twenty years, to provide time to pay off bonds that are sold backed by the pledged taxes.

In late 2006, we were looking for additional ways we could be supported with public tax dollars. We had begun to get state tax funds from the slot machines at all Louisiana racetracks before Katrina, and that had expanded significantly when the Fair Grounds casino came to fruition after the storm. While the state had stepped up to support the park, the city, other than through capital contributions, had not dedicated any tax dollars to us. We decided that we could try the tax increment approach by dedicating city and state sales taxes generated in the park back to the park. This approach for this financing tool had not been tried in the state before. All the funds generated by the tax would benefit a public body and not a private development.

To enact tax increment financing, specific legislative authority must be granted, which then allows the state as well as local governing bodies to participate should they choose. Working through our delegation again and with the help of Darrell Hunt, the Friends' legislative liaison, and Meredith Hathorn of the Foley & Judell law firm, who volunteered her time to help prepare the legislation, we secured passage of Act 266 of the 2007 legislature. This act created the City Park Taxing District and allowed the park to receive both the city's 2.5 percent sales and use tax collected within the boundaries of the park as well as the state's similar share. The act provided that the funds be spent on public works and infrastructure improvements. The board of the Taxing District was to be made up of the president of the New Orleans City Council; the secretary of the Department of

Culture, Recreation and Tourism; and both the president and the CEO of the City Park Improvement Association.

Once the enabling legislation passed, we secured the support of Mayor Nagin and the City Council, and on December 18, 2007, the City Council authorized city participation in the Taxing District for a period of ten years. The initial baseline of tax funding was established at $83,543, with the park receiving any collected funds above that base. The park received the first funds from the Taxing District in November 2008. Since that time, received funds have ranged from a few hundred thousand dollars in the early years to nearly a half-million in 2020. All told, as of June 2019, we had received $2,758,000 in TIF funding. In February of 2014, the City Council renewed the city's participation in the Taxing District, and in November of 2019, a further reauthorization was approved until January 2026.

Unfortunately, the state has never chosen to participate, citing a never-ending budget crisis. However, City Park continues to try.

Private Fundraising

Even though our fundraising efforts consisted largely of work by John Hopper, our chief development officer; various board members; and myself, the national attention focused on New Orleans meant that many opportunities came to us without us having to reach out with limited communications. In 2005 and 2006, we raised approximately $7,000,000 from a host of sources. Over the next three years, we raised approximately $8,500,000, for a total of almost $16,000,000 between 2005 through 2009. The list of donations always starts with our board members, who, despite relocating or having to repair their businesses, were always the first to step up and donate for the recovery. Many individuals donated as well, and, in the aggregate, they gave hundreds of thousands of dollars. Some gifts were unrestricted, and others were designated for specific areas of the park or certain types of aid, such as equipment or operations. The following is a list of those organizations and individuals who contributed funds between 2005 and 2009. While the park has obviously continued to raise money each year, I have listed those organizations who gave funds during those first five years and the purposes of their money because it is always important to recognize and remember those who came to the aid of the park in its darkest hour.

2005-6

Board giving—unrestricted	$71,000
Anonymous donors	$55,000
Individual donors—unrestricted	$422,9952
(This listing includes thousands of individual gifts)	
Donor-advised fund at Greater New Orleans Foundation	$5,000
Saks Fifth Avenue—operations	$24,000
Azby Fund—garden/sports/driving range	$1,264,000

Fore!Kids Foundation—operations $10,000
Shell—operations/carousel $150,000
Hibernia Bank—unrestricted $25,000
Selley Foundation—equipment $50,000
German newspaper readers—operations $35,000
(This donation was facilitated by the Times-Picayune)
New Orleans Garden Clubs—landscaping $40,000
Pro-Max—landscaping $25,000
Maritz—Botanical Garden cash and in-kind services $100,000
Freeport-McMoRan Foundation—Christmas event $100,000
Montgomery Watson Harza—Storyland $25,000
Helis Foundation—Botanical Garden $50,000
NYC Central Park Conservancy—trees
Donnelly Fund—trees $10,000
Square D by Schneider Electric—new train $275,000
Toler Foundation—carousel $100,000
Tauck Family Foundation—Pavilion of the Two Sisters $40,000
Howrey LLP—operations $25,000
National Association of Realtors—unrestricted $15,750
Capital One—Amusement Park $50,000
Haspel Family—Robert B. Haspel Stage in garden $50,000
Emmis Communications—Amusement Park $92,000
U.S. Tennis Association—Tennis Center repairs/operations $149,000

Northrop Grumman—cash and in-kind $500,000
Reggie Bush—Tad Gormley field $86,000
Cathy Tai—carousel $25,000
Rejazz New Orleans—Tad Gormley Stadium $10,000
Libby Dufour Fund—equipment $25,000
Clein-Lemann Esperanza Foundation—trees/grounds $10,000
Stanley Rosenthal—volunteer department $15,000
Rotary Clubs of New Orleans and Baton Rouge—Lelong Drive $140,000
(The Rotary Clubs, while not large, doggedly pursued donations from Rotary membership in the U.S. and around the world)
Morgan Buildings—volunteer supplies $10,000
Southern Pine—flooring for carousel $24,500
Swan Secure Products—screws for carousel floor $2,000
American Forests—trees $45,000
Merrill Lynch—operations $20,000
National Geographic Society—Couturie Forest $150,000
Junior League—landscaping $10,000
Coca-Cola—football $51,000
Shell employees—drinking fountains $18,000
Sugar Bowl Committee—Tad Gormley Stadium $800,000
Bertucci Contracting Company—concrete removal $5,000
Lafarge North America—unrestricted $20,000

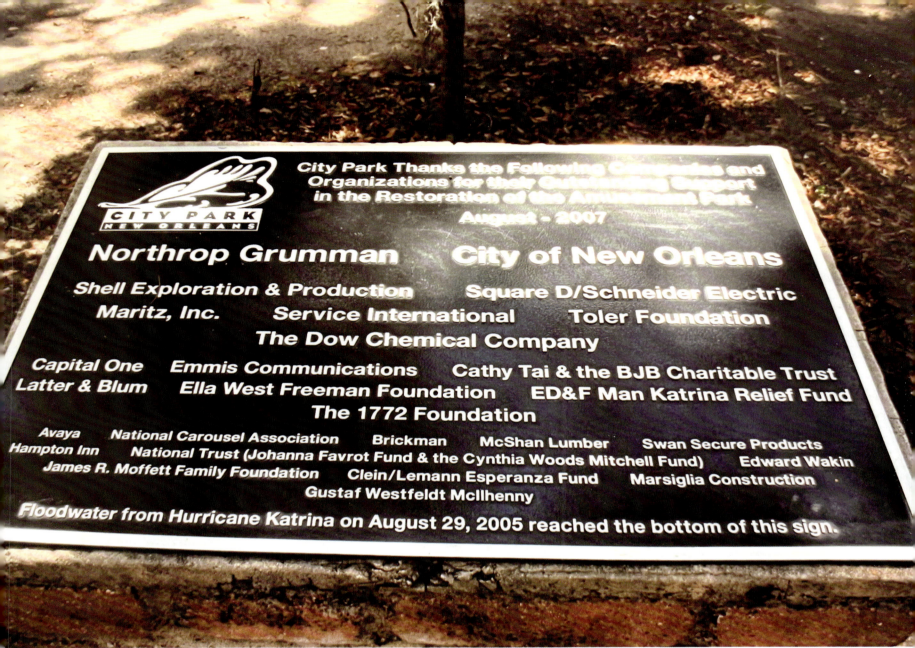

City Park Thanks the Following Companies and Organizations for their Outstanding Support in the Restoration of the Amusement Park

August - 2007

CITY PARK NEW ORLEANS

Northrop Grumman   City of New Orleans

Shell Exploration & Production   Square D/Schneider Electric
Maritz, Inc.   Service International   Toler Foundation
The Dow Chemical Company

Capital One   Emmis Communications   Cathy Tai & the BJB Charitable Trust
Latter & Blum   Ella West Freeman Foundation   ED&F Man Katrina Relief Fund
The 1772 Foundation

Avaya   National Carousel Association   Brickman   McShan Lumber   Swan Secure Products
Hampton Inn   National Trust (Johanna Favrot Fund & the Cynthia Woods Mitchell Fund)   Edward Wakin
James R. Moffett Family Foundation   Clein/Lemann Esperanza Fund   Marsiglia Construction
Gustaf Westfeldt McIlhenny

Floodwater from Hurricane Katrina on August 29, 2005 reached the bottom of this sign.

This plaque honors many of the donors who support the Amusement Park

Pinckelope Foundation—WPA restorations
$10,000
Harrah's Casino-City Council designation—volunteers
$16,000
Trust for Public Land—Big Lake
$2,000,000

(The Trust raised funds during 2006 and 2007 for improvements at Big Lake. Some of the foundations and companies who gave money to the Trust were Allstate Insurance, the Zemurray Foundation, and the Goldring Family Foundation. Boh Bros. Construction Co. built the improvements at cost.)

Keller Family Foundation—operations
$10,000
Gildea Foundation—operations/equipment
$25,000
Jan Marie Hayden—unrestricted $10,000
Bruce and Carol Bryant—operations
$10,000
W. D. Sanchez—unrestricted $5,000
LIG Inc.—unrestricted $10,000

2007
Board giving—unrestricted $64,000
Individual donors—unrestricted $119,265
Selley Foundation—equipment $10,000
Krewe of Hermes scarf sales—unrestricted
$26,000
Starbucks Foundation—shelter/play equipment $250,000

(One day in 2007, several people showed up at our trailer and asked to speak to someone representing the park. They said they wanted to help New Orleans and tried to engage with someone at the city's recreation department, but they could not find anyone to talk to. Someone at the city then recommended they make their way to City Park, which they did. They were from the Starbucks Foundation and gave money for shelter renovations, new play equipment, and site furniture next to the Amusement Park!)

Shell—trees/operating expenses/Botanical Garden $145,000
Helis Foundation—Botanical Garden
$50,000
Rejazz New Orleans (Capital One)—repairs/renovations $20,000
Starwood/Sheraton—Popp Fountain
$100,000
New Orleans Track Club—drinking fountains $30,000
Bayou Tree Service—trees and in-kind
$18,000
Movie company—operating expenses
$5,000
James R. Moffett Family Foundation—amusements $5,000
Libby Dufour Fund—equipment $25,000
Donald and Larry Garvey—operations
$20,000
Cahn Family Foundation—operations
$15,000
NFL Youth Football Fund—artificial turf, Pan American Stadium $550,000
Tolleson Family Foundation—unrestricted
$10,000
Phelps Dunbar—concert series $5,000
Getty Foundation—Botanical Garden
$120,000
Loughlin Fund—operations $5,000
Garden Clubs of America—bayou

improvements $25,000
COM.IT.ES—Storyland $4,000
NOLA Foundation—staff support $50,000
Coalition to Restore Coastal Louisiana—
greenhouse $42,000
Brees Dream Foundation—Pan Am Stadium
$15,521
Merrill Lynch—unrestricted $25,000
SDT Waste & Debris Services—unrestricted
$5,000
L'Oréal—operations $10,000
Stanley W. Ray, Jr. Trust—endowment
pledge over four years $250,000
Burger King—Friends of City Park $25,000
Mulvihill Family Foundation—unrestricted
$25,000
BJB Charitable Trust—carousel $25,000
  (Beau Bassich took a personal challenge to raise all the funds necessary to restore the carousel, the only park building listed on the National Register of Historic Places)
Dow Chemical—purchase of a Ferris wheel
$400,000
Duplantier Family—unrestricted $10,000
Circuit City—in-kind $10,000
Hayden Family—unrestricted $10,000
Almar Foundation—planting trees on Wisner
$50,000
ISO—in-kind $6,000
Peter A. Mayer Company—trees $20,000
Nancy Marshall—trees/landscaping
$5,000
Gildea Foundation—carousel $10,000
Azby Fund—unrestricted $5,000
Bryant Family—unrestricted $10,000

New Ferris wheel, sponsored by Dow Chemical

Sanchez Family—unrestricted $10,000
Lelong Family—endowment $105,000
Johnson & Johnson Company—unrestricted
in-kind $25,000
Motiva Enterprises—Friends of City Park
$20,000
Ed Mathes—unrestricted $5,000
Margaret Bridwell—Botanical Garden
$15,000
Helis Foundation—Botanical Garden
$50,000

2008
Board giving—unrestricted $66,500
Individual donors—unrestricted $183,000
Coca-Cola Bottlers—Big Lake construction
$20,000
New Orleans Track Club—Botanical Garden
$7,200
Jones Foundation—Botanical Garden
$10,000
Friends of City Park—Popp Fountain
$300,000
Rotary International—sidewalk repairs
$51,000
Goldring Family & Woldenberg
Foundations—Great Lawn $2,000,000
Selley Foundation—equipment $60,000
Rotary International—softball/soccer
lighting $150,000
1772 Foundation—carousel $50,000
General Mills—landscaping $7,500
Greater New Orleans Foundation—Harrison
bike path $25,000
Shell—trees/landscaping $60,000

Keep Louisiana Beautiful—Couturie Forest
$15,000
Purina Dog Chow—dog park $4,000
National Association for the Education of
Young Children (NAEYC)—landscaping
$10,500
BJB Charitable Trust—carousel $25,000
Deuce McAllister Catch 22 Foundation—Pan
Am Stadium $16,000
NOLA.com—Tad Gormley Stadium $12,000
Laughlin Fund—operations $5,000
Johnson Controls—amusements $15,000
Starbucks Foundation—Tad Gormley
Stadium and Wisner path $67,000
Selley Foundation—equipment $15,000
Coca-Cola—T-shirts/Tad Gormley Stadium/
family trail $105,600
*(Coke paid for commemorative T-shirts, which
the park sold as a fundraiser)*
Pepsi—endowment for Tennis Center paid
over four years $1,000,000
Helis Foundation—park and Botanical
Garden $50,000
Lelong Fund—Lelong Drive $5,000
Bryant Family—unrestricted $5,000

2009
Fore!Kids Foundation—golf $25,200
Contributions to carousel endowment
$75,000
Jones Foundation—carousel $15,000
National Football League—Tad Gormley
Stadium turf $709,000
Shell—trees $60,000
American Bar Association—trees $7,500

The Great Lawn, a $2 million gift from the Goldring Family &
Woldenberg Foundations

Selley Foundation—WPA restorations
$15,000

McDonald's Corporation—unrestricted
$40,000

Redwood Creek Wine—trees $50,000

Monteleone Hotel—carousel $5,000

Rotary (Algiers)—Lelong Drive $10,000

Almar Foundation—pump house and
endowment $100,000

Trailways—Couturie Forest $80,000

These gifts do not include funds raised by the Friends of City Park at their major annual event, Lark in the Park, or proceeds from the annual Celebration in the Oaks. It is also clear that a variety of foundations have been consistent supporters over the years. Examples of those include the Selley Foundation, Helis Foundation, Azby Fund, and Shell.

Of course, not all private or public fundraising solicitations were successful. We struck out with the Kingdom of Saudi Arabia. In December 2005, both the PGA of America and the Golf Course Superintendents Association of America turned down our request for assistance. In 2007, encouraged by local Coca-Cola representatives, we prepared an extensive request for support totaling $10 million. Unfortunately, Coke officials in Atlanta directed the company's gift to Habitat for Humanity, clearly a worthy cause but not one that benefited us. We applied to the Bush-Clinton Katrina Fund but were turned down.

In January 2006, the Louisiana Department of Culture, Recreation and Tourism requested $670 million from the Louisiana Recovery Authority for what they called a Louisiana Rebirth Plan. This plan included $13.9 million for City Park. It was never approved.

Endowments

The City Park Endowment Fund was created in 1992 and is held by the Greater New Orleans Foundation, our local Community Chest. However, in spite of repeated recommendations over the years that the park build a substantial endowment for both capital improvements and operating support, there was only $48,702 on deposit in July 2001. It became a priority of our plan to build a much more robust fund for the future. In 2002, I approached the local Azby Fund and proposed a matching plan in which the park (through the Friends of City Park) and the Azby Fund would each contribute $25,000 a year to maintain the Pavilion of the Two Sisters and the Conservatory of the Two Sisters in the Botanical Garden, both of which the Azby Fund helped build. They agreed, and we created a separate fund for that purpose. Because of the small value of the endowments, we decided not to tap into any of the funds to allow them to grow with the market.

In 2007, we recruited the local Stanley W. Ray, Jr. Trust to donate to a fund to maintain the park's main playground, which we renamed the Stanley Ray Playground. In 2008, we held a fundraiser to endow our historic carousel. Through the next couple of years, we added endowments for our Botanical Garden, Pump House, and Arbor Fund. The Friends of City Park dedicated the proceeds of their Lark in the Park event to the general Park Endowment Fund, and we continued to add to the fund from a variety of sources.

Perhaps our biggest endowment success came with our new tennis complex. We had secured funding from the state to construct a new, twenty-six-court complex in accordance with our plan, and it opened in March of 2011. We also wanted to build an endowment large enough to properly maintain it. In 2008, we spoke to Bill Goldring, a longtime supporter, and he said he would talk with Pepsi about a donation, as he had a relationship with the company through his family's liquor business. He told them that Coca-Cola had been a large supporter of the city following Katrina, and it was essential that Pepsi become competitive in that regard. They stepped up and signed a pledge agreement for a $1 million endowment to be payable over four years beginning in 2011.

At the beginning of 2020, the park had eleven separate endowment funds totaling $6.4 million. It was not until 2019 that we finally made a draw on any of the funds, to cover needed capital improvements. The latest fund was created in 2019 in support of the park's forest. The annual Heart of the Park Hat Luncheon sustains this fund. The park splits the proceeds with the New Orleans Town Gardeners, a horticultural organization with a history of supporting City Park.

Other Fundraising Efforts

Since Sen. Mary Landrieu had secured our reentry passes in the early days after the storm, I had kept in touch with her office to see what other support she could lend to our recovery. We were hoping for funding from a variety of federal sources to implement pieces of the master plan. In 2006, Senator Landrieu initiated a $1 million appropriation, to be placed in the federal Department of Transportation budget under the Transportation, Community, and System Preservation (TCSP) Program, for the construction of a main parking lot between Victory and Dreyfous. This amenity was key to our master plan, because it provided a 259-space lot to serve the Botanical Garden and the Casino Building in the most utilized part of the park. Despite the appropriation, it took until May of 2010 before a bid of $1,087,742 was awarded to a local contractor. Part of the delay was caused by the fact that the Federal Highway Administration, which was administering the grant through the Louisiana Department of Transportation and Development, was so slow in moving it through their design and implementation stage that the federal government's funding formula was reinterpreted to be 80-20 percent instead of 100 percent. This meant that the park had to provide more than $200,000 in matching funds. Fortunately, Walter Brooks at the New Orleans Regional Planning Commission offered to assist us with unrestricted funds that the commission had for transportation improvements. With that commitment, the state awarded the bid, and we built the parking lot.

In 2010, Senator Landrieu was able to secure a second transportation earmark with an appropriation of $1,948,000 in the budget of the Federal Highway Administration.

The Great Lawn, Casino Building, and parking lot

These funds were designated for a variety of improvements, including demolishing broken sidewalks, installing new lighting fixtures along Victory and Dreyfous, replacing broken drainage pipes on Victory, reworking the entrance to the Botanical Garden across from the Great Lawn, paving the plaza at the Peristyle, and building a parking lot and plaza adjacent to the proposed miniature golf course. We supplied the matching funds of $367,000 with proceeds from the slot tax.

In total, Senator Landrieu secured approximately $3 million in federal funds to advance the master plan. When combined with projects undertaken with other funds (such as the private fundraising that paid for miniature golf), this resulted in the complete transformation of the front of the park from an athletic venue with tennis courts to an entertainment, cultural, recreational, and amusement venue.

Utilizing the Master Plan as a Blueprint for Recovery

While these grants and donations made it possible to implement the master plan in the front of the park, we also used the plan as a guide to capital investments and fundraising for improvements elsewhere on our acreage. We secured funds in the state's capital budget to build a new tennis complex on Marconi near Zachary Taylor. This allowed us to not only build a first-class tennis complex in a

more appropriate space but released the former tennis area for its transformation into an entertainment and recreation venue, with the investments in the Botanical Garden and Amusement Park and the addition of miniature golf.

Big Lake

Likewise, we were determined to use the closure of the more than eighty acres of the South Golf Course to implement other parts of the master plan.

One key to this strategy was to convert the area around the Big Lake into an informal, passive people area devoted to walking or jogging among enhanced landscaping and decorative features, such as fountains and park furniture. We hired the same team that created the master plan, Laura Burnett of Wallace Roberts & Todd and Carlos Cashio of Cashio Cochran LLC, to develop the detailed plan and construction drawings.

At the same time, the Trust for Public Land (TPL), through its local director Larry Schmidt, approached us about raising funds to provide a substantial park improvement. Susan Hess, a park board member and chair of TPL's New Orleans Advisory Council, had been lobbying the national TPL board to do something significant for the park. Initially, the Trust had been thinking about building a completely new park, but after seeing the devastation City Park had suffered, and with the strong urging of Hess and Schmidt, they decided to implement a project in our park that was a part of our master plan. Transforming land from a former golf course into a brand-new area with a completely different focus intrigued the Trust's leadership, and they decided to partner with us. They devoted the front page and substantial text in a monthly publication to urge support for the project from across the nation.[3] The park signed a memorandum of agreement with the Trust in June of 2007 to secure their assistance with the funding, design, and construction of the City Park Big Lake Trail and Meadow. With local and national funders and the offer of one of Louisiana's largest construction companies, Boh Bros., to build the project at cost, the construction began in December of 2008 and the trail opened in October of 2009 with the New Leviathan Oriental Foxtrot Orchestra playing at the dedication. In addition to a walking path and massive regrading and landscaping, the project included a pier for the renting of boats, a Louisiana Native Garden and education area, and a decorative fountain near the museum. The park moved a building that had been located on the small lake behind the museum, and it became the headquarters for both the boat rental and new bicycle and surrey rental operation. The total project cost was $1,660,372, with the Trust raising $1,114,765 and City Park contributing $478,721.

Festival Grounds

The park's master plan also called for transforming a larger portion of the South Golf Course into a Festival Grounds in the area between Christian Brothers School and the railroad tracks that bisect the park. This part of the plan was going to be expensive since the site lacked basic utilities, particularly drainage.

In early October of 2005, I attended the previously scheduled annual conference of the Louisiana Chapter of the American Planning Association in Shreveport. It was obviously a distressing time for all of us from South Louisiana, but since I had to go back to Dallas to retrieve my dogs from my daughter's house, I made it a point to attend the conference for a day. A variety of speakers tried to make sense of the situation in New Orleans and to see how they might be able to help the city. The guests included consultants and "experts" who saw the opportunity of a lifetime to influence the redevelopment of a major American city but also to earn significant fees.

One person who attended the conference was Dr. Ed Blakely, a widely published academic who headed the Urban and Regional Planning Program at the University of Sydney in Australia. While I did not have an extensive conversation with him, I did introduce myself and made a note that this was an ambitious person likely to be seen again.

In early 2007, Mayor Nagin named Blakely as the city's Recovery Czar. Dr. Blakely was a highly controversial figure almost from the outset. He once described New Orleans as a "Third World country" and its residents as "buffoons." (He also famously predicted that he would have "cranes in the sky" by September.) Dr. Blakely lasted until July of 2009 but, in that time, had a significant impact on the city's recovery. He created a series of seventeen target zones in order to focus dollars in areas that had the best opportunity for quick recovery and made other strategic investments in infrastructure throughout the city.

We submitted a funding request to his office for $4 million to transform the old South Golf Course into a Festival Grounds in conformance with our plan, and in March of 2007, Blakely expressed a desire to visit the park. He arrived with some of his staff and several park board members, and I participated in a bicycle trip around the park and in particular around the proposed Festival Grounds. He invited us to attend a half-day workshop the next month on the city's recovery plan, and I was appointed to the Government Relations Subcommittee of the newly created Recovery Council.

Perhaps Dr. Blakely was impressed by the fact that our project was a part of an overall existing master plan or that the park was led by an urban planner, or he recognized the transformational impact that rebuilding the park could have on the community. Whatever the reason, in October of 2008, he recommended that the Festival Grounds project be approved for Community Development Block Grant (CDBG) funding for $4 million as one of his major recovery projects! This was a huge step forward in implementing our plan. While it took years to go through the formal approval process, hire a designer (Ace Torre of Torre Design Consortium), complete plans, and bid the project, the new Festival Grounds opened in December of 2012.

CHAPTER 10

Uses Never Realized

Just as important as the uses that were repaired or newly introduced in the park in the wake of Katrina are the uses that someone or some group proposed that never made it into the plan or into construction. Following a disaster as profound as Hurricane Katrina, all ideas seem to be on the table. Anyone can propose some use of land that to them may seem totally logical and justified, while to others, the suggestion makes no sense. The following are some of the uses that have been proposed for the park since August of 2005.

Treetop adventure walk—A group of potential investors wanted to build a tower on top of Couturie Forest (the highest point in the park) and a zip line across Harrison Avenue.

Observatory—One would-be scientist submitted a proposal for the construction of an observatory on Harrison Avenue.

Science museum—Several science enthusiasts asked the park board to reserve a site off Harrison Avenue for a science museum. While our plan had provided for building an additional cultural facility, we decided to pursue the Children's Museum instead.

International School—In December 2005, the International School of Louisiana wanted a two-year lease to place portable classroom trailers on two to three acres of land.

Cyclo-cross track—In 2015, bicycle advocates presented a proposal to build a cyclo-cross track, stating, "Tens of thousands of fans pack the courses creating a festival like atmosphere that combines the speed and frenetic energy of competitive bike racing with mud, sand, beer and cowbells, generating a spectacle that is as fun for the racers as it is for the spectators."

Mobile home park—While previous plans and recommendations have suggested that a recreational vehicle park would be a compatible land use and revenue generator, this proposal suggested the construction of permanent sites for anchored mobile homes—a nonstarter for us.

Beach volleyball—Beach volleyball has been suggested on many occasions as a recreation activity that would be in perfect harmony with the park. This idea became especially popular after the Army Corps of Engineers had to remove the popular Coconut Beach volleyball courts at West End Park in order to build a permanent drainage pump station on Lake Pontchartrain. We went so far as to have a feasibility study completed for a sixteen-court Beach Volleyball Complex, and we scouted several locations for the activity. The concept would also include parking, restrooms, and a "clubhouse" or bar popular in most beach volleyball complexes. While not built yet, it could be considered in the future.

Mountain-bike course—This idea is similar in nature to the cyclo-cross track concept.

Extreme sports venue—There was also a proposal to dedicate a section of the park to extreme sports, including a variety of bike and motorcycle courses, CrossFit training, and IRONMAN-type endurance venues.

Human foosball—A version of the popular tabletop game, human foosball takes place in a permanent or temporary "rink." Inside, people are spaced as in table foosball, with the objective of kicking the ball into the other team's goal. The rink can be built indoors or outdoors!

Pickleball and paddle tennis—The game is somewhat like tennis, except it is played with a kind of Wiffle Ball and paddles on a smaller court. Very popular with older players and those with limited mobility, it is one of the country's fastest-growing sports. It is something that the park is very interested in pursuing when a source of funding becomes available.

Water Whipping course—Proposed for Bayou St. John, this is a concept that uses a cable to "whip" people across the waterway, similar to waterskiing.

Axe-throwing venue—A recreational axe-throwing venue was proposed, where competitors aim for targets inside metal cages to protect visitors from flying hatchets. This use is usually combined with a sports bar or other activities.

Ice rink—City Park experimented with a real ice rink during the colder season. It was combined with a kind of toy store. However, not surprisingly, it was difficult to keep the ice cold enough for easy skating, and the experiment was not repeated. Years later, we tried a type of silicon skating surface during our holiday light show. It also did not provide a very satisfying skating experience. But the idea periodically resurfaces.

Bike polo—This version of polo is played on a small hard-court surface with bicycles instead of horses.

Polo—There have been several proposals for the park to build a polo field to host fundraisers and to bring a completely different type of interest group to the park. The large size of the field and the necessity of keeping it in perfect condition to avoid injury to the horses has made consideration of the suggestion difficult.

Rowing complex—The New Orleans Rowing Club has proposed building a rowing center on Bayou St. John. In the past, the club has rowed in one of the city's drainage canals. The center would include a building and dock.

Bocce court complex—There are individuals and groups who believe that a complex of several bocce courts would be very successful, as the game is very popular in some areas of the country.

Cross country course—Since Katrina, the high-school cross country community has wanted to build a permanent racing course in City Park. Immediately after the storm, they were permitted to run on a course constructed on the site of the old South Golf Course, just north of Christian Brothers School. For the last few years, they have run on the site of the old East Golf Course, between Harrison Avenue and Zachary Taylor. Since cross country meets usually occur only for a few months in the year, the park board has favored a temporary course over a permanent one that would impact other potential park uses.

Wife-carrying course—Originally popularized in Finland, in this sport, as the name implies, competitors carry teammates across a course, advancing against opposing teams. There is even a North American Wife Carrying Championship.

Topgolf—A popular "play" off golf, Topgolf combines an updated version of the traditional golf driving range with a sports bar to create a recreation/entertainment complex. While our staff closely examined this use, the extremely large building and net complex required to host the activity have made it incompatible with the park as currently designed.

Baseball stadium—In 2011, Loyola University proposed building a home baseball stadium adjacent to the Softball Quadruplex along Diagonal Drive. The proposal would also have renovated the quadruplex into a small girls' softball stadium. After much consideration, the park felt that the baseball complex was out of scale with the area.

Horse park—Equest Farm, the current tenant occupying the park's Equestrian Complex on Filmore Avenue, explored the concept of creating a forty-acre horse park that would provide an expanded area for horse shows, demonstrations, and auctions. After careful study, we concluded the concept would require a significant contraction of the North Golf Course to provide the necessary acreage for the horse park.

Boathouse restaurant—The park explored the potential of locating a restaurant on Big Lake, similar in concept to Tavern on the Green in New York City's Central Park. A feasibility study was conducted in 2012, and a master plan amendment approved for the location, but no further action has occurred.

NOLA Flightline—This zip-line concept was proposed for the Orleans Canal.

Fuel depot—In early 2006, the park was approached by an entrepreneur who wanted to take advantage of the fact that there were very few gas stations open in the city. He requested land to build a fuel depot in the park.

CHAPTER 11

Full Recovery Mode, 2006-19

Never let a good crisis go to waste.
—Winston Churchill

Over the course of the next ten years, FEMA continued to ramp up their payments for damage claims, we continued raising money, and our operating budget stabilized as we were able to repair and open our facilities. Our staff increased from twenty-two to thirty-six in January of 2007, to forty-five full-time positions by April, and eventually to around ninety employees in 2009, where we stabilized for several years. We began to open and build new facilities at a rapid rate. Basic building repairs, funded by FEMA, began with one contractor working primarily on damaged buildings south of I-610 and separate contractors working on repairs to Tad Gormley Stadium and Pan American Stadium.

iconic playground, and on March 4, we held the first wedding in the repaired Pavilion of the Two Sisters. Pat O'Shaughnessy, our catering director and chef, cooked dinner on a barbecue grill in the service yard and made pasta in a gumbo pot. In September, we were able to reopen Tad Gormley Stadium after extensive electrical repairs and hosted twenty football games there. We received a donation from the Sugar Bowl Committee, which allowed us to make improvements to the bathrooms, concession areas, and locker rooms. On a personal note, I finished my dissertation and comprehensive examinations and received my doctor of philosophy degree from the University of New Orleans in May.

2006

In March 2006, we opened the fully restored Botanical Garden and scheduled over sixty weddings and events for that year. In the same month, we opened Storyland, the children's

2007

In 2007, we secured funding from the City of New Orleans to supplement what they were already spending on repaving Robert E. Lee Boulevard (now Allen Toussaint Boulevard), and we built a bike path along the boulevard from the federal agricultural research station to Marconi. A major initiative of our master plan involved building more biking and jogging trails, as, before 2007, there were no sidewalks or pedestrian paths along Wisner Boulevard, Robert E. Lee Boulevard, or Marconi Drive. We began repairing buildings in the Amusement Park and ordered new rides to replace those heavily damaged. In June of 2007, we completely landscaped Lelong Drive. The various oak species that lined Lelong were near the end of their life and suffered heavy wind damage from the storm. We made the difficult decision to completely remove the remaining trees and replant with live oaks and single-stem crepe myrtles. Construction of the Wisner Bike Path began in June while the path on Robert E. Lee was under construction. It ended at the interstate, but ten years later, the state built a new bridge over the interstate and railroad tracks. It included a dedicated bike line, thus allowing anyone to travel from Robert E. Lee to Esplanade Avenue without being in the street. A new Japanese Garden opened in the Botanical Garden, and we opened a few repaired picnic shelters. Our historic carousel building was repaired, and the carousel animals were returned from refurbishment in New Jersey. We opened it in November, just in time for Celebration in the Oaks, our holiday light show.

The Friends of City Park restarted their newsletter in 2007 and began to build their membership from 300 in October of 2005 to the more than 4,000 they had before the storm. We dedicated the Haspel Stage and began our highly successful "Thursdays at Twilight" concert series in the Botanical Garden.

We also continued building back various events, such as Lark in the Park and Ghosts in the Oaks, both Friends of City Park fundraisers. Other events such as Voodoo Music + Arts Experience and road races and runs also began to resume.

Master Plan Amendment 2007

In 2007, the first formal amendment of the City Park master plan since its adoption in March of 2005 was approved. Two years into the park's recovery, we considered three specific requests to modify the plan. Two came from organizations looking for space in the park and another from the nonprofit Bayou District Foundation, which had a new vision for the golf complex.

The two organizations looking for space were the Louisiana Children's Museum (LCM) and Louisiana Public Broadcasting (LPB), in conjunction with WLAE Public Television.

The 2005 master plan had designated several sites for future cultural facilities in accordance with the study conducted by the Trust for Public Land. LCM proposed an extensive project called an "Early Learning Village," which not only contained a children's museum relocated from the Central Business District but also a variety of related facilities in a campus-like setting. Those proposals included a children's public library, parenting center, childcare center, visual and performing arts building, early learning center for nonprofits, higher-education building, charter elementary school, charter high school, bookstore, playgrounds, picnic areas, parking, and discovery trail. This extensive proposal would have required thirty-five acres of land and cost more than $200 million.

We informed the LCM that the proposal was too large for the park, and we did not wish to host additional schools on the grounds. Public comments on the proposal ranged from those in support of the relocation to those who opposed its move, arguing it would take up scarce green space. After further discussions, the request was reduced to twelve acres, and a two-year reservation of that land was approved to allow time for the concept to solidify and fundraising to occur. The concept was scaled down again in the face of fundraising challenges.

Louisiana Public Broadcasting sought a site in one of the areas designated as a future cultural site to locate a studio. We informed LPB that we were not interested in a broadcast studio as that could be in many locations and did not qualify as a "cultural facility." They later modified their proposal to add a Louisiana Music Heritage Museum, 4D theater, 200-seat theater, and audio-recording studio. They offered to partner with us to broadcast park events and activities, including hosting public-policy forums, movies, and interactive movies. While some people expressed support for this proposal, at the formal public hearing on the plan, a majority of the comments opposed locating the broadcast studio in the park since it was not serving a primary park purpose and could easily be at other locations in the city. After considering all the information, the park board decided not to reserve a site for these uses.

The Bayou District Foundation (BDF) golf proposal dramatically modified the one contained in our plan. They envisioned a three-course complex with a hierarchical distribution of the fifty-four holes, including high, medium, and lower-end courses. The BDF proposal included two championship eighteen-hole courses and a nine-hole executive course, all located between Filmore and Zachary Taylor. The North Course would be converted from golf into soccer fields. This proposal would also require the police horse stables to move from the park, and Scout Island would have been incorporated into the golf complex.

The BDF plan also proposed that the foundation would lease the grounds, operate the new complex, and pay the park a percentage of net income.

Residents in the subdivision adjacent to the North Golf Course opposed this proposal, as the soccer fields potentially would bring traffic, noise, and light pollution into their neighborhood. It also depended on moving the police horse stables, which the city showed no inclination in doing. After considerable analysis, the park board decided that any redevelopment of golf should occur primarily within the existing golf footprint and that a golf strategy had to be developed jointly with the park to address market conditions and maintain some degree of "affordable golf" in the plan. The board authorized further negotiations with the BDF based on these parameters.

The plan amendments proposed relocating the dog park from Marconi between Roosevelt Mall and the railroad tracks. The original location was a proposed by the Society for the Prevention of Cruelty to Animals (SPCA) in order to accommodate a pet adoption center on the property. However, post-Katrina, the SPCA was no longer interested in such a center, so a site on Marconi was no longer necessary for its visibility. A new location was proposed on Zachary Taylor, which incorporated an existing shelter. The park board approved the site.

The amendments also moved the site for a proposed Skate Park from Tri-Centennial Place to a location on Palm Drive and for a slight modification of the North Golf Course to accommodate an expansion of the equestrian complex. The board also approved the Christian Brothers School's plan to add a gymnasium and classroom space, provided it all occurred within their currently leased area. Finally, a modification of the capital financing strategy included in the 2005 plan was proposed to include financing from the recently approved slot tax.

We held a public hearing on all the proposed amendments on September 25, 2007, and the plan was formally amended on November 27, 2007.

2008

At the beginning of 2008, we opened one new and one refurbished playground. The Stanley W. Ray, Jr. Trust provided funds to repair and add play equipment to the playground adjacent to the Casino Building, and Starbucks built a new playground in the picnic grove next to the Amusement Park. We removed the antique car ride in the Amusement Park and repurposed the buildings into a birthday village, which provides increased revenue. In March, we began to replace the bleachers at Pan American Stadium and opened it for games in August. We received a grant from the Louisiana Recovery Authority in 2008 for the construction of a fishing pier on Marconi. The North Golf Course was repaired and opened in September, and in October, the Wisner Bike Path was completed and opened. We repaired the Casino Building and opened the Parkview Café on the ground floor, and in the Amusement Park, we installed a new Ferris wheel bought by Dow Chemical.

2009

In 2009, the park completed renovations at Tad Gormley Stadium using funds from the Sugar Bowl Committee, and we installed artificial turf for the first time, which allowed much greater play and reduced operating

The trail around Big Lake

costs. The trail around Big Lake opened, and we dedicated our volunteer center in the "demonstration house" on Harrison Avenue.

The next several years were huge in terms of park repairs and the introduction of new activities. In 2008, Jackie Shreves (a park board member) and I searched the park for potential locations for a new dog park. Shreves, Kathleen Schrenk, and many others saw the need for a place where dog owners could let their dogs run off-leash in a safe environment, so they formed NOLA City Bark with the goal of raising funds for its construction. After looking at various sites, we agreed that property between Zachary Taylor Drive and Magnolia Drive incorporating a damaged picnic shelter would make a good location. It contained approximately three acres of land. NOLA City Bark hired Ace Torre Design to develop the plan and began to solicit funds for its construction. The park also chipped in, and in March 2010, we dedicated the dog park. NOLA City Bark created strict rules for a permit program and at present has over two thousand permit holders. Groups all over the nation have looked to our dog park for its design and operating parameters as a model for the industry.

Master Plan Amendment 2009

The 2007 amendments to the master plan essentially designated the same amount of land utilized by golf before Katrina, except for the South Golf Course, which was closed before the storm. Following this action, we determined that we should prepare a new master plan for golf within these constraints. The State of Louisiana then agreed to amend the contract of the landscape architect hired to develop a new plan for the East Course with golf course architect, Bobby Weed, to carry out a master plan study. When Weed decided not to continue with the project, Torre subcontracted with the internationally known Rees Jones Golf Course Architects to assist in developing the plan. While I will discuss the process in more detail in the chapter devoted to golf, suffice it to say that a new master plan was developed. The clubhouse was proposed to move off Filmore and onto a site accessed from Mirabeau. Phase I of the plan would have constructed a new championship course with a new clubhouse, driving range, and maintenance facilities. The North Course would remain open in the first phase. A second phase would have constructed a second eighteen-hole course and a nine-hole course. The board retained Economic Research Associates to undertake a market and feasibility study to determine whether the proposed plan would be economically successful and would cover not only everyday operating expenses but generate a net profit.

A major conclusion of the study was that the park would have to seek financial backing outside of the secured public funding in order to implement the plan. This set the stage for a formal Request for Proposal to be issued for entities interested in making a capital investment in the courses and providing management services for the complex.

Comments at the public hearing held on

March 10, 2009, ranged from people who liked the concept, to those who thought the new golf courses would be too expensive to play, to park users who did not want the damaged courses repaired as they enjoyed utilizing the space passively in its "natural state." Clearly, the areas were not in a natural state, as they were former golf courses and had been from almost the moment the land was incorporated into the park (the East Course being built in 1933 and the West Course in 1957). Still, some members of the public wanted it left alone.

The park board decided to adopt the entire plan but only proceed with Phase I. They directed management to put out a Request for Proposal to solicit private contributions and stated that should insufficient funds be available to implement Phase I, the park should upgrade the East Course with the public funds on hand.

The plan amendments adopted on May 26, 2009, moved us closer to eventually developing and implementing a final golf plan and gave more realistic estimates for the capital cost of various alternatives and their financial impact. The public-hearing comments also made clear that different users of the park held wildly divergent views of how the damaged golf-course land should be used.

2010

With the help of volunteers from the Friends of City Park and throughout the U.S., historic Popp Fountain was cleaned, restored, and re-landscaped in 2010. The city repaved Harrison Avenue through the park and added a dedicated bike lane that connected with the Wisner Bike Path, adding another link in the master plan's program for dedicated and shared bike lanes. Hundreds of volunteers helped plant more than two thousand trees in Couturie Forest, the park's arboretum. In addition, volunteers removed or killed hundreds of invasive tallow trees, whose seeds had come into the forest during the flooding.

In October of 2007, we submitted a proposal to the Goldring Family & Woldenberg Foundations that contained four options for their consideration. One was to fund the Great Lawn, a major master plan project in the area the tennis courts currently occupied, as they were scheduled to be relocated. The Great Lawn was the centerpiece of this reimagined part of the park, which we had named Tri-Centennial Place. We were invited to make a presentation to their foundations' board and added to our list of possibilities an endowment for our tennis complex that had been funded by the state. The foundations liked the Great Lawn project for its impact in the center of the park and pledged $2 million toward its design and construction. We hired Cashio Cochran LLC to prepare design drawings, and the project was put out to public bid in March of 2009. We opened the Goldring/Woldenberg Great Lawn in March of 2010. The $2 million gift remains the largest private gift in our recovery.

In 2010, we repaired the driving-range building, removed our temporary trailer, and opened it as the driving range and North Golf Course headquarters. We bought a new "thrill" ride for the Amusement Park, the Musik Express, and opened the new Marconi fishing pier in September. Finally, we completed the new parking lot and its central bio swale in time for the 2010 Celebration in the Oaks event.

Since park staff returned from the storm, we had been in a combination of rented office trailers, the old tennis clubhouse, and the Botanical Garden. After some fits and starts, including FEMA initially determining that our administrative offices could just be repaired after taking on four feet of floodwaters, they agreed in 2010 to declare the building a total loss and pay for a new one. Of course, FEMA refused to pay for the building to be raised higher than the base flood elevation, in spite of the fact that the actual flood of record was at least a foot above that. The park ended up paying for the building to be elevated an additional foot, since we knew that if the levees failed again, that would be the height of the floodwater. We moved into the new building, designed by the local architectural firm of Waggonner & Ball, in January 2011.

2011

In March of 2011, the City Park/Pepsi Tennis Center opened on Marconi, with Pepsi ceremoniously presenting a check for $1 million to endow the facility. City Park board president Robert Lupo pronounced the complex one of the finest in the South, with sixteen hard-surface courts and ten clay-surface courts. In September 2011, we opened the new Arbor Room reception facility in the same location as Popp Fountain. Prior to the storm, the park purchased a large tent so weddings could be held with the fountain as the backdrop and the actual reception in the tent. Obviously, the storm annihilated the tent. When we discovered that FEMA assessed the tent damage at over $800,000, we decided to make the reception facility a hybrid between a permanent building and a tent. The kitchen, bathrooms, and brides' room were all permanent buildings, and the covering of the reception facility was a tent since FEMA would only pay to replace like with like facilities. The Friends of City Park donated $500,000 of funds from Lark in the Park and retained earnings, completing the funding package. Possibly the most unique reception facility in the region, the Arbor Room has hosted hundreds of weddings and special events since 2011.

Master Plan Amendment 2011

In 2011, we came to a final resolution of how much of the park's land would be devoted to golf. Since 2010, we continually reexamined the course plan with an eye to reducing the golf footprint as much as possible to make land available for other park uses. The 2011 plan amendments included: 1. Create two eighteen-hole courses instead of the forty-

City Park Tennis Center

Arbor Room damage before the 2011 reopening

five-hole plan approved two years earlier, 2. Locate a new golf clubhouse in the area of the former clubhouse on Filmore, as opposed to a site off Mirabeau, and 3. Reduce the footprint of golf from 526 acres in the 2009 plan to 383 acres by limiting the new championship course to land north of Harrison Avenue.

In response to the Request for Proposal called for in 2009, the Bayou District Foundation, a local nonprofit, submitted a proposal to provide external capital and management expertise. They promised $8.9 million in capital funding and brought PGA Golf Properties to the table as the proposed manager of the complex.

Finally, we felt we had decided upon a solid direction for the redevelopment of golf!

2012

In 2012, another big year, we celebrated the renovation of the historic Peristyle, one of the oldest buildings in the park, and Grow Dat Youth Farm opened on seven acres we leased to Tulane University on Zachary Taylor. We opened three of the diamonds in the Softball Quadruplex. Since the storm destroyed the park's maintenance facilities, that department had been operating out of the quadruplex clubhouse, with all our equipment stored on one of the fields. The situation stayed this way until October of 2017 when we moved maintenance into a location in Tad Gormley Stadium while we pressed forward with the design of a new

maintenance complex. With the generosity of Bobby and Lori Savoie, we built a new soccer pavilion on Marconi, which we completed in December 2012. Also in December, we dedicated the Festival Grounds, which we built with CDBG funds provided by the city's recovery program. At the same location, we opened a complete fitness center and a wetland to filter stormwater. Equest Farm, the tenant operating the equestrian facility on Filmore, began construction of a large, covered rink that was completed the next year.

2013

We began 2013 by hosting several major events associated with the Super Bowl held in New Orleans. Tom and Gayle Benson, owners of the New Orleans Saints football team, put on an elaborate party for the NFL owners in the picnic area next to the Amusement Park, including constructing a wooden deck over the entire picnic grounds and tenting almost the whole site. In addition, the NFL practiced the halftime festivities in Tad Gormley Stadium, and ESPN held their Super Bowl party in a tent covering the entire stadium field.

In 2013, we began more building projects in the Amusement Park, including the construction of new bathrooms and the conversion of an existing shelter into an enclosed, air-conditioned café. The Voodoo Music + Arts Experience moved to the Festival Grounds, and on July 3, we inaugurated a concert series honoring the signing of the Declaration of Independence with the Marine Band playing on the Great Lawn. Julie LaCour, our special events director, created the event, and it has become one of the most popular annual events in the park.

In 2011, we began to explore the construction of a miniature golf complex in Tri-Centennial Place. This project was another central piece of the 2005 Master Plan, located adjacent to the Great Lawn between the Peristyle and Storyland. We conducted a feasibility study, which determined that there was a market at this time for this type of recreational entertainment. We developed a financing plan that included funds from the park, proceeds from the 2011 Lark in the Park Friends fundraiser, and other private donations. Since the complex included two eighteen-hole courses, we decided to seek sponsors for each of the thirty-six holes, an individual sponsor for each course, and an overall sponsor. The complex also included a "clubhouse" with two birthday rooms. We hired a local architect, Steve Rome, to design the clubhouse and a Tennessee company specializing in miniature golf courses to design and build the complex. One course had holes named after Louisiana cities, and the other had a New Orleans theme, with each hole named after a famous street. "City Putt" opened in May 2013. We ended the year with resurfacing Filmore Avenue with dedicated bicycle lanes, completing the covered rink at the equestrian complex, opening a boating and bicycle rental concession on Big Lake, and reroofing our old maintenance buildings to keep them from deteriorating further while we developed a reuse plan.

The end of 2013 also saw another one of the strange happenings that occurred endlessly. City Park, in the 1990s, had secured federal Land and Water Conservation Fund (LWCF) capital to construct ten additional courts at the tennis complex, which, at the time, was located in the front of the park between Victory Avenue and Dreyfous Drive. Of course, since that time, we had demolished those courts and moved the entire complex to its current location on Marconi Drive, in accordance with our 2005 Master Plan. In December, I got a letter from the Louisiana Office of State Parks, the agency charged with monitoring the spending of local LWCF appropriations. It said I needed to put up a sign in an area of high visibility to recognize the LWCF funding for improvements in the old tennis complex. I wrote back saying the area that was approved for the federal funds was no longer there, so there was no point in putting up a sign recognizing a project that was gone. State Parks replied that a sign was required nonetheless, and I should place it where the courts used to be! I wrote back saying that was a ridiculous request that would simply confuse people. I offered to put up a sign at the new tennis location to signify we had received federal funds for the previous tennis complex, but that apparently did not satisfy the requirements. After several more pieces of correspondence, I filed the proposed sign in our archives for another day.

2014

The Amusement Park was the big beneficiary of improvements in 2014. We opened Parker's Café in the area of the new Musik Express amusement ride, which converted a former open-air shelter into an air-conditioned food and refreshment facility.[1] In addition, we opened the new bathrooms adjacent to the café. The city's capital budget paid for both facilities, and they opened in May. Finally, after years of effort on the part of our CEO, Rob DeViney, FEMA agreed to pay for a new rollercoaster to replace the "old" Ladybug, after we proved that floodwaters had compromised the structural integrity of the ride. It opened in February of the next year.

Other highlights of 2014 included the construction of a ropes course by students at Tulane's City Center and a new pedestrian-bridge entrance to Couturie Forest. I also received a Lifetime Achievement Award from the Bureau of Governmental Research.

For many, the year was capped off when we celebrated, in September, the fiftieth anniversary of the Beatles playing a concert in what was then City Park Stadium (renamed Tad Gormley Stadium) in 1964! Despite rainy weather, the Beatles tribute band, The Fab Four, played the night away with everyone wearing their 1960s finest.

Master Plan Amendments 2014

The amendments to the plan proposed in February of 2014 were mainly housekeeping, designed to relocate some of the components as well as remove others that had not proved feasible.

The most important amendment moved the proposed Splash Park from a location near City Park Avenue and Marconi Drive to one closer to the Administration Building on Palm Drive. We felt that with the continued redevelopment of the front section of the park, placing a popular water feature in the same area would overburden the parking and roadways. The new location would give us the opportunity to build adequate parking and minimally impact other uses.

A second amendment proposed building a maintenance complex adjacent to the Celebration in the Oaks warehouse alongside the railroad tracks near the interstate, rather than renovating the damaged 1930s buildings. This was consistent with the master plan strategy of locating park support structures against the tracks to minimize their impact on park users.

The amendments also removed the concept of building a new catering complex along the service corridor and eliminated a proposed baseball diamond along Diagonal Drive and Harrison Avenue. It was also recommended that we remove the proposed Skate Park and Multipurpose Building from a specific location in the plan, as no funding had been identified for these projects to determine their exact size and character.

Finally, we reaffirmed that the Children's Museum would be located on the property made available by closing the South Golf

The Softball Quadruplex was a temporary location for the maintenance department after the storm destroyed their facility. It was also temporarily located in Tad Gormley Stadium.

Course and reducing its size to approximately 51,000 square feet and an eight-acre site.

These amendments were adopted on February 18, 2014.

2015

In 2015, through the generosity of the Brees Dream Foundation and the National Football League, we replaced the deteriorating synthetic field that had been installed at Pan American Stadium. When part of the field began to unravel, we sought its replacement as a warranty issue. When the company protested, we called in the 800-pound gorilla, the NFL, to persuade them that the problem was their faulty installation, and they replaced it. That year also saw work beginning on the Tri-Centennial Place improvements paid for with the federal grant secured by Sen. Mary Landrieu. Thanks to the generosity of the Helis Foundation and the cooperation of the daughter of Mexican artist Enrique Alférez, we built and opened a new exhibit in the Botanical Garden displaying many of his WPA sculptures. With funds from the city, the Friends, and the Oscar J. Tolmas Charitable Trust, we opened a new entrance to the garden and the adjacent Storyland by renovating an existing building and constructing new bathrooms and a giftshop.[2]

Finally, in 2010, there was a huge oil spill in the Gulf of Mexico when a blowout preventer in a British Petroleum (BP) drilling platform failed, spilling hundreds of millions of gallons of oil into the water and killing eleven workers. Years of litigation ensued, with many individuals and organizations claiming damages. City Park, like many New Orleans organizations, filed a claim under expansive guidelines approved by the company. Even though the park is 110 miles from the gulf, the loss of revenue caused by the impacts of the spill resulted in the park receiving a settlement of $845,000 in 2015, which we deposited into our reserves. The Friends of City Park, who had also filed a claim, received $581,327.

We purchased new bins that effectively divided trash from recyclables, and we placed them around the park. We continued our tree-planting program, having planted more than six thousand trees since Hurricane Katrina. By virtue of a telephone survey, which we began prior to the storm and continued in each subsequent year, our attendance grew from basically zero in September of 2005 to over one million distinct visitors making multiple visits to the park, resulting in over ten million park visits.

Finally, in 2015, we started construction of the new championship South Golf Course on ground previously occupied by the old East and West courses. There is much more about this in a later chapter.

Beau Bassich, the park's longtime volunteer executive director, passed away in August of 2015, and his family asked for donations to be made to the Carousel Endowment in his memory.

2016

We completed the Tri-Centennial Place improvements in 2016 and made extensive drainage improvements in the Festival Grounds. We also completed an arrival garden in the Botanical Garden as part of the new front entrance. The golf-course contractor, Duininck Golf, finished the major construction of the course, and we began to grow into it. Construction also began on a new golf clubhouse and maintenance complex by the Bayou District Foundation, our partner in the golf complex.

In addition to all the events and activities[3] we had been bringing back, we displayed a new special exhibit in the Botanical Garden of exotic lighted Chinese lanterns from February through May. The exhibit was very successful and drew people who had previously been unaware of the park's progress.

This year also marked the 120th anniversary of the City of New Orleans and the State of Louisiana entrusting the City Park Improvement Association with the stewardship of City Park.

2017

In 2017, we completed two important pedestrian and biking projects: the Marconi Bike Path, from Robert E. Lee Boulevard to Harrison Avenue, and the new Wisner overpass, with a dedicated bike and jogging lane. These projects continued the implementation of the healthy living portion of our 2005 Master Plan by allowing walking, jogging, and biking virtually uninterrupted along Wisner Boulevard, Robert E. Lee Boulevard, and Marconi Drive. Taken together with the dedicated bicycle paths on Filmore and Harrison, the park, with the assistance of the state and the city, has completed more than three miles of these paths.

After years of negotiations and dedicated fundraising by the Louisiana Children's Museum (LCM), including substantial funding from the State of Louisiana, the LCM began construction on a 50,000-square-foot museum on the site of the old South Golf Course in 2017.

Master Plan Amendments 2017

Since we had adopted the final plan for golf in 2011, the fate of the former East Golf Course in the area surrounded by Wisner, Zachary Taylor, Diagonal, and Harrison, approximately ninety acres, remained unresolved. It was clear that members of the public familiar with the parcel overwhelmingly favored a passive recreational use there, as opposed to an active sports use. A committee of the CPIA board studied the property, solicited public comments on alternate proposals, and concluded that this former golf-course site offered a tremendous opportunity to create a very special area unlike any other in the park. Developing the site for passive, open space would give people an important alternative to the more active areas of the park. A passive designation would permit non-structured, casual activities with minimal impact on the natural habitat. Removing the sports designation of the area would greatly increase the percentage of park land devoted to passive recreation and natural-resource protection while reducing land designated for sports and festivals. The park board decided that approval of the change would allow for development of a detailed plan for tree planting, lagoon enhancements, path reconfiguration, drainage, and stormwater holding, as well as any accessory uses such as shelters or bathrooms.

The plan amendments were presented at a public hearing on September 26, 2017, and adopted by the CPIA board the same day.

2018

In 2018, the exterior renovation of one of the park's damaged maintenance buildings along Henry Thomas Drive was completed. Also, the "Hat Luncheon," an annual fundraiser for the park's forest, was inaugurated in the Arbor Room at Popp Fountain. The park splits its portion of funds raised at this event between ongoing tree-care efforts and building a permanent endowment for our trees.

2019

For several reasons, 2019 was a momentous year. Renovations to the Casino Building were completed by new tenant Café Du Monde, and the second phase of the Besthoff Sculpture Garden opened in May. We also finished an outdoor kitchen in the Botanical Garden and total renovation of the iconic children's play area, Storyland, with park board members, other individuals, and companies sponsoring individual exhibits. The Louisiana Children's Museum opened on August 31, 2019, with Gov. John Bel Edwards and his wife, Donna, in attendance. This fulfilled another major initiative of the park's plan by adding a cultural attraction to complement the New Orleans Museum of Art, the Besthoff Sculpture Garden, and the New Orleans Botanical Garden. Closing the South Golf Course on the July Fourth weekend of 2005 eventually made the LCM possible.

Unfortunately, June 2019 saw the death of George Parker, the park's chief administrative officer, who had held a variety of positions in his long tenure at City Park.

The highlight of the year occurred in May, with voters approving the first-ever dedicated property-tax millage for City Park!

CHAPTER 12

Golf[1]

The most important shot in golf is the next one.
—Ben Hogan

Historical Background

Golf has always played an important role in the history and development of City Park, beginning with the construction of the South Course in 1902. In the early years, the park leased land for golf play as a concession to the private New Orleans Golf Club, generally located between Lelong Drive and Friedrichs Avenue. The club built a clubhouse overlooking Bayou St. John, along with other facilities such as a boathouse and pavilion, stables, and a hitching shed. They wished to expand the original nine holes to eighteen, but there was little space for growth. Finally, the club purchased land, which today is the New Orleans Country Club, and relocated to that site, leaving the City Park Improvement Association to manage the future of the sport in City Park.

In 1920, the park sold acreage it had west of the Orleans Canal (providing a site for what is today Delgado Community College)

and used the funds to purchase several parcels of land north of Friedrichs Avenue. This provided the land necessary to expand the South Golf Course from nine to eighteen holes, eventually adding another nine holes for a total of twenty-seven.

From the very beginning, golf generated significant revenues for the park. By the 1920s, greens fees from the course as well as income from renting golf clubs and selling balls totaled over $13,000 a year. Golf was a particularly popular recreational activity and one that the park board felt was compatible with the natural environment. It also delivered constantly increasing revenues, which made it a high priority for the association.

In 1934, the federal Works Progress Administration built the East Course between Zachary Taylor and Harrison and in 1938 added a golf clubhouse on Zachary Taylor. After additional land purchases made expansion to the north possible, the park built the West Golf Course in 1957 in the general area between Filmore Avenue and Harrison

Avenue. The final course, the North, was built in 1968 between Filmore Avenue and Robert E. Lee Boulevard. A new golf clubhouse was also built on Filmore, replacing the one built in 1938.

At one point, more than 200,000 rounds of golf were played on the four courses, and City Park was home to a stop on the PGA Tour, with the first "New Orleans Open" held in 1938. The tournament was played in City Park on and off for twenty-five years.

Golf requires large land areas for its play. By the time the North Golf Course was completed in 1968, golf, as a land use, accounted for more than 500 acres or 39 percent of the park's 1,300 total acreage.

South Course	100 acres
East Course	159 acres
West Course	135 acres
North Course & Driving Range	114 acres

The only justification for occupying so much park land was the financial contribution it made to the overall operating budget. The financial importance of golf did not just relate to the revenue it generated but also to the profit the courses produced. This operating profit was increasingly used to support other areas of the park that generated little to no profit. Parts of the park that were free and open to the public did not produce any revenue to cover their maintenance. Activities such as trash pickup and grass cutting and overhead expenses such as insurance and utility payments had to be funded from other park activities, as the state and city provided no public support.

By 2002, golf-course fees, rentals of golf carts, and income from the driving range produced a total revenue of $3,355,098 and had expenses of $2,165,757, yielding a net operating income or profit of $1,189,341.[2] This net income then supported other areas of the park. Impressive as this was, the total golf play and profit had been declining since the late 1990s. By 2002, the number of rounds had decreased from a high of 200,000 to 130,000 and the percentage of total park revenue reduced from 40 percent to 30 percent. While much of this decline related to competition from other athletic activities, it was also clear that utilizing golf profits to support other areas in the park meant that virtually no funds were available to reinvest in the courses, carts, driving range, and clubhouse. This had caused the courses to deteriorate and forced the park to neglect some of them in order to make whatever little investment was possible in the East and West courses, which generated the most revenue. With the clubhouse and driving range in what might best be described as a death spiral, the golfing experience became increasingly substandard, leading to decreased revenues.

As early as 1983, the plan that the EDAW design firm produced foresaw the need to provide land for other park activities and had recommended that the South Golf Course be closed to provide for those uses. This conclusion was reached again, in our 2005 Master Plan. The closing was necessitated not only to provide land for other uses but in consideration of the local golf market, which had other low-cost courses available, and a desire to streamline operating costs. While the proposal was very unpopular with some older golfers who had learned to play on the easy South Course, it was obvious that the combination of declining play, the decreasing net income being generated on the four courses, and the need to provide land for other activities made the closing of the South Course a crucial first step in implementing the newly adopted plan. Thus, 103 years after it was constructed, the South Golf Course was closed over the July Fourth weekend in 2005. Two months later, Hurricane Katrina flooded all the courses.

Golf Plan Pre-Katrina

Even prior to the adoption of the 2005 Master Plan, we began to plan for improvements to the courses. In order to stop their continued deterioration because of the park's lack of funds to invest in them, we sought help from the state through their Capital Outlay process. In 2003 we applied for funds to renovate the East Golf Course, and in 2004, the state approved $400,000 for planning and design for those improvements. The state hired Ace Torre and Bobby Weed as the architects for the restoration.

Seeking an overall vision for golf in City Park, the state engaged Economic Research Associates (ERA) in February 2005 to prepare an analysis of preferred investments for the sport. ERA concluded that the South Golf Course should be closed immediately, and as previously discussed, that recommendation was an instrumental part of the 2005 Master Plan. ERA also determined that the positioning of each of the Bayou Oaks courses (Bayou Oaks was the name of the entire golf complex) was relatively homogeneous, offering similar golf experiences, all at a low price.

ERA recognized the need for the State of Louisiana to invest in golf in City Park and felt that the refurbishment being designed by Torre and Weed would reposition the East Course as a higher-quality course. ERA recommended that the West Course receive improvements and a higher level of maintenance, offering a better experience but at a price still below the East Course. The North Course should receive some modifications to appeal to the less accomplished and more price sensitive golfer and preserve its current price structure. They felt that all upgrades could be completed by 2010.

In 2005, based upon this three-course planning, the park applied for, and the state approved, $6.6 million for rehabilitation of the East Golf Course. After additional design work and cost estimates, the park applied for $3.3 million more for the project.

While we sought funding for physical improvements, it was also necessary to improve the management of the complex. In 2001, City Park had a contract with KemperSports, a private golf-course management company. However, this arrangement proved to be unpopular with City Park staff and unproductive in the care and maintenance of the courses. It was essential to unify the staff by transferring all the park golf employees to the private management company. As CEO, I sought approval from the State Civil Service Commission and offered an economic incentive to the park employees to give up their state employment and transition to private employment. Civil Service permission was granted, and the staff moved en masse to private employment. At the time Katrina struck, KemperSports employed the entire golf staff.

Katrina's Impact on Golf

While brackish water from Lake Pontchartrain flooded almost the entire park, the golf complex was particularly hard hit. Floodwaters there reached between three and eight feet, with the higher range occurring above Filmore, on the North Course. Because it took the U.S. Army Corps of Engineers weeks to seal off the floodwall breaches that caused the flooding and weeks to pump out water from the park and surrounding neighborhoods, the damage was extensive. The brackish water killed all the grass; buried the sprinkler systems; inundated the clubhouse, driving-range headquarters, and maintenance buildings; and destroyed all the golf equipment.

Eventually, the damage claims we submitted to FEMA comprised nine individual Project Worksheets and totaled $8.5 million. We divided the claims into ones for the East and West courses and clubhouses and ones for the North Course. Total funds for the former were $7,724,863; the latter amounted to $841,586. It took years before these claims were even approved for expenditure, and I previously described the difficulties we had with FEMA documenting the total damages and having to arbitrate their refusal to pay for grass damage. FEMA initially estimated damage to the courses themselves at $300,000, while we thought it approached $2,500,000. I commented on FEMA's concept of restoring golf in an article in the *Times-Picayune* in June 2006: "FEMA's idea of restoring the courses is to resod some of the greens and replace some of the pumps, . . . that's it, nothing toward the irrigation system, nothing to the tees or fairways to fix the ruts that the cleanup contractors have caused. FEMA goes out and looks at a tee box and sees grass and says, 'Let's cut it and play on it.' Our former golf course superintendent says the root stems are contaminated because the grass has been under water for weeks and has to be removed and replaced."[3]

KemperSports immediately sought to terminate its contract with the park, as the complex was unusable and unable to generate any revenue. It took several years to resolve

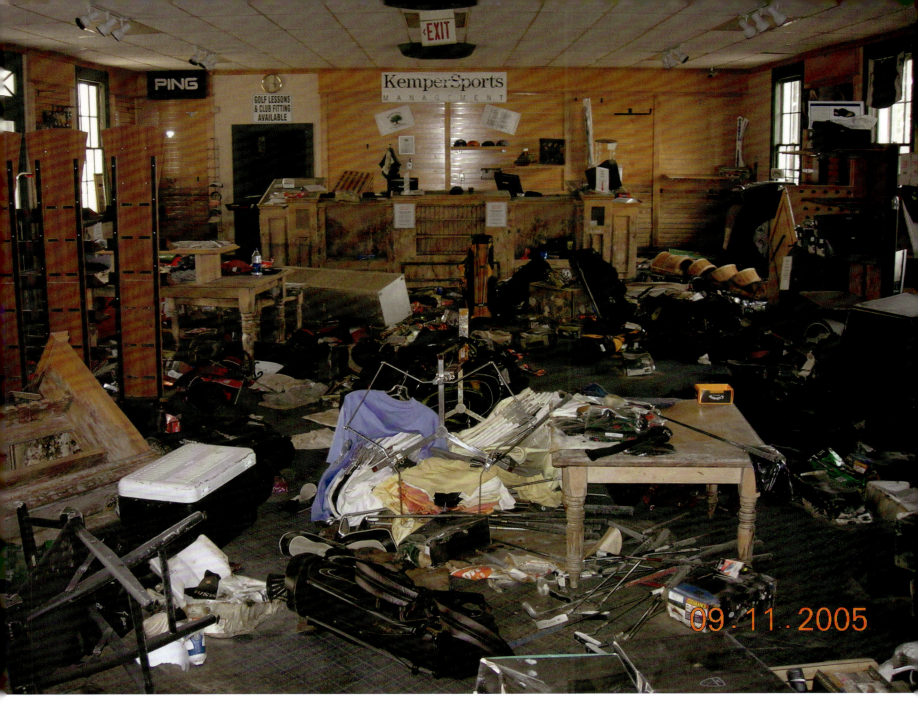

Damage in the golf clubhouse

Flooded golf equipment

issues such as who was responsible for the inventory of the clubhouse and pro shop.

After the storm, the state suspended all renovations of the East Course that had been under way. Despite that action, the legislature, in their 2006 session, approved the additional $3.3 million for the project that the park had applied for the previous year, bringing the state's investment to $9.9 million.

In order to generate some revenue, we opened the driving range out of a tent in February 2006. Subsequently, we rented an office trailer as a substitute for the damaged driving-range building until April 2010, when we were able to repair that building and put it back in use.

We decided to renovate the North Golf Course with the damage funds we received from FEMA. We were able to reopen the course in September 2008.

New Golf Concepts Emerge

The complete destruction that Hurricane Katrina visited upon City Park provided an opportunity to rethink many aspects of the our plan—particularly regarding golf. That portion of the 2005 Master Plan focused on offering three courses with different price points and levels of experience. In July 2006, the Fore!Kids Foundation, a nonprofit organization that utilizes golf to provide life lessons to underserved children, presented the park board with a radical new concept for golf in City Park.

Their concept still envisioned three golf courses. However, they proposed two championship eighteen-hole courses and a nine-hole executive course. All the courses would be constructed between Zachary Taylor Drive and Filmore Avenue. The North Course would no longer be needed for golf purposes and would be converted into soccer fields and a relocated Softball Quadruplex. Moving the quadruplex made it possible to return land that had originally been part of the East Course to a golf use. This proposal also expanded the footprint of golf to include the police horse stables and Scout Island.

Concurrent with the submission of the Fore!Kids Foundation plan was the formation of the Bayou District Foundation (BDF) in 2007, to serve as the overall coordinating and management entity for the golf project. The BDF membership came from the Fore!Kids Foundation and several other partners, including an affiliate of the Baton Rouge Area Foundation.

The BDF's model for its proposal was the East Lake neighborhood in Atlanta, which it succeeded in improving through golf. In Atlanta, a developer named Tom Cousins saw the opportunity to invest in a rundown course and use the revenues for housing, education, and social programs in the surrounding low-income neighborhood. The unfortunate flooding of the St. Bernard Housing Project by Hurricane Katrina, and its subsequent abandonment by the Housing Authority of New Orleans, presented the BDF with the opportunity to see if the concept that worked in Atlanta would work in New Orleans.

The basic idea was to create a new mixed-income community, with schools as a centerpiece along with recreational and social program amenities replacing the old housing project. The BDF engaged the East Lake Foundation as an adviser for the concept. Federal housing funds would support the mixed-income community, and proceeds from a revitalized golf complex would fund the social programs.

Just as important as the physical transformation proposed in the plan was the management proposal. The BDF offered to lease the entire golf complex and pay the park a rental fee plus a percentage of any profits that would be generated, and they would provide management services to operate and maintain the assets. This concept was for a public-private partnership where City Park would provide the land and contribute funding for golf improvements included in the state capital budget, plus whatever damage claim funds that would come from FEMA, and the BDF would fundraise for the rest of the physical improvements.

We included the Fore!Kids/BDF proposal in a public hearing devoted to considering other amendments to the park's master plan in September 2007. There were favorable comments from golf enthusiasts as well as opposition to the idea of converting the North Golf Course into soccer fields. Residents from the Lake Vista neighborhood just across Robert E. Lee Boulevard were concerned about increased traffic and light pollution from the soccer fields. Discussions with the City of New Orleans revealed that they were not interested in moving the police horse stables, a component of the proposed plan.

Because the plan was such a dramatic departure from the three eighteen-hole course plan approved just two years earlier, the park and Bayou District Foundation retained Economic Research Associates to evaluate the demand for golf in the New Orleans market and comment on the Fore!Kids/BDF concept. ERA, which had studied the golf market before Katrina, undertook a post-storm analysis and concluded that there was limited potential for success in appealing to either a high-end or low-end market. The greatest potential was in the midmarket range. They also concluded that a nine-hole course would likely be unsuccessful. Finally, ERA determined that neither City Park nor the Fore!Kids Foundation had a record of successfully managing golf complexes, and they recommended that a third-party operator be considered.

The objections to the expansion of golf beyond its current location led the City Park board to conclude that any redevelopment of golf should occur within its existing footprint. They also decided that any golf strategy should include hierarchical golf assets: high end, moderate, and affordable. The board found merit in the concept of a public-private partnership with the Bayou District Foundation and authorized management to continue negotiations to come up with an acceptable proposal. The board also required that a new master plan for golf be created, to determine precisely how the land set aside for golf would be utilized. The park board adopted these actions in its 2007 master plan amendment.

In September 2008, renovations and repairs to the North Golf Course were completed. In preparation for returning golf play to the park, we signed a contract with Billy Casper

Golf Course & Club Management to operate the North Course and driving range. In a bit of irony, fifty years earlier, professional golfer Billy Casper defeated Ken Venturi in a playoff to win the Greater New Orleans Open Invitational on our West Course! Now Casper had his own golf management company and was returning to operate our course. Mr. Casper came to City Park to inaugurate the opening of the North Course in September.

The 2009 Golf Plan

The park moved forward to initiate a new golf master plan, which would be in the same golf footprint north of Zachary Taylor Drive. In April 2008, the state approved changes in the Torre contract to conduct a master plan study. Rees Jones, Inc. replaced Bobby Weed as the golf-course architect to produce the plan utilizing the input from the 2007 process, particularly the conclusions reached by Economic Research Associates.

Their proposed plan was presented to the park in February 2009 and was the subject of a public hearing held the following month. While there were some similarities to the 2007 concept, there were also significant differences. The main similarity was the proposal for two eighteen-hole courses and a nine-hole course. The differences included:

- The golf clubhouse was to be located off Mirabeau and Wisner as opposed to a location on Filmore Avenue.
- Scout Island and the police horse stables were not a part of the plan.
- The sports fields proposed to be located on what was the North Course were eliminated from the plan, keeping that course in place.
- Land located east of Mona Lisa Drive that was not a part of the old East Golf Course was included in the golf plan. Mona Lisa Drive had traditionally separated golf from Couturie Forest. Thus the eight-acre tract, while not developed with golf holes, was considered part of the golf course.
- The proposed nine-hole course was reduced from an executive course to a par-3 course.

Because the estimated total cost of the reconfigured course was approximately $46 million, the plan was broken out into two phases. The first phase would include a championship eighteen-hole course (called the number 1 course) roughly between Zachary Taylor and Harrison Avenue. Phase I would also include a relocated driving range, new maintenance building, a new clubhouse and access road off Mirabeau Avenue. Phase II would include the second eighteen-hole course (called the number 2 course) plus construction of the nine-hole par-3 course. The first phase was estimated to cost approximately $24 million and the second $22 million. The plan provided for the North

Course to continue to operate, albeit with improvements. Upon completion of the plan, the total acreage footprint of golf would be reduced from 508 acres to approximately 429, primarily from the closing of the South Golf Course. This reduction in park acres devoted to golf was the first decrease since golf was introduced in the park in 1902. Finally, ERA projected that just the Phase I plan of the new championship course combined with the existing North Course would generate 62,000 rounds by 2016.

Public-hearing comments came mainly from golfers who objected to what they presumed would be higher costs to play the courses, from golfers who favored at least one high-level course, and from people who currently used the damaged courses for passive recreation such as walking, biking, or walking their dog. Several submitted written comments positing that pedestrians on the courses far outnumbered potential golfers. Park management countered that it had conducted a count of people using the damaged courses on a Saturday and Sunday, and the total for both days was approximately 550 people. At the same time, it was not unusual on a typical day for a course to accommodate over 225 golfers, hardly "far outnumbered" by the walkers. Comments were also made that people enjoyed experiencing a natural area and did not want it "converted" to a golf course. We explained, as we had for several years, that the subject area was not a natural area but a golf course that had been damaged, and the proposal was to restore the area to what it had been before the hurricane. Nevertheless, the continued interest by a number of park users to have a portion of the park set aside for a natural passive area was noted and eight years later was enshrined into the park's master plan by setting aside a large part of the old East Course for that purpose.

The park board decided to adopt the proposed plan but only to proceed with Phase I. In addition, they directed the park staff to prepare a Request for Proposal to secure a public-private partnership that would bring additional capital to the plan. Those actions were approved in the May 2009 amendment to the master plan. Park staff began to prepare a Request for Proposal that was reviewed by the Louisiana Attorney General's Office, who advised that the RFP should not only include a solicitation for capital contributions but also for management services. It took almost a full year to produce a final RFP, but in December 2009 the park issued the proposal.

The Final Modification

We received three responses to the RFP seeking external capital and a manager for the proposed golf complex: one from Honours Golf, one from Billy Casper Golf, and one from the Bayou District Foundation. A committee of City Park board members ranked all proposals and selected the BDF as the most responsive, primarily because they were the only bidder offering to bring capital funding for the implementation of the golf plan.

In addition to the RFP effort, the board continued to examine the physical layout of the 2009 plan and the total park area devoted to golf as a result of that plan. We looked at the plan with six objectives:

1. To minimize the land that would be necessary to implement the plan, to make previously used golf acres available for other park uses.

2. To determine whether two eighteen-hole courses and one nine-hole course were still the best use of golf assets.

3. To minimize the impact of implementing the plan on the park's urban forest.

4. To be certain the park could continue to offer a range of hierarchical golf experiences.

5. To be certain that the plan was able to maximize the revenue potential for the park.

6. To settle on a final golf plan that was affordable and implementable.

As a result of this review, we decided that a significant modification of the adopted golf plan was necessary.

The major proposed change was to develop two eighteen-hole courses but no nine-hole course. One of the courses would be the North Course, which would continue to offer a moderately priced experience, while the other course, named the South Course, would be a high-end championship course for those seeking a more challenging experience. The area for this new course would be reduced from 310 acres to approximately 250 acres. Accompanying this change was the decision that the golf clubhouse, which had been demolished following flooding by Katrina, would be rebuilt generally on the site of the former clubhouse and not off Mirabeau. Finally, the driving range would be improved on its current site and not relocated to the south side of Filmore.

As a result of these decisions, the high-end South Course would not utilize land south of Harrison Avenue, freeing up this acreage for other park uses. Another major advantage of concentrating the new course north of Harrison Avenue was that the land there had substantially less tree cover than the area south of Harrison, meaning that many fewer mature trees would be affected by the construction.

We would greatly save costs by rebuilding the clubhouse and improving the driving range on their previous sites, because they were already served by existing utilities and we could cluster maintenance and golf-operation activities near the clubhouse. This advantage would be maximized by having the South Golf Course near the clubhouse, maintenance facilities, and driving range.

Finally, the recommended changes to the golf plan did not alter the economics of the golf complex, as the park's economic consultant estimated that after three years of play, the entire complex would generate approximately $4 million of gross revenue.

The adoption of this new plan, when considered alongside the previous closing of the South Golf Course, would reduce the footprint of golf in City Park from roughly 508 acres, or 39 percent of the total park acreage, to approximately 316 acres, or 24 percent of total park acreage. This reduction allowed nearly 200 acres to be transitioned from golf to other park uses designated in the master plan!

Comments at the public hearing were very favorable to the proposed amendments and the decrease in acreage devoted to golf.

This plan was translated into a series of amendments to the master plan's land-use categories, and on March 22, 2011, the City Park board unanimously approved the amendments.

With the passage of the "final" golf plan, we had only to finish negotiations with the Bayou District Foundation, secure final authorization from the state to commit the funds from the Capital Outlay bill, finish design drawings, complete any necessary environmental permitting, bid the golf course, construct the course, and open for business. It seemed simple enough.

Negotiations with the Bayou District Foundation

First up was the drafting of an agreement between the Bayou District Foundation and City Park enshrining the particulars of the BDF proposal. The Attorney General's Office suggested that this take the form of a Cooperative Endeavor Agreement (CEA) as opposed to a standard lease, and our attorneys proceeded to develop a draft by early 2012. A management agreement with BDF also had to be drawn up, outlining the specifics of a management plan and proposed staffing.

What seemed relatively simple was not and it took over two years of drafting to come up with a CEA that was satisfactory to both parties. The basic framework of the CEA provided for the following:

- The agreement's term was thirty-five years.
- The BDF's capital contribution was set at $8.9 million.
- City Park would contribute $17.5 million, composed of $9.9 million in state funds and $7.6 million from the park's damage claims from Hurricane Katrina.
- In return for raising and contributing $8.9 million, the BDF was allotted a share of the net operating income from the golf complex. Up to $1,150,000 of the net operating income that would be generated was to be divided, with 75 percent coming to the park and 25 percent to the BDF. Income exceeding $1,150,000 was to be divided 55 percent to the park and 45 percent to the BDF.
- In recognition that golf revenues at City Park had been historically

syphoned off to cover other park operating expenses, leaving little to reinvest in golf, the agreement provided that prior to any net income being divided, an operating reserve of $250,000 would be established. When that account was fully funded, a capital reserve account would then be established of an equal amount.

- The BDF was named as the official manager of the golf and would be responsible to grow in the course after the contractor had completed basic construction and for all startup costs.
- Finally, PGA Tour Golf Course Properties Inc. would hire the director of golf, while other golf employees would be employees of the BDF.

In March 2014, the City Park board approved and signed the agreement. Subsequently, both parties inked management and operating agreements in July 2016.

Securing Release of State Funding

As previously described, state funding for golf improvements began before Hurricane Katrina and eventually totaled $9.9 million. These funds were contained in what is called House Bill #2, the Capital Outlay bill. The state allocated dollars from these funds for the Torre/Jones team to complete the design drawings for the new course and prepare bidding documents. The plans were finished and ready to bid in October 2013.[4] We petitioned the state to release the remaining funds so that the bid process could begin, but the state refused to do so. What was the problem?

As 2014 moved along, we were unable to get the state to release the funds and unable to understand the reason why. As the 2014 legislative session began, there was still no movement on what should have been a routine legislative act to reapprove the funding allocation to allow the project to be bid.

Word finally got back to us that Sen. John Alario, perhaps the most powerful man in the legislature and a longtime park supporter, had asked Gov. Bobby Jindal not to release the funds or move the project forward because of his fear that the PGA's New Orleans tournament, called the Zurich Classic, would move from its current home in Avondale to City Park. The Zurich Classic had been held at the Tournament Players Club Louisiana course in Jefferson Parish since 2007. Senator Alario had been instrumental in developing the championship golf course on the west bank in his district. He had also been instrumental in luring the PGA Tour back to the New Orleans area after a long absence, and he rightly was concerned that the new course in the central location of City Park would eventually cause the PGA to move the signature event.

Finally, there was clarity about the issue. Darrell Hunt, the Friends lobbyist, reached out to Alario, whom he had known for years, to discuss a solution to the dilemma. After all, if Senator Alario had wanted to scuttle the entire City Park golf project he certainly was able to do so, but that was not his goal. He simply wanted to protect the project he had worked so hard to secure for his district.

Darrell discussed the issue with me. We decided to reassure Alario and the rest of the Jefferson legislative delegation by inserting language in the capital appropriation bill that the tournament would not move to City Park. It read in part: "Due to the State's current investment in TPC Louisiana and the financial support it provides to the PGA TOUR event currently played at said facility, the funding of the City Park Golf Complex Improvements project . . . is conditioned upon said PGA TOUR event not being played at New Orleans City Park Golf Complex without prior agreement of the Commissioner of Administration and the Jefferson Parish Council." With this assurance, Senator Alario released his hold on the project and the funds were released in the summer of 2014.

Permitting

In September of 2011, with the master plan amended to incorporate the new course on a reduced park footprint and with preliminary design plans far enough along that the layout of the course could be determined, we began the process of securing the appropriate permits for eventual construction. We submitted a Joint Permit Application to both the Louisiana Department of Natural Resources/Office of Coastal Management and the U.S. Army Corps of Engineers for work in the Louisiana Coastal Zone. Later that month we were notified that a Coastal Use Permit was not required as a result of our project being in a fast land, a determination that was good for two years. In 2013, we resubmitted the Joint Permit Application.

Because part of the funding was coming from FEMA, an Environmental Assessment had to be performed in accordance with the National Environmental Policy Act of 1969 (NEPA) before the federal funding could be released. The submitted project included excavation of approximately 40,000 cubic yards to enlarge existing water bodies and 22,000 cubic yards of fill to provide for culvert installations. It was noted that the project converted 5.5 acres of previously unused park space (not part of the old East Course nor part of Couturie Forest) into a buffer for a new golf hole. It was also noted that the project converted 96 acres of golf course land (part of the old East Course) into accessible open space for park visitors. FEMA prepared a FONSI (Finding of No Significant Impact) in May 2013 with opportunity for public comment. The FONSI was approved and signed in June 2013. Believing that all appropriate permits had been secured, the state put the project out to bid and a construction contract was awarded in November 2014 for $13,180,000.

Duininck Golf was the lowest of four bidders, and following a ceremonial groundbreaking on February 12, 2015, construction began.

Not So Fast

Once Duininck erected a construction fence around the site and access was cut off for the walkers and nature enthusiasts who had used the area since it was damaged by Katrina, opposition to the construction galvanized. Email chains were started; signs were put up on the construction fence expressing opposition, some using very obscene language; parts of the construction fence were repeatedly torn down; and sand was put into some of the contractor's equipment. Demonstrators picketed park events and several climbed oak trees on the site in the hopes that sitting in the trees would prevent them from being removed by the construction. Protestors appeared at park board meetings to present their case.[5] In March 2015, an opposition group, City Park for Everyone Coalition, filed a federal lawsuit against the park and FEMA alleging that the Environmental Assessment conducted on the project two years earlier was inadequate.

The opponents convinced the U.S. Army Corps of Engineers to inspect the area of the construction adjacent to Hole #5, which was in the process of being cleared of vegetation to provide a buffer for the hole, to determine whether jurisdictional wetlands were present on the site. The Corps visited the site three times and observed ponding water in several areas, including in ruts left by construction equipment. They made several more in April and it was clear that the Corps felt pressure from opposition groups to find wetlands in the area. The Corps asked that the architect inform the contractor to stay completely out of the area until a wetland determination had been made. The state and the park pointed out to the Corps that the area in question was not a naturally occurring wetland and did not naturally connect to any body of water but was made wet by a leaking water pipe nearby and persistent rains. However, the Corps felt that the condition of the site, regardless of how that condition occurred, justified a formal evaluation of whether jurisdictional wetlands existed.

The park's attorneys hired the respected environmental health and environmental liability management company U.S. Helm to conduct the formal wetland evaluation and present those findings to all parties. The evaluation was conducted in May 2015, while construction of the course continued in all other locations except the area in question. U.S. Helm concluded that approximately 1.31 acres out of the contested 5.5 acres exhibited wetland characteristics in accordance with Army Corps standard practice. The Corps accepted U.S. Helm's finding and concluded that a swale on the eastern side of the wetland that was five inches deep and 3 feet wide and ran 100 feet constituted a "water of the

United States." This finding was made despite incontrovertible evidence that the wetland area was created by a leaking water pipe, and the so-called "water of the United States" was simply a drainage swale. Nevertheless, the Corps issued a cease-and-desist order on July 10, 2015, an unnecessary action since the contractor had stopped working in the contested area in April.

In further discussion with the Corps, it was determined that the state and park would apply for an After-the-Fact (ATF) Permit, as City Park had not applied for appropriate permits under the Clean Water Act before initiating work. (We had not applied as we were unaware that any wetlands existed on the site.) FEMA, after an analysis of our ATF application, concluded that the failure to secure the appropriate wetland permit prior to initiating work did not substantially changed the environmental conditions addressed in the original Environmental Assessment. As a result, the Corps issued the ATF Permit for the 1.31 acres of wetlands in January 2016, approximately one year after construction had started.

A condition of the permit provided that some form of mitigation for the damaged wetlands be obtained. After negotiations with the Corps, it was determined that City Park and the State of Louisiana would purchase mitigation credits in a wetland bank in another part of the state. In October 2015, 1.6 acres of credits were purchased in the Weyerhaeuser NR Company Gum Swamp Mitigation Bank. A sum of $19,600 was paid for the credits, effectively ending the permit process.

The litigation continued, however, and it was not until November 2016 that federal judge Sarah Vance dismissed the lawsuit against FEMA (City Park having been previously dismissed from the suit). The course was completed, grown in, and opened and the new clubhouse dedicated in April 2017.

The Odyssey of Golf

In 2020, golf at City Park turned 118 years old, making it one of the longest continuously operating sporting venues in the park. The sport has seen four golf clubhouses (one private and three public) on three different sites, with one clubhouse cut in half by an interstate highway and another destroyed by Hurricane Katrina.

There has been a dizzying variety of golf-course configurations, beginning with a nine-hole course in 1902 in the southern portion of the park below the current interstate and railroad tracks and ending with two eighteen-hole courses north of Harrison Avenue. The driving range has been in two locations, and the courses have been managed by park employees, a combination of park employees and private management, and now totally by private management. We went from playing 200,000 rounds of golf on four courses to zero rounds for three years after Katrina. The courses have held amateur and professional championships and of course innumerable charity events. The complex has been disrupted by construction of an interstate highway and been the subject of lawsuits, arbitration claims, flooding, and protests.

The golf complex has gone from occupying almost 40 percent of park land to a little less than 25 percent and from generating almost 40 percent of the park's total income to approximately 25 percent today. Hall of Fame golfers such as Ben Hogan, Sam Snead, Byron Nelson, and Gene Sarazen played in City Park, while Hall of Famer Tiger Woods never has.

I expect that through it all, Ben Hogan's famous saying about the next shot will be true of golf at City Park. The next shot golf takes will be the most important!

CHAPTER 13

The Beauregard Monument[1]

I think it wiser, moreover, not to keep open the sores of war but to follow the examples of those nations who endeavored to obliterate the marks of civil strife, to commit to oblivion the feelings engendered.
—Former Confederate general Robert E. Lee on a proposal for a monument in Gettysburg, September 3, 1869

In July 2015, then-mayor Mitch Landrieu appeared before the New Orleans City Council to request that they begin the legal process to remove four post-Civil War monuments dedicated to "heroes" of the Confederacy. In doing so, he was continuing a debate begun in Charlottesville, Virginia, over the role of an estimated seven hundred public memorials, plaques, and fountains in the history of this country and the difficult history that is the legacy of the Civil War.

The four monuments Landrieu asked to be removed from public spaces were statues of Robert E. Lee, Jefferson Davis, Gen. P. G. T. Beauregard, and a memorial to the Battle of Liberty Place. These monuments were all erected during what some historians characterize as "The Cult of the Lost Cause." The National Park Service gave this description of the Cult of the Lost Cause in its consideration of City Park's 1999 nomination of the Beauregard statue to the National Register of Historic Places:

The Cult of the Lost Cause has its roots in the Southern search for justification and the need to find a substitute for victory in the Civil War. In attempting to deal with defeat, Southerners created an image of the war as a great heroic epic. A major theme in the Cult of the Lost Cause was the clash of two civilizations, one inferior to the other. The North, "invigorated" by constant struggle with nature, had become materialistic, grasping for wealth and power. The South had a "more generous climate" which had led to a finer society based upon "veracity and honor in man, chastity and fidelity in women." Like tragic heroes, Southerners had waged a noble but doomed struggle to preserve their superior civilization. There was an element of chivalry in the way the South had fought, achieving noteworthy victories against staggering odds. . . . A particularly popular form of veneration was the memorial, of which the north-facing Confederate soldier was the most common type.[2]

Other favorable theories for the monuments suggested that they were merely elegant works of art, or war memorials to veterans.

For those individuals and groups arguing that the statues and other symbols of the

Confederacy be removed, another narrative holds prominence. In this view, the monuments intend to glorify a rebellion and serve as symbols of intimidation, inspiring hate and bigotry. These statues, opponents argue, ignore the real reason for the Civil War, which was the South's fight to preserve slavery.

These two strongly held and diametrically opposed opinions of the purpose of the monuments have led to vigorous debates in recent times. In some places where elected leaders proposed their removal, riots and violence have resulted.

Public parks have seen their share of these debates and demonstrations, as many of the monuments and plaques are located in or adjacent to parks and other open spaces. Such is the case with the statue that stood at the entrance to New Orleans City Park in 2015.

General Beauregard

Pierre Gustave Toutant Beauregard was born on May 28, 1818, on the Contreras plantation in St. Bernard Parish (a suburb of New Orleans) but grew up in New Orleans. Before the Civil War, he attended West Point, graduating second in his class in 1838 and eventually becoming superintendent for a short time. He served in the U.S. Army Corps of Engineers as well as earning awards for bravery in the Mexican-American War. He later returned to New Orleans, where he ran unsuccessfully for mayor. He was involved in the reconstruction of the United States Custom House on Canal Street and served as a supervisor for the Louisiana Lottery.

General Beauregard resigned his commission in the United States Army to join the Confederate army in 1861 and was appointed as the Confederacy's first brigadier general. According to the National Park Service, "The high point of his Civil War service was probably his command of the Southern forces at Charleston, including his responsibility for ordering the bombardment of Fort Sumter on April 12, 1861. . . . His other important contributions to the war effort included commanding roles in the battles of First Manassas (June 1861) and Shiloh (April 1862), command of coastal defenses in Georgia and South Carolina (September 1862-April 1864), direction of the defense of Petersburg (June 1864) and command of the Military Division of the West (October 1864)."[3]

Supporters of General Beauregard's legacy point out that after the war, he was an early proponent of reconciliation between the races and an advocate of equal rights for previously enslaved peoples. He chaired a committee of prominent New Orleanians that called for integrated schools, public places, and transportation years before the United States Congress passed legislation to guarantee those rights.

General Beauregard died in 1893, a war hero to many Southerners while Northerners remember him as having committed treason against the United States and for starting a war to perpetuate slavery by firing on Fort Sumter. As in so many debates about Civil War "heroes," supporters and critics of General Beauregard's legacy each mount arguments they believe best support their case. However, at the end of the day, as the famous football coach Bill Parcells once said, "You are what your record says you are."

Erection of the Statue

On the day General Beauregard died, the New Orleans chapter of the United Confederate Veterans met and decided to form a separate association to raise funds for "the erection in New Orleans of a monument commemorative of the patriotic deeds and noble achievements of the great Louisiana soldier and General."[4] They then incorporated the Beauregard Monument Association (BMA). Raising sufficient funds turned out to be a difficult and very slow process. Various entities including the United Daughters of the Confederacy, the Sons of Confederate Veterans, the Ladies Confederate Memorial Association, and the Louisiana Historical Society all contributed funds.

The BMA solicited sculptor Alexander Doyle of New York to design the statue, as he had already completed monuments of Robert E. Lee at Lee Circle and Albert Sidney Johnston in Metairie Cemetery, both in New Orleans. In 1895 the BMA even staged a mock Civil War battle in City Park using units of the Louisiana National Guard.

Having secured a sculptor for the monument, it was then necessary to find a site. In 1905, the BMA approached the City Park Improvement Association, which offered a site to be selected when the BMA was ready to start construction.[5] Time dragged on with periodic reports to the CPIA on the progress of fund raising. In 1907, fourteen years after General Beauregard's death, the park agreed to contribute $1,000 toward the building of the foundation, mound, pedestal, and base only. That payment was not actually made until 1915. Finally, in 1908, the CPIA tendered a specific site in front of City Park at what would be the intersection of Esplanade Avenue and Wisner Boulevard. (The question of whether that property was actually owned or controlled by the park is confusing and not resolved. It remains one of the issues in pending lawsuits.) At the site's dedication, Judge John St. Paul said: "Well, indeed, may they worship at his shrine, for he was one, and not the least, of that galaxy of heroic men whose glorious deeds have placed their age and the struggle in which they took part among the grandest that adorn the annals of all times."[6]

In 1908, a contract with sculptor Doyle and the Beauregard Monument Association was executed, and in 1912 a contract to construct a foundation and pedestal was awarded to a local marble company, with the pedestal being completed the next year. In 1913, a time capsule was entombed in the base for future generations to find. Finally, on November 11, 1915, the completed statue was dedicated at

Statue of Confederate general P. G. T. Beauregard erected by the Beauregard Monument Association in 1915

an elaborate public ceremony.

Doyle's statue consists of Beauregard mounted on a horse and is sixteen feet high. When placed on the pedestal, the entire monument rises to a height of twenty-seven feet, making an imposing presence at the front entrance of City Park at the terminus of Esplanade Avenue. The bas-relief inscription on the pedestal reads:

> *G. T. Beauregard*
> *1818-1893*
> *General C.S.A.*
> *1861-1865*

In 1919, the BMA offered the City Park Improvement Association $2,000 to take responsibility for the perpetual care of the monument. However, payment was never made, and the association never accepted such responsibility.

The next significant event in the history of the monument occurred in 1997, when the City Park Improvement Association nominated it for the National Register of Historic Places. As applications for National Register status require an entity to assume ownership of the statue, the City Park board president asserted in the application that the CPIA was the legal owner of the sculpture. With that declaration, the National Park Service, finding that the statue was a representative example of the Cult of the Lost Clause, placed the statue on the National Register in 1999.

Extensive examination of the record,

however, does not reveal any documentation that City Park ever received title to the statue from the Beauregard Monument Association nor from any other entity. In fact, as previously mentioned, City Park board minutes document that the park never agreed to maintain the statue, which was funded solely by gifts to the BMA. Thus, we can add the ownership of the statue to the list of issues yet to be resolved.

After the dedication in 1915, the Beauregard monument created little or no controversy and stood at the entrance to City Park in relative obscurity despite its prominent location. That continued until 2015, 100 years later.

The City Removes the Beauregard Statue

Following Mayor Landrieu's appearance before the City Council to ask that that body to declare the four monuments public nuisances and order their removal, a period of intense debate occurred within the city as the meaning of the Civil War and the role of statues honoring Confederate war heroes became a major topic of public discourse. In December of 2015, the City Council, in a 6-1 decision, declared the monuments public nuisances and ordered them removed. Over a year and a half passed before the city was able to marshal the resources to have the statues taken down. Because of the controversy, various companies declined to sign any city contract to remove the monuments because of threats of violence against their workers.

During this time, people opposed to the removal began to argue that the CPIA should exercise its rights as "owner" of the Beauregard statue to prevent its removal.

In 2017, the city began the process of taking down the monuments. In early May, the city attorney informed the CPIA that the city intended to follow through on the City Council's order to remove the Beauregard statue. Also in early May, the Lt. Gov. Billy Nungesser and the attorney general of Louisiana, Jeff Landry, wrote Mayor Landrieu saying that ownership issues regarding the statue should be resolved before the city seized it. They asserted that if it turned out that the CPIA owned the Beauregard monument and the city removed it, the city could face an obligation to restore it to its former location.

The Monumental Task Committee, which opposed the removal of the Beauregard statue, filed for a temporary restraining order to stop the city from taking down the monuments. However, an Orleans Civil District Court judge refused to issue such an order.

On May 16, 2017, the City Park Improvement Association issued the following statement regarding the imminent removal of the statue.

The issues regarding the Beauregard Monument and its location are complicated. New Orleans City Park Improvement Association is not aware of any definitive evidence that the NOCPIA owns the General P. G. T. Beauregard Monument. Following the passage of an ordinance approved by the City Council and signed by Mayor Landrieu in December of 2015, a decision was made by the city to remove the century old monument from its current location. Mayor Landrieu has clearly indicated that the removal of the monument is imminent, and we hope it will be done safely and that all parties, while exercising their first amendment rights, respect the laws of our city and state. The City has acknowledged NOCPIA's authority to own, manage, and maintain New Orleans City Park property. The NOCPIA has asserted its right on this matter, including the property upon which the monument sits, and the dialogue regarding those rights with the City is ongoing.

That same night, May 16, 2017, with a large contingent of police present, an anonymous contractor and other city personnel, all masked to protect their identity, removed the statue and carted it away to a location in the eastern part of the city. The city did not remove the pedestal nor comment on the ultimate acceptable site for the statue's relocation.

In November 2017, a New Orleans citizen and a reformulated Beauregard Monument Association (the original association having long ago disbanded) filed suit against the City Park Improvement Association, arguing that the land under the monument falls under the jurisdiction of and is owned by the CPIA and that a previous board president had asserted that the park owned the statue in its application for National Register status. The suit further claimed that City Park was not compensated by the city when it seized the statue and that the city unlawfully took the property of the CPIA. Finally, it asserted that the CPIA breached its fiduciary duty when it failed to object to the city's taking of its property. The city responded in a legal brief that City Park did not own the statue. The litigation is still in a suspended status.

Since the time of the filing of the lawsuit, protests in various forms have intermittently continued. Periodically protestors have appeared at board meetings or held signs and walked up and down outside the park's Administration Building. Stones painted with the names of Confederate leaders have been thrown onto the circle where the statue once stood, and alternative news magazines occasionally run stories about the city's "unlawful seizure of the statue."

Numerous City Park board members have also been impacted by the controversy, as they have acquaintances or friends who are on one side or the other of the debate. Steve Pettus, the president of the board in 2017; Paul Masinter, chair of our legal committee; as well as many members of our board were impacted by the tensions in the community. They received phone calls, emails, and visits to their homes as they tried to balance friendship with upholding the authority of the CPIA and the future of the park.

As the face of the park, I also experienced my share of difficult correspondence and public confrontations. One day, shortly after the monument was taken down, my phone rang with an unknown number. I decided to answer it, despite the fact that the controversy had impressed upon me the need to send any

Stones thrown onto Beauregard Circle at the front of City Park by supporters of Confederate monuments, 2019

This voodoo doll was among the protest objects thrown onto Beauregard Circle

unrecognized numbers to my voicemail. The caller shouted at me that I was allowing the city to seize a piece of the South's history and that I should be embarrassed to call myself a "son of the South." I had to explain that I was not born in the South and therefore could not be considered a "son of the South." He hung up.

In 2018, after waiting nearly a year for the city to complete their removal of the base and pedestal, and noting the unsightly appearance of the statue-less pedestal at the front of the park, the CPIA informed the city that it would remove and store the pedestal while we continued to work for the permanent relocation of both the statue and pedestal. The pedestal continues to be stored on City Park grounds, and the park has made temporary landscape improvements in the traffic circle where the monument had resided.

During the process of removing the pedestal, the time capsule placed in the foundation over one hundred years ago was recovered and provided to the State Museum. Unfortunately, mistakes made in the initial placement of the time capsule allowed water to penetrate the box, significantly damaging the contents. The State Museum is still working to restore some of the artifacts.

Since the statue's removal, Mayor LaToya Cantrell, who succeeded Mayor Landrieu, and the city have shown little interest in placing it in an alternate site. Any action the city takes, whether to keep it in a warehouse or place it someplace else, will again stir up the controversy. So, for the time being, no action either by the city or by the citizens who filed suit seems likely. The mayor seems content to keep the statue hidden and pass the problem along to future administrations. Likewise, after years of efforts to find a solution, the park will wait until the city has a renewed interest in a permanent solution.

Lessons for Today

Several lessons can be taken from City Park's experience with a Civil War monument.

First, more than 150 years after the Civil War, for some individuals the wounds of that great conflict are not only still present, but they are used to justify many behaviors, from peaceful demonstrations to violent clashes.

Second, while some monuments are truly works of art in and of themselves, many others are unremarkable pieces of stone or bronze that are either symbols of white supremacy or solemn reminders of assumed past glory, depending on your point of view.

Third, while Mayor Landrieu made clear the reasons he sought removal of the four monuments, he had absolutely no plan for the ultimate disposition of the statues. He left that for the future. But by doing so,

he allowed the wound to fester. The lack of closure continues to tie up time and resources and does not contribute to healing the wounds that the removal has caused in various communities. Had there been a plan, it is possible that the removal and relocation could have been accomplished without the rancor and discord that characterized the removal of each of the monuments. It is hoped that a permanent location for General Beauregard, in keeping with the conditions imposed by the City Council, can be achieved in the future and this difficult episode in the history of the park concluded.

Finally, our experience with the Beauregard statue is just a microcosm of a larger debate over history, how it should be interpreted, and to what extent the removal of Civil War monuments and plaques is righting a terrible wrong or an attempt at rewriting history, just as the early proponents of these artifacts hoped to do. Inevitably, there will be people and organizations caught in the middle of the debate for which there is almost no conclusion that would satisfy all sides. The city has moved ahead with renaming streets, parks, and schools that were named for Confederate heroes, as it tries to erase the glorification of those who were slaveholders or who fought to preserve slavery.

CHAPTER 14

The Tax

Rivers know this: there is no hurry. We shall get there some day.
—A. A. Milne, *Winnie-the-Pooh*

Since at least 1896, when Act 130 of the Louisiana Legislature mandated that the Common Council of New Orleans appropriate $15,000 annually for the support of City Park, the park has been making the case that the citizens of New Orleans needed to provide it with consistent public tax support. In the 1980s, the park proposed a two-mill property tax in order prevent further deterioration of the park and as an alternate to the unpopular idea of leasing some of the park's land for residential purposes to create that consistent income. This idea gained no traction.

The 2005 Master Plan included as part of its financing scheme a three-mill property tax, which would have yielded approximately $6 million to be split between capital and operating expenses. While we were successful in obtaining state support through the tax on slot machines at the Fair Grounds with a maximum of $2.2 million allowed, we could not get the City of New Orleans to commit to its share of operating funding.

Following Katrina, we argued strenuously that funding from both the state and the city was necessary to provide a base of public tax support, which could then be augmented through earned income and fund raising. We stressed that the park's financial future would always be in jeopardy without that public support. Once the state rescued the park by providing operating funds through the slot tax, we sought many times to persuade the city to provide an equal amount of funds. On numerous occasions we met with Mayor Mitch Landrieu to secure his support, but he never embraced the idea that the city could provide funds for a park operated by a state agency, even though he was once the lieutenant governor of the state and was intimately familiar with our situation.

Failure of the Audubon Tax Proposal

In late 2013, Bill Hoffman, our president, and I went to see Ron Forman, president of the Audubon Nature Institute and my former boss, to discuss the possibility of collaborating on a tax proposal. We believed that together we might have a stronger chance of securing passage of some type of property tax. Ron, however, felt that he was better off going to the voters by himself than cooperating with other park agencies. He believed that the success of the Audubon Nature Institute along with the support of Mayor Landrieu and other influential New Orleanians would guarantee a successful election. We left that meeting thinking we would have to find other partners.

In March 2014, however, New Orleans voters rejected a proposal to extend two Audubon tax millages for fifty years. The proposition would have consolidated the two taxes (one for the zoo and one for the aquarium) into one, increased the combined millage rate from 3.31 mills to 4.2 mills, and allowed the proceeds of the millage to be used at any of its properties as opposed to being dedicated to the zoo or the aquarium. The proposal was not just defeated; it was crushed 65 percent to 35 percent. Fortunately, if that can be a term for a devastating loss, the millages to be combined would not expire until 2021 and 2022 respectively, so there was time for a reconsideration.

The millages were defeated by a grassroots, social-media effort orchestrated by a loose-knit combination of neighborhood groups unhappy with Audubon's management of Audubon Park and a newly formed group, Parks for All, who felt that Audubon was not responsive to community needs. (Certain actions that Audubon had taken over the years, such as rebuilding the Audubon Park golf course and proposing playing fields for an area that was general open space, were some of the reasons for unhappiness among some constituents.) Audubon put together an aggressive campaign featuring prominent New Orleanians and television and social-media endorsements from a wide segment of the community. However, the opponents mounted an equally aggressive digital campaign, which eventually resulted in the lopsided defeat.

Work Begins on a More Acceptable Plan

Following the March 2014 defeat of Audubon's proposal, we began to discuss with Audubon, the city's Parks and Parkways department, and New Orleans Recreation Development Commission (NORDC) an alternate approach to securing equitable funding for all of the most prominent recreation agencies. A powerful incentive for a cooperative effort was the fact that not only were supporting tax millages for Audubon expiring in the future, but millages supporting NORDC and Parks and Parkways were also expiring at the same time. Loss of those millages would have been devastating to the budgets of all three entities. Our incentive was clear—we had no property-tax millage from the citizens of New Orleans, and we urgently needed to find another source of public operating revenue.

The "partners" decided that the best course of action would be to enlist an independent third party to study recreation funding in the city and develop alternatives to address the lack of funding. We proposed engaging the Trust for Public Land, a nationally recognized nonprofit land-conservation organization that advised a variety of communities on public financing options for parks and recreation areas. We, of course, had used the TPL to initially study City Park's financial status, ultimately leading to the adoption of our 2005 Master Plan, which called for a city property tax to support the park.

Each entity contributed approximately $13,000 toward a $140,000 financial feasibility study, with the remaining funds coming from local philanthropic foundations. In 2017, the TPL published its findings in a report entitled *The Park Agencies of New Orleans: Existing Conditions Report and Recommendations.* The report noted that if you exclude the federally managed Bayou Sauvage National Wildlife Refuge on the eastern edge of the city, the four park agencies controlled about 2,900 acres of park and recreation land in New Orleans, or 85 percent of its total acreage. Other park and recreation lands were controlled by other entities such as the Lakefront Management Authority, the Orleans Public School Board, and the Orleans Levee District. The report contained several major findings.

- The current revenue sources funding the park agencies were inadequate to sustain and grow a comprehensive New Orleans Park system. The report also noted that current millages for NORDC, Parks and Parkways, and Audubon would all expire in 2021 and 2022, leaving a $20.8 million hole in recreation funding.
- The report expressed concern about the lack of coordination and communication among numerous park agencies and made recommendations for a more formalized approach to collaboration.
- The report noted that there was some confusion among citizens trying to report problems without knowing which agency had responsibility, along with some overlap in park services.

Also in 2017, the city, after years of effort by the New Orleans City Planning Commission, adopted an amended City Master Plan, which called for more effective collaboration and management of parks and green spaces. It called for a variety of recreation initiatives, including the development of a new recreation master plan for the community.

Creation of a Specific Tax Proposition

In May of 2018, LaToya Cantrell became mayor of New Orleans. Here was an opportunity to interest a newly elected mayor in the funding of parks and recreation. We began to engage the new administration through the transition team she established to advise her on a wide range of issues facing the city. We impressed upon the team that not only were several important millages going to expire toward the end of the mayor's first term and that the loss of those millages would severely damage the entire recreation system in the city, but that City Park was in serious need of another source of public funding or it faced being unable to maintain the improvements made after Hurricane Katrina. Reiterating the findings of the Trust for Public Land, the team stated, "The New Orleans Park system is at significant risk of deterioration due to the lack of sustainable funding for maintenance, park safety, programming and capital improvement."

In June, what had come to be called the "Park Partners" (City Park, Audubon Nature Institute, Parks and Parkways, and NORDC) met with Mayor Cantrell to secure her support for a potential election to renew the expiring millages and to provide funding for City Park. The mayor expressed interest in the proposal and urged our group to develop a specific plan for a more equitable distribution of the dollars going to parks and recreation.

Following this meeting, the Park Partners began convening regularly with the mayor's staff and the local representative of the Trust for Public Land, who brought in national staff members for consultation.

We decided early on that a property-tax increase to sustain recreation would not garner significant support. However, a "redistribution" of existing millage among the partners that did not require a tax increase had a much better chance of voter approval. To achieve the goal of no tax increase, it was clear that the Audubon Nature Institute would have to give up some of its mills so they could be reallocated. Audubon had used some of its tax millage to retire bonds sold to build the aquarium and make improvements at the zoo, and these bonds were due to be fully retired in 2020. Therefore, a portion of the current Audubon millage could be made available to other entities if approved by the voters.

In 2019, the millage supporting parks and recreation agencies was divided as follows:

Audubon Nature Institute—3.31 mills (comprised of 2.99 mills dedicated to the aquarium and related facilities and .32 mills dedicated to the establishment and maintenance of a zoological garden in Audubon Park). The aquarium mills expired at the end of 2021 and the zoo millage expired at the end of 2022. Together the 3.31 mills produced approximately $10.8 million in revenue.

New Orleans Recreation Development Commission—1.5 mills generating approximately $5 million in revenue.

Parks and Parkways—1.5 mills generating approximately $5 million in revenue.

New Orleans City Park—no mills and thus no revenue.

All told, the 6.31 mills dedicated to parks and recreation produced approximately $21 million.[1]

I developed an initial concept of redistributing part of the Audubon tax millage, with City Park receiving a first-ever allocation and NORDC and Parkways each receiving an increased amount. Audubon would receive less but still enough to support their various facilities. That formula was debated over the summer and fall months of 2018, as the city agencies and City Park sought to maximize the funding they would receive while Audubon attempted to minimize the amount it would have to give up. The Park Partners also decided that the term of the redistributed tax would be twenty years, as the fifty-year term sought by Audubon in 2014 had proved to be unpopular with the voters.

Finally, after much discussion, a final formula was agreed upon. Audubon's millage would be reduced from 3.31 mills to 1.95 mills, a reduction of 1.36 mills, amounting to a loss of approximately $4.4 million. That millage and those dollars would be redistributed as follows:

New Orleans Recreation Development Commission would change from 1.5 mills or $5 million to 1.95 mills or $6.4 million, an increase of $1.4 million annually.
Parks and Parkways would change from 1.5 mills or $5 million to 1.8 mills or $6 million, an increase of $1 million annually.
New Orleans City Park would go from 0 mills or no funds from the city to .61 mills or a little over $2 million annually.

SUMMARY CHART OF MILLAGE CHANGES

Agency	Current	Proposed	Change
Audubon	3.31 mills	1.95 mills	-1.36 mills
NORDC	1.5 mills	1.95 mills	+.45 mills
Parkways	1.5 mills	1.8 mills	+.3 mills
City Park	None	.61 mills	+.61 mills

While we certainly could have used more money coming out of the millage redistribution, City Park would receive 2 million more dollars than we were currently getting. Combined with the nearly $2 million we received from the slot tax at the Fair Grounds, this would give us almost $4 million in public funding, or nearly 20 percent of the park's $22 million 2019 operating budget. In addition, the city property-tax assessments would potentially increase over time, and we felt good that we had substantially advanced the park's financial position. Now all we had to do was convince the New Orleans City Council to put the matter on the ballot and the citizens to pass the measure!

The Cooperative Endeavor Agreement

After reaching agreement with the city on the basic terms of the tax redistribution, we along with our partners began meeting with members of the New Orleans City Council to brief them and to secure their support to put the measure on the ballot. Because language for tax propositions must be approved by the secretary of state as to form, it was necessary for the City Council to adopt final ballot language long before an election date. After considering a number of dates, it was decided to set the election early in 2019 and not wait until the fall, when other ballot measures might have led to a higher voter turnout. By proceeding in May, we felt we had time to get our message out, and the mayor, only one year into her term, would hopefully still be very popular. Her support for the proposition along with that of the City Council would be critical to its success since it is virtually impossible to pass any kind of tax measure if you have elected-official opposition. People do not need much incentive to vote no.

In October we met with each City Council person to fully explain the proposal. The council felt it was necessary to lay out details regarding how the funding would be spent, how citizens would be involved, and how improved coordination among the park agencies would translate into specific actions. While that level of detail could have been accomplished with a Mayor's Executive Order, the council felt that an agreement would be more effective if it was referenced in the ordinance calling for the tax election. The various park citizen advocates were also lobbying the mayor and council demanding that there be an ordinance and Cooperative Endeavor Agreement before they would lend their support.

A Cooperative Endeavor Agreement (CEA) between the City of New Orleans and the partners consisting of the Audubon Commission, the City Park Improvement Association, and the New Orleans Recreation Development Commission) was selected as the appropriate vehicle. (Parks and Parkways, being a department of city government, was not included in the CEA.)

The CEA provided for the following:

- Establishing an interagency coordinating council composed of the park agencies to coordinate programming and capital improvements, share best practices, and collaborate in professional development and training.
- Holding quarterly meetings of the agencies and, twice a year, public meetings to communicate the activities of the agencies and secure public input. The CEA requires executive-level participation of the agencies at the quarterly and semiannual meetings.[2]
- Producing an annual report describing the year's activities of the agencies.
- Providing guidance and reasonable funding to the city for the development of a citywide recreation master plan, to be facilitated by an outside consultant with national park-planning experience.
- Each agency providing an annual audit, showing its use of the funds.

The agreement would last the term of the tax or twenty years.

The creation of an interagency parks and recreation coordinating group was a key recommendation of the Trust for Public Land's study. While acknowledging that the park agencies do collaborate on an informal basis, the TPL felt that a more structured arrangement would lead to more efficient and effective delivery of services and possibly to such things as establishing uniform park design and maintenance standards.

After the initial draft of the CEA was completed and reviewed with the park agencies, the Mayor's Office studied it with Parks for All, the nonprofit recreation-advocacy group that had headed the effort against the Audubon tax. Parks for All, along with similar organizations, endorsed the draft agreement with minor modifications. The recreation-advocacy groups lobbied for other additions to the agreement, such as dedicating funding from the tax to their groups and creating a broad-based oversight council. However, those proposals were not approved, and the City Council formally accepted the CEA on February 21, 2019. It was executed by all parties, and an election was called for May 4, 2019.

The Campaign

With the distribution formula and the CEA approved, the focus turned to informing the public about the proposition and how it would affect recreation in the city. As with all tax elections, this effort would take many avenues and it would also be expensive. Even a totally social media campaign is costly, so one that had to reach hundreds of thousands of voters and provide descriptive information would definitely be so.

A separate fundraising organization was established to support the public-information effort, while leaders of the partners and the city developed an extensive list of groups to visit, make presentations to, and then ask for their endorsement. The fundraising effort was carefully segregated from the activities of civil servants to ensure no one could raise any ethics or campaign-finance issues. City Park board president Larry Katz led the fund-raising effort along with officials from Audubon and the NORDC private foundation. With the funding raised, a polling expert was retained along with social-media consultants and advisors skilled at getting out the vote on election day. These election experts helped craft a campaign strategy, from messaging to voter turnout.

Yard signs, T-shirts, flyers, PowerPoint presentations, and other campaign materials were produced and distributed. I, along with Rebecca Dietz of Audubon, Emily Wolff of the mayor's staff, Larry Barabino, Jr., of NORDC, and Ann Macdonald of Parks and Parkways, assumed the role of explaining the proposal to many organizations throughout the city. The city organized five Council District meetings to be sure the plan was presented to all the citizens. Mayor Cantrell came to each meeting and, after expressing her support and answering questions, stayed during the entire presentation. Her enthusiasm for the ballot measure—the first tax proposal of her administration—cannot be overstated.

Another extremely important event was securing the first of many neighborhood endorsements, from the Faubourg St. John Neighborhood Association. These groups often do not wish to be out front on many citywide issues, opting instead to join in once other associations have publicly expressed their opinion, so it was important to get an initial endorsement. Having worked with the Faubourg St. John association for many years and knowing several of the board members, I thought they would be the ideal group to back the effort. I contacted Linda Landesberg, the president of the association, and she immediately placed the matter in front of her board. They unanimously voted to support the citywide parks millage and transmitted that opinion to Mayor Cantrell. That led to the endorsement of a wide range of similar groups, such as the Lower Garden District Neighborhood Association, the St. Charles Avenue Neighborhood Association, the Pontchartrain Park Neighborhood Association, and the Audubon Riverside Neighborhood Association, among others.

In addition, we solicited support from a variety of business and "good government" organizations such as the Urban League, the Friends of Lafitte Greenway, and the Business Council of New Orleans and the River Region. After meeting with the editorial board of the *Times-Picayune/Advocate* newspaper, we secured their endorsement, as well as from publications such as *Gambit*, the *New Orleans Tribune* (a minority-owned publication), and *New Orleans Magazine.* Various elected officials, including every City Council person and many senators and representatives in the Louisiana Legislature, lent their support.

Another extremely important endorsement came from the Bureau of Governmental Research, a private nonprofit, independent research organization that analyzes all tax measures put before the public, in addition to other public-policy issues. The bureau performed a thorough analysis of the proposal and recommended its approval with the following explanation.

New Orleans parks and recreation facilities support citizens' quality of life. They also draw many visitors from around the region and beyond. But the existing property taxes fund too narrow a range of entities and purposes. The proposition gives voters a chance to rebalance the tax revenue. It emerged from a process that evaluated and prioritized agency needs. Without increasing taxes, the millage would provide greater funding to the New Orleans Recreation Development Commission and the City's Department of parks and parkways, helping them to improve their services and programs. It would provide City Park with its first-ever property tax revenue, helping to stabilize its budget and enhance park amenities. And it would enable the Audubon Commission to retain a smaller but more flexible source of revenue for its Zoo, Aquarium and other facilities. In addition to rebalancing tax revenue, voter approval of the proposition would put into effect an agreement among the park agencies and the City intended to foster greater planning, coordination, and public accountability.[3]

While there was some opposition to the proposal, it was minimal and not enough to sway public opinion.

On May 4, 2019, despite constant rain, which usually diminishes voter turnout, the proposal to redistribute the existing property-tax millage and give City Park the first-ever funding from the citizens of New Orleans passed easily. With slightly less than 10 percent of the registered voters turning out, the proposition passed 76 percent to 24 percent. The vote in favor was not only overwhelming; it was almost universal across the city's 351 precincts.

The night of the election, we held a victory celebration along with our partners and various park supporters at our golf clubhouse. It was a long time in coming!

A Win for City Park

All the park agencies gained something from the tax redistribution. Even though Audubon lost a significant portion of their previous millage, they secured a base level of tax support for another twenty years and a new freedom to use their millage across all their facilities, not only the zoo or aquarium.

NORDC and Parks and Parkways secured an increase in their funding and guaranteed it for another twenty years. But in my humble opinion, the big winner was City Park.

First, it validated all the planning that the park had undertaken since the turn of the twentieth century. All during the next 120 years, plan after plan and study after study of the park had decried the lack of public funding and made recommendation after recommendation that support from the city was absolutely necessary. Eventually this message was received.

Second, we secured over $2 million in New Orleans property-tax funds beginning in 2021 for a 20-year period. When added to the support from the state tax on slot machines at the Fair Grounds, we finally obtained a base level of public financial support, something that took 169 years to achieve (1850-2019). Funds from the state recognize that ours is a regional park run by a state agency and provides facilities and services for everyone throughout Louisiana. Funds from New Orleans recognize that the park sits in the city and derives almost half of its visitation from its residents. While the park will still have to raise 70 to 80 percent of its operating revenue through activities in the park, it is far better than needing 100 percent to come from earned income.

Third, there is significant reason to believe that the participation of City Park as a millage recipient was crucial to the passing of the ballot initiative. While it may be a reach to say that City Park "carried the election,"

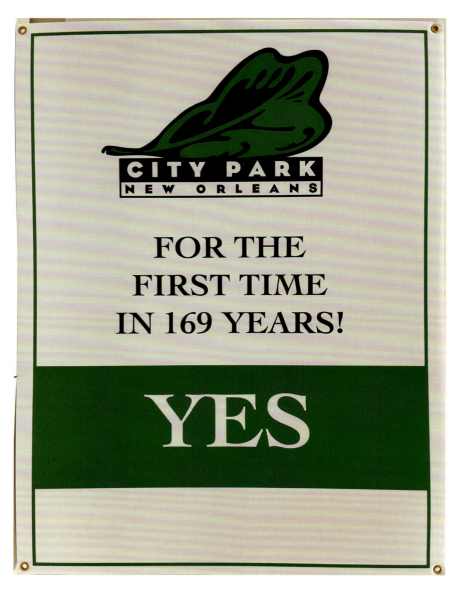

A park sign celebrating passage of the tax proposal

the countless meetings we held since 2001 on the park's financial condition, the public participation we solicited regarding the 2005 Master Plan and its various amendments, all of the improvements we implemented since Katrina, and the obvious fact that the park had been left out of city funding would support that conclusion. As Mayor Cantrell frequently declared when speaking about City Park not receiving funding in its 169-year history, "You can't make this up!"

And as Winnie-the-Pooh said, "We shall get there some day."

CHAPTER 15

COVID-19: Global Pandemic

Flattening the curve, social distancing, essential persons, quarantining, phased reopening, overwhelming the healthcare system, masking up, hydroxychloroquine, ventilators, community spread, and other terms we became familiar with!

I Contemplate Retirement

Following the passage of the property-tax redistribution initiative, I began to ponder retirement. I felt that securing city funding for the park was a highlight of my tenure, and even though the funds would not come until the first quarter of 2021, the park could now plan for the future with some certainty.

In May 2019, Pat and I had four children who had given us eight grandchildren and none of them lived in Louisiana—or anywhere close, for that matter. Dallas, Texas; Ann Arbor, Michigan; Dublin, Ireland; and Louisville, Kentucky were home to our children and grandchildren, and my wife and I wanted badly to spend time with them. Pat was also contemplating retirement from her teaching career, and thus the stars seemed to be lining up.

I began to discuss retirement with the board president and some members of our executive committee. I told them I would stay on through a succession process and provide orientation for a new chief executive officer. With funds from a local foundation, the president engaged the executive search firm of Ralph Andersen & Associates to organize a process to find a successor. In the fall 2019 employee newsletter, I informed my staff of my intention to retire and congratulated them on their spectacular success since Hurricane Katrina.

The search firm interviewed park staff, board members, and some of the long-term tenants in the park to develop a job description and a list of talents and skills they would like in a new leader. I prepared a series of briefing papers on various topics such as our finances, the master plan, organization, and authority, among other important areas that I felt should be considered when reviewing resumes. In the papers, I laid out my opinions on the most significant challenges the park faced in each of the selected areas so the board would have the benefit of my experience and thinking on these matters.

It was not until early January 2020 that the search firm advertised nationally and locally for my position in all the relevant publications and through their own network. When the resume process closed on February 17, over 120 applications and letters of interest had been received. Ralph Andersen & Associates narrowed down this list to ten and eventually to the six most impressive from the large pool.

In early February, my team and various board members began preparing for the upcoming session of the state legislature, which was to begin on March 9, by holding a lunch for key lawmakers and presenting the park's legislative agenda. We continued this effort in the first week of March by meeting with the commissioner of administration in Baton Rouge to ask for support for including park projects in the Capital Outlay bill (the construction bill) and discussing our request for state funding of our insurance program.

Unbeknownst to us, an incident that began nearly eight thousand miles from New Orleans in the late fall of 2019 was to upend all our careful planning!

COVID-19[1]

Sometime, mostly likely in November 2019, a coronavirus, which is common in many different species of animals, including camels, cattle, cats, and bats, "jumped" from an animal species to humans in Wuhan, China, most likely in a "wet" or animal market in that city. (In spite of some conspiracy theorists, no solid evidence has emerged that the virus originated in a laboratory and somehow escaped into the population.) The transmission of viruses from animals to humans has happened before and relatively recently and includes the MERS-CoV and SARS-CoV. COVID-19 likely originated in bats and was transmitted to humans through an intermediary species, possibly a pangolin. When a new coronavirus appears and has not previously been identified it is given the title of a "novel coronavirus."[2] According to the Centers for Disease Control and Prevention, there are many types of human coronaviruses, some of which cause mild symptoms such as a common cold and others that cause more severe upper-respiratory-tract infections. COVID-19 is a new disease not previously seen in humans and is thought to spread primarily from person to person, mainly through respiratory droplets produced when an infected person coughs or sneezes.

Although information is still inconclusive, it is likely that China knew there was an outbreak of some sort but delayed informing the World Health Organization (WHO) while it sought to bring the outbreak in Wuhan under control. For all intents and purposes, China closed a city of nine million people and enforced a quarantine, restricting all movements in and out of the city. News of the infection began to spread to other countries, although some thought the disease could be easily controlled, including the United States.[3]

As the reach of the virus grew, the WHO declared the outbreak a Public Health Emergency of International Concern on January 30, 2020.

The extent of the coming disaster was not completely understood by Mardi Gras in late February, so Pat and I traveled to WaterColor in the panhandle of Florida for a week's vacation and met old friends, including Minette Bruce, my former CFO whom we had not seen in a long time. We had dinner at a City Park board member's house in the same development and Ron Forman and his wife, Sally, were also guests. Ron and I joked about who would retire first.

When we returned from Florida, it was clear that concerns over the impact of the virus were becoming much more serious. The first Louisiana resident tested positive for COVID-19 on March 9 and the WHO declared a worldwide pandemic on March 11, 2020. On March 13, I met with Board President Larry Katz and we decided to suspend the search process indefinitely, as the park's worsening financial position would not have made an ideal environment for bringing in a new CEO. Larry asked me if I would stay on to help guide the association through the crisis and I agreed to stay until the situation stabilized or at least for a year. Within the space of a few weeks, we had gone from a situation where my job was highly desirable, attracting over one hundred candidates, to one where no one wanted it!

Closing the Economy

On the same day that the WHO declared the existence of a pandemic, Gov. John Bel Edwards, using authority granted his office under the Louisiana Health Emergency Powers Act, declared a statewide public health emergency "as a result of the imminent threat posed to Louisiana citizens by COVID-19, which has created emergency conditions that threaten the lives and health of the citizens of the State."[4]

The declaration instituted travel restrictions for state employees, empowered the Department of Health to take any and all actions necessary to respond to the crisis, prohibited price gouging on goods and services, and ordered the Civil Service Commission and Division of Administration to develop guidelines for state employees who become infected.

In subsequent Executive Proclamations (Proclamation Number 30 and 33 JBE 2020) on March 16 and 22, Governor Edwards enacted the following restrictions in response to the pandemic.

- Closing all state office buildings.
- Prohibiting all gatherings of ten or more people except for at locations such as airports, medical facilities, grocery stores, or factories.
- Requiring citizens to stay at home unless performing an essential activity such as obtaining food or medicine, obtaining non-elective medical care and treatment, or going to and from home, a workplace, or the home of a family member.
- Prohibiting restaurants from allowing

on-premise consumption (allowing a continuation of drive-thru and takeout business) and closing businesses such as movie theaters, bars, bowling alleys, fitness centers, and casinos.

Additional restrictions prohibited the opening of playgrounds, museums, event spaces, dog parks, and a variety of other types of businesses. (An important omission to the closing orders were golf courses.)

Essentially, the governor shut down the economy of the State of Louisiana and with it the economy of City Park. Mayor Cantrell was quick to follow suit and, in some instances, enacted regulations more restrictive than the state's guidance.

Now What Do We Do?

Up until early March 2020, we were experiencing a very good year financially. A combination of pleasant weather benefiting our outdoor revenue generators and favorable contracts with event and food and beverage purveyors had given us a healthy surplus compared to our budget and I was looking forward to leaving the park with an excellent balance sheet. COVID-19 changed that in a matter of a month.

With the restrictions closing virtually all our revenue-generating operations, we went from a projected surplus in March to losing $700,000 in income. In April we lost $975,000 and in May $800,000. It had the eerie feeling of Hurricane Katrina all over again, in that one day you had a stable operating budget and the next day you had no revenue!

While we could not do much about the catastrophic loss of income over a short period of time, we could reduce our expenses to minimize the damage to our financial position.

Our chief financial officer, Keith Hemel, and Rob DeViney, the chief operating officer, and I began to examine every contract and service the park had with a third party. We looked for any contract that could be considered nonessential or that we could postpone. We canceled such things as bottled-water service to various departments and the cleaning of building entrance mats. We eliminated the contract cleaning of our office buildings and put the burden on office staff to clean the buildings and empty the trash. We postponed the hiring of part-time contract employees that we usually retained in the summer to help with grounds maintenance, and we delayed ordering supplies and materials. However, as with most organizations, the bulk of our funding was for payroll and benefits for our employees. We knew we had to reduce those expenses.

I closed the park offices on Monday March 16 and formulated a plan for payroll and benefit reductions. Beginning with the next payroll, on March 24, I took the following actions.

- Furloughed all the part-time employees. (This action does not separate them from service but does discontinue their salary and allow them to apply for unemployment.)
- Froze hiring.
- Stopped the park's contribution to the employees' 457 retirement plan.
- Reduced the salaries of all employees making under $50,000 by 15 percent and all employees making over $50,000 by 20 percent. I reduced my salary by 25 percent.

These actions, if in effect for a full year, would have saved approximately one million dollars in payroll and benefit costs. I tried to explain to my employees that these actions were necessary to immediately address our huge revenue loss and that I was taking these steps to preserve as much cash as possible and keep as many people as possible getting a paycheck, even if it was much reduced. It was a difficult message to deliver and an even harder one to receive. Two-thirds of our employees were still working in the park, as opposed to staying at home, and they were exposing themselves to the virus while taking a pay cut.

The last possible action I wanted to take on my way to retirement was to implement a large payroll and benefit cut to our employees. But it was necessary, and we did it.

The CARES Act

The restrictions imposed by state and local governments to halt the spread of the virus had the immediate impact of millions of Americans losing their jobs, as large and small businesses sought to limit the financial damage of closing and having their revenue completely cut off. In short order the national unemployment rate went from a historic low of around 4 percent to a high of nearly 15 percent, and by the end of June nearly forty million Americans applied for unemployment.

In order to address this catastrophe, Congress passed in record time the Coronavirus Aid, Relief, and Economic Security Act (CARES Act), which was signed into law on March 27, 2020. The act provided direct aid for families and businesses impacted by the pandemic. Payments up to $1,200 were to be sent to eligible recipients and a $150 billion fund was to be established to assist state, local, and tribal governments affected by the loss of sales taxes as well as the cost of business fees. Perhaps the most widely anticipated part of the CARES Act was the Paycheck Protection Program. This provided forgivable loans to businesses and nonprofits with fewer than five hundred employees for eight weeks. Applicants would borrow money from local lending institutions approved by the Small Business Administration and have the entire loan forgiven if 75 percent went to protect paychecks. (In June, the amount would be reduced to 60 percent.) The remaining funds could be used for rent, utilities, and other costs of running businesses.

We immediately began investigating to see if government agencies were eligible. We and our attorneys picked through every page of the act looking for any provisions that would allow us to apply. We contacted several local banks to determine if they would lend us money and reached out to the Small Business Administration to review the rules of the program. While the larger national banks were not interested, community banks were making loans to businesses across our region. We were not eligible. Even though we earned 90 percent of our income from operating businesses in the park, the fact that we were a state agency prevented us from securing a loan. For months we had to respond to park supporters asking why we did not seek a PPP loan that we were ineligible.

Since we were shut out of assistance from that portion of the CARES Act, we concentrated on asking for funds from the pool of money given to states for relief. We transmitted our request for $2 million in emergency supplemental state aid before the end of the state fiscal year on June 30 and $5 million in aid for the next fiscal year beginning on July 1, 2020. We felt that since the State of Louisiana had received approximately $1.8 billion as its share of the $150 billion set aside for state and local governments, we could expect some form of financial aid. We also submitted our request for an appropriation through the Lieutenant Governor's Office directly to the governor's administration, as the legislature was going to convene in May.

Another provision of the CARES Act required all employers to provide up to ten days of paid sick leave to any employee who requested it. For private-sector employers, the act provided tax credits to pay for that leave. Unfortunately, since public-sector agencies were not eligible to take tax credits, it meant that the park had to absorb the cost of this federal mandate without any possibility of being reimbursed.

In addition, during the governor's stay-at-home order, we had to continue to pay any staff who had either vacation or sick leave. Employees who stayed home and for which there was no work as a result of the closure of our businesses continued to receive a full paycheck as long as they had a leave balance. When that balance was exhausted, they would no longer receive a paycheck and would be furloughed so they could apply for unemployment benefits, which under the CARES Act were extremely generous. (People applying for unemployment benefits received $600 weekly in addition to the normal benefit paid by the State of Louisiana. For some employees, this was more than they would normally receive in their regular paycheck.)

We kept careful records on leave payments in the hopes we could apply for reimbursement for those paid benefits. On March 13, 2020, the president of the United States declared the COVID-19 pandemic a National Emergency, making certain expenditures to prevent serious harm or injury, financial or otherwise, as a result of the disease potentially eligible for reimbursement by FEMA. We had gone down this road before with FEMA during Hurricane Katrina, so we knew the importance of documentation.

Closing Down

In the meantime, we focused on actions we could undertake.

1. We restricted access to park administration buildings to 20 percent of their normal occupancy and developed schedules for employees working in the buildings to be sure the capacity limits were enforced.

2. We ordered and issued personal protective equipment to all of our staff.

3. Our human resources staff developed a manager's guide to use with employees returning to work that emphasized workplace safety and protocols for employees who became sick.

4. We placed signs throughout the park exhorting people to practice social distancing while in the park.

5. We closed and wrapped in orange plastic fencing all our playground equipment and "bagged" all our water fountains.

6. We established guidelines for those employees working from home and impressed upon our department managers to be certain the hours those employees were recording on their timesheets could be justified.

7. In anticipation of a loosening of restric-tions, we prepared reopening guidelines for each facility and transmitted them to the department heads and the city, which had requested them.

8. All during the month of April, I repeatedly sent updates on the park's financial condition to our legislative delegation and the commissioner of administration, Jay Dardenne. Darrell Hunt, the Friends lobbyist, made repeated contact with those legislators we considered most influential and who sat on important committees, to inform them of the park's deteriorating financial status.

9. Our sales and catering staff sought to convince clients to postpone their weddings or shelter rentals, as opposed to canceling the events outright. By May, 158 events had been adversely impacted by the closure orders and 78 had been able to be rescheduled. This was a remarkable feat since we could provide no assurance that a future date would, in fact, be available.

10. Keith Hemel, our CFO, developed a financial model, which projected how long our cash would hold out with our reduced expenses. With all our revenue shut off, we thought we had enough money to last through August or September.

11. As most of the conditions for reopening facilities focused on limiting capacity, we began to calculate the capacity of all of our facilities. For some this was relatively easy— 26,000 seats in one of our stadiums, 104 players on our twenty-six tennis courts, etc. For other facilities, we had to calculate the

square footages of, for instance, our Botanical Garden, Dog Park, and Amusement Park and then reduce the useable area to 25 percent, which was the guidance in the Phase 1 opening regulations.

12. We repurposed staff. Since our athletic facilities were closed, we moved our staff who maintained those fields to our grounds department to supplement their staff. The latter had been depleted by employees choosing to stay at home because of fear of becoming sick. Employees who worked in our main office building were assigned to help with trash collection or even getting on a lawnmower and cutting grass. Once some facilities were allowed to reopen, staff from other departments began to fill in taking tickets, selling snoballs, or operating miniature golf. This effort reminded everyone, once again, of the crisis created by Hurricane Katrina, when employees essentially worked in whatever departments needed help and everyone performed "duties as assigned."

13. In early March, we developed Workforce Guidance for our managers so they would be prepared to address various workplace occurrences caused by COVID-19. This covered what to do if an employee appears sick, what to do if an employee says he/she tested positive for the virus, under what conditions can they approve a request to work from home, etc. State Civil Service also issued guidance on what to do if:

a. Employee is visibly sick and/or exhibits symptoms of COVID-19 and refuses to leave work.

b. Employee is presumptively or positively diagnosed with COVID-19.

c. Employee was possibly exposed to COVID-19 and has no symptoms of illness.

d. Employees have compromised immune systems.

e. Employees have dependent-care issues arising from state proclamations. And on and on.

Fundraising

In addition to doing everything possible to reduce our operating expenses, we knew we needed to seek new and additional financial support while our "old" revenue was closed. Our board; the board and staff of the Friends of City Park; our chief development officer, Casie Duplechain; and I took the lead engaging in the following:

- We solicited donations from our current and past board members, many of whom made their yearly donation early or increased their donations.
- We reached out to our traditional supporters the Friends of City Park and the Botanical Garden Foundation and secured pledges of $270,000 over a six-month period. These funds would support specific sections of the park such as the Botanical Garden

and our Development and Public Relations Department.

- We also reached out to foundations and organizations who traditionally support the park and received donations from groups such as the Tolmas Trust and the Azby Fund.
- Where possible, we raised prices on open facilities such as miniature golf and the Botanical Garden to cover the expenses of additional cleaning and sanitizing.
- We examined the park's various endowment funds. Where we had a balance of interest we could legally withdraw, we did so, to support the grounds and tennis departments.
- We also secured the return of funds being held by the state for a long-canceled capital project and dedicated them to repay deposits and down payments for events that were canceled.

In addition, Casie and her staff launched an aggressive public outreach to solicit donations from users of the park and traditional supporters. I wrote a letter to the editor of the *Times-Picayune* discussing the park's dire situation and the need for donations. We sent direct emails to thousands of people on our list. We posted signs throughout the park making the public aware of the opportunity to donate online. Through the beginning of June, that campaign had secured over nine hundred donors (43 percent of them new ones) for a total of $225,000. This was a remarkable effort considering the widespread economic disaster the closure orders had visited on the city.

Phased Reopening

The governor extended his stay-at-home orders through several proclamations limiting all gatherings larger than ten people and closing all nonessential businesses through the middle of April. Strangely enough, golf-course play continued to be allowed, subject to a variety of social-distancing guidelines. It is ironic that our South Golf Course, which just four years earlier had been the subject of protests with some stating it would not be an economic benefit to the park, was in fact the only park asset (besides our other course—the North) generating any revenue and taking care of approximately 25 percent of the total park property!).

The closures implemented to contain the virus throughout the country had a devastating impact on the national economy, throwing millions into unemployment, causing a drop in the stock market of over 7,000 points in just a few days, and posing a threat of bankruptcy to tens of thousands of small and large businesses. As the country struggled to contain the virus, it was clear that the economy could not remain closed forever. The CDC issued guidelines in the middle of April on how the country could begin a phased reopening. The guidelines emphasized that for all phases, basic policies would have to be followed including enforcing social-distancing requirements, providing protective equipment to employees, conducting temperature checks, and most importantly, implementing enhanced testing for the virus.

The CDC recommended a three-phased reopening process that would gradually increase the type of businesses that could reopen and the capacity or number of customers allowed in businesses.

The state and city adopted the basic tenets of the CDC guidance, although the city's policies were, in some cases, more restrictive than the state's. The state implemented a Phase 0 approach beginning on May 1 and permitted, in addition to essential businesses, restaurants to open for takeout service only. Phase 1 started on May 15.

Phase 1

Beginning on May 16, we began to open some of the park facilities that had been closed since March. We determined that we could open our Botanical Garden, tennis courts, playground, Storyland, miniature golf, and non-contact sport fields. (Unfortunately, the state and city considered almost all sporting activities contact sports and therefore not permitted. Only baseball and beach volleyball appeared to satisfy the non-contact criteria. According to the guidelines, permitted sports included tennis, golf, biking, swimming, archery, curling, running, softball, and baseball, all without spectators. Soccer was considered a contact sport, as were football and rugby.) All of these would open with a 25 percent capacity limit and with strict social-distancing procedures in place. We implemented the reopening guidelines we had previously prepared, including providing all employees with masks, sanitizing products, and protective screens as well as posting signs to encourage visitors to wear masks and conducting enhanced cleaning of the venues. The Botanical Garden, Storyland, and miniature golf operated under new hours and were closed on Mondays and Tuesdays, where before they were closed just on Mondays. The reduced days and hours were necessary as we could not predict how many people would use the facilities when they could reopen, and we had to operate with virtually no part-time staff. The garden also began to offer a Sunday brunch prepared in its Outdoor Kitchen and plant sales at our greenhouse.

We were not able to open our Amusement Park, hold weddings or special events, or have live entertainment. The closing of our catering business with the prohibitions on weddings, and not being able to open the Amusement Park, had a major negative financial impact.

While we were principally concerned with opening our own facilities, we were also paying attention to the restrictions on casinos, since our only public funding was coming from the state tax on slot machines at the Fair Grounds. Unfortunately, casinos were permitted to open in Louisiana with restrictions but not in New Orleans. As a result, the state reduced its projections of how much revenue the park could expect to receive from the tax in the next fiscal year from $1.9 million in May to $1.6 million in June, when the Fair Grounds casino was allowed to open on a limited basis.

Phase 2

Satisfied with the efforts to limit the virus, the state decided to move into Phase 2 in early June, and the city followed suit on June 13, 2020. Under Phase 2 state guidelines, all businesses that were previously allowed to be open were able to increase their capacity from 25 percent to 50 percent, while still maintaining six feet of distance amongst patrons. Events, such as weddings, could happen at 50 percent of capacity with a 250-person limit, while amusement parks remained closed. Unfortunately, the city's guidelines for events and sports required special-event permits and a limit of 100 persons. They also required the presence of one "crowd control" officer for every 50 people. In addition, no dancing or live music were permitted.

These limits were extremely unfortunate for our wedding business. Almost all the weddings that we were scheduled to hold and had postponed were for more than 100 people. In addition, most people wanted live entertainment at the event and, of course, dancing. We lost a few of the weddings we had scheduled to adjacent parishes that did not have the 100-person limit and did permit live entertainment and dancing outside of a building.[5]

The state allowed outdoor "controlled" playgrounds to open, meaning surrounded by a fence, although the city's guidance permitted all playgrounds to open. We informed the city that their decision involved fewer restrictions than those imposed by the state. The city quickly acknowledged the error and corrected their guidance. Since we only had one controlled playground, Storyland, our playgrounds remained closed through Phase 2.

The Virus Hits Close to Home

From the beginning of the pandemic and with the closure of virtually all activities in the region, the park experienced a large increase in people coming for exercise or a mental-health break. Even without open facilities, the park's green spaces were a huge attraction. Our employees did their best to keep up with the increased usage, even as our staff began to shrink. People were taking other jobs because of the salary reductions and our forced furloughs for staff who had no work because of the closure of our businesses.

Then on June 13, one of our grounds employees reported that he tested positive for COVID-19. Because the grounds employees occupied the same building for check-in and break, we were forced to quarantine the entire group of around twenty people. This staff is responsible for trash pickup and grass cutting. The quarantine meant there was no one to pick up trash on one of the busiest weekends of the year, due to a tremendous number of people seeking relief from the COVID restrictions. On Monday, we mobilized the central office staff to pick up trash throughout the park while we arranged for contract employees to begin trash pickup for the fourteen days the quarantine period was in effect. You have not really experienced trash patrol until you have picked up tons of garbage including crawfish shells, fast-food wrappers, beer bottles, and condoms in ninety-four-degree heat! The following Thursday, we learned that one of the employees in our sales department tested positive and we had to quarantine that staff for a total (with the grounds staff) of around twenty-five people or 25 percent of our entire staff! In preparation for their return, we deep cleaned the grounds building and our Administrative Building, which holds the sales staff.

The Legislature Meets

The Louisiana Legislature, its session disrupted by the virus, was supposed to finish its work by the end of May. The most important job the legislature faced during this period was passing the annual operating and capital budgets. Unfortunately, the legislature was so distracted by battles with the governor over tort reform legislation that it failed to finish the budgets by May 31 and was forced to call a special session beginning on June 1. For us this was not necessarily a bad thing, since the appropriations bill the legislature was working on did not contain an emergency appropriation for the park, something we had been advocating for since March. Starting over gave us an opportunity to redouble our efforts to convince representatives and senators to include an appropriation for City Park in the operating budget. In April we had submitted a formal request for $5 million to address the dramatic decline in revenue that we had experienced.

Continually during the special session, we lobbied for support. We had board members and Friends of City Park members contact lawmakers they knew to urge their support for City Park. They supplied the Friends lobbyist with a steady stream of updates on the park's financial status. On June 10 we traveled to Baton Rouge to a breakfast that Lt. Gov. Billy Nungesser hosted for legislators, so we could speak directly to them about our needs.

In the meantime, challenges at the park mounted. In early June, I closed the park in anticipation of Tropical Storm Cristobal. Protests that had been occurring nationwide as a result of the killing of George Floyd in Minneapolis arrived in City Park, when hundreds of people gathered near our miniature golf facility and marched down Esplanade Avenue to the First District Police Station.

When the special session ended on Tuesday June 30, we were not included in the legislature's appropriation bill for any funding from the state's general fund. While we did receive Capital Outlay funding for expansion of our tennis complex and renovations to our maintenance buildings damaged in Katrina, and we also received $1 million in Community Development Block Grant funding for improvements, we did not receive what we needed most—funding for our damaged operating budget.

Year-End Financial Status

When we compiled our numbers for the fiscal year ending June 30, we had a deficit of $303,045. Given the fact that we lost $4.4 million in budgeted revenue since February, I considered this shortfall to be a major victory. All of the measures we had put in place (including personnel actions) had helped us cut our operating expenses by over $4 million, resulting in what was a minimal loss on a $22 million operating budget. The board, recognizing the extreme hardship borne by our employees in an effort to keep our end-of-the-year loss manageable, adopted a new operating budget on June 9, allowing us to begin to restore the salary reductions to

full-time employees by the end of July. This was done in anticipation of receiving state operating assistance in the new fiscal year. The news was met with great enthusiasm and appreciation.

The operating budget for the new fiscal year projected a loss in revenue from $22 million in FY 19-20 to $17.5 million for FY 20-21, with a concomitant reduction in expenses. Given what we knew about the pandemic-caused restrictions, we were hopeful we could meet the budget goals.

Further Efforts

As we entered the new fiscal year (July 1, 2020-June 30, 2021), prospects for the park were clouded with uncertainty. On July 1 we had $2.9 million in cash and reserves. We owed approximately one-half million dollars in deposits we had received for canceled events. In spite of every cost-cutting measure we could implement, our monthly expense budget was about $600,000. We had appealed to all the park's traditional supporters, and while their response was gratifying, it was not nearly enough to make a substantial difference. We projected we had enough reserves to last through September before further dramatic cuts in personnel had to be implemented, which would only help us get through perhaps October. Even those forecasts were thrown into doubt when on June 11, the governor tightened the restrictions in Phase

2 by reducing public gatherings to 50 people from 250 and requiring facemasks to be worn by all residents while outdoors.

With no help coming from the state administration and legislature as had been provided during Katrina, I decided to try to see Gov. John Bel Edwards directly and make a last appeal for support.

Phase 2 Continues

Unfortunately, the governor's staff suggested that we have a telephone call with the commissioner of administration and the governor's chief of staff, Mark Cooper. Larry Katz, Keith Hemel, Rob DeViney, and I had a conference call with them on July 16 and pressed home our need for funds to address lost revenue. While they were sympathetic, no help was promised. They did promise to brief the governor, but taking no chances, I wrote to him separately.

On July 24, Mayor LaToya Cantrell further tightened restrictions, limiting gathering size to twenty-five persons in New Orleans.

While the salary cuts helped reduce our expenses, I concluded that we had to actually decrease our workforce at the end of July to meet our budget goals. These staff reductions constituted 30 percent of our full-time employees, going from 116 at the first of the calendar year to 80. These actions allowed us to reduce the monthly payroll from approximately $575,000 to $350,000

and obviously were very helpful in cutting our overall expenses.

All departments were affected. Grounds went from 21 employees to 19 and the catering staff from 10 to 1. Some departments were eliminated, including concessions and planning, construction, and sustainability. I also made permanent the reduction in our seasonal staff, who had been furloughed in March. This involved layoffs of 273 people.

All these reductions, particularly those of our full-time employees, were extremely painful to me and our senior staff. These were people we had worked with, some for many years. I always said that following Katrina, I would not lay off any more of our staff. I was wrong, and knowing that these layoffs may not be the last made the process all that more painful.

We began to institute additional management initiatives to deal with the situation. We continued repurposing our athletic staff (who had no fields or stadiums to prepare for play) into our grounds department to help with the increased litter we were seeing as a result of more people coming to the park for a mental-health break, for exercising, or to visit one of the few attractions we had open. Additionally, we decided to expand our once-a-month plant sales in the Botanical Garden to every weekend, and we put half of the horticulture crew into the greenhouse to supplement the regular staff to prepare the plants. In August we began to show scary movies at the Arbor Room, which were limited to fifty people. We sold out almost immediately at thirty-five dollars a person.

Full-time staff filled in for most part-time positions in miniature golf or Storyland. Using tax district funds, which can only be used for public improvements or equipment, we purchased two new police cruisers to replace our aging fleet and cut down on costly repairs.

In August we submitted our eligible COVID-19 expenses for reimbursement through the city. Through June we submitted $504,922, which if approved in their entirely would be a huge lift for the operating budget. We also began to prepare a new educational and fundraising campaign, which we expected to launch before the end of August. Stalled talks between the Democrats and Republicans on the national level on a new COVID relief package (which we hoped would contain additional aid to state and local governments, improving our chances of getting a supplemental appropriation) was discouraging news. We had hoped that with the announcement of a new federal initiative, we could combine a renewed effort directed at the governor and state legislators with a more broad-based campaign to generate operating funds. We entered August with about $2.6 million in reserves. We projected we could make those last, combined with new revenue and reduced expenses, until the first of the year, provided our forecasts of earned income materialized. As the pandemic raged, we realized how little control we had over projections, as further restrictions or market resistance were real possibilities.

On August 12, the president of the board and I met with Mayor LaToya Cantrell and her staff to brief her on the status of the park's finances. She promised to call the governor and express her concern over the lack of state support as well as discussing the matter with the legislative delegation. We asked if the city could "advance" payment of its property tax, the first payment of which was supposed to come at the end of February 2021, but she was unable to commit to that as she was not sure the city could collect the tax on schedule. We were thankful that the mayor understood the consequences if we were unable to maintain the park.

Hurricanes and Tropical Storms

Hurricane forecasters had already predicted that the 2020 season would be a very active one. Of course—COVID-19 was not enough! As we approached the fifteenth anniversary of Hurricane Katrina on August 29, we already had over ten named storms, although only one of those affected us directly.

This changed with the development of Tropical Storms Marco and Laura, and by late on Sunday August 23, the effects of Marco were being felt in our area. We completed our storm preparations that day, and I closed the park on Monday and Tuesday, with the great likelihood we would also close on Wednesday if Laura, the more dangerous of the systems, came ashore close to the city.

Marco became a non-event even as it moved along the Louisiana coast. Laura, on the other hand, developed into a ferocious Category 4 hurricane, which homed in on Cameron Parish and the Lake Charles area. The National Weather Service issued a warning that the storm surge connected with Laura would be "unsurvivable," reminiscent of similar warnings before Hurricane Katrina made landfall. While the predicted storm surge did not materialize, the 150-mph winds devastated the southwestern coast of Louisiana, topping the damage sustained in Hurricane Rita just fifteen years earlier. Recovery will take years.

Before the storm hit the coast, the governor extended Phase 2 of recovery from COVID-19 to September 11, hoping that the Labor Day weekend didn't see a surge in cases that would cause him to further push out the reopening of the economy. We also received the bad news that our reimbursement request would likely not be funded, as the city had already received all the funding it was eligible for. This was extremely disappointing, since the commissioner of administration had advised us to apply for the repayment. If he knew that the city had already received everything to which it was entitled, why did he encourage us to apply? Now we would have to switch gears and apply to FEMA for reimbursement of eligible COVID costs, which at best would only reimburse up to 75 percent.

By the middle of September, another storm began to take shape in the Gulf of Mexico—Sally. Sally was projected to come ashore as a Category 1 or 2 hurricane, directly into New Orleans after crossing Florida and turning north. On Sunday, September 13, with predictions of 100-mph winds and catastrophic rain and storm surge, I informed the staff that we were closing at noon the next day and staying closed until at least Wednesday. Preparations were made according to the hurricane plans that each department had developed. Fortunately, Sally turned eastward and came ashore near the Alabama/Mississippi line. We had dodged another bullet. By the end of November, there had been thirty-one named storms in the Atlantic and Caribbean basins and New Orleans had been in the "cone of uncertainty" seven times. Before the hurricane season was over, I had closed the park on October 9 for Hurricane Delta and again on October 28 for Hurricane Zeta. The Atlantic hurricane season for 2020 set a record for the most active season ever!

Phase 3

On Friday September 11, Governor Edwards announced that the state was moving into Phase 3 of recovery from COVID-19. While everyone was still required to wear a mask and practice social distancing, there were some significant liftings of the onerous restrictions present in Phase 2. Crowd sizes were increased to 75 percent of capacity of a facility, which would allow the park to restart our wedding business. Stadiums and arenas hosting athletic events could hold spectators up to 25 percent of their capacity. While amusement parks and festivals were still not permitted, the ability to resume hosting weddings and athletic events was significant for generating revenue. Unfortunately, the City of New Orleans chose to remain in Phase 2, thus negating the state's revised rules. Our wedding business continued to migrate to sites in Jefferson Parish, which chose to follow the state's restrictions. Sports teams that would have played in our facilities moved to stadiums and fields in Jefferson Parish.

One clear impact of the governor's decision to allow local jurisdictions to enact COVID-19 rules more restrictive than the state's was that millions of dollars of revenue that would have come to the park under the state's guidelines were lost when uses were prohibited under the city's guidelines. Since the virus does not respect political jurisdictions, it seems in retrospect that the state should have considered placing entire regions under the same regulations. This would have recognized that regions could have different capacity and use limits based on their relative geographic isolation. Parishes in the same market area would be treated similarly, thus removing the artificial barriers put on commerce that might benefit one parish over another.

Mayor Announces Phase 3

Mayor Cantrell, under mounting pressure from business interests, announced that the city would move into Phase 3 starting October 3. The city broke it into three parts, beginning with Phase 3.1. Unfortunately, this still did not provide relief to the park's finances, as the restrictions on holding weddings were basically the same: only 50 people permitted at an indoor event and 100 people at an outdoor event. Stadiums were limited to 500 spectators and amusement parks remained closed.

On October 15, the mayor announced the city would move into Phase 3.2 two days later, but again it did not offer relief from the restrictions that most impacted City Park.

However, a much more important action occurred than the announcements of phased reopenings by the state and the city. The Louisiana Legislature called itself back into session!

Concern by some Republican legislators that the governor overstepped his emergency authority with the length and extent of restrictions on activities and that that overreach had damaged the state's economy unnecessarily was the main reason the legislature went back into session. Other issues to be addressed included the destruction caused by Hurricane Laura in Southwest Louisiana (and eventually compounded by Hurricane Delta) and the near bankruptcy of the state's unemployment compensation fund. Whatever the reasons, we saw a final opportunity to secure state support for our operating budget.

In September we had begun a media blitz to alert the community to our dire financial condition. I appeared on many television and radio shows, and we launched an aggressive social-media campaign. The aim was to educate the public and our legislators about our condition, seek volunteers who could help our depleted staff maintain the park, and obtain new financial contributions to bolster our budget. Coordinating with Darrell Hunt, we contacted specific legislative champions to press our case. A Supplemental Appropriations Bill was introduced to add funding to what was approved during the first special session in June. The bill was nothing more than a shell, with no specific appropriations mentioned.

On the first of October, I received a call from Barbara Goodson, the deputy commissioner of administration and the chief architect of the state's operating budget. She said the state understood our plight. She knew we had been asking for $5 million in supplemental financial assistance but "that wasn't in the cards." She said the administration could support an appropriation of $2.5 million, which she felt could get us to the next regular session of the legislature in the spring of 2021. A longer-term solution to our financial situation could be developed then. For the first time, the state administration had taken a position that would help the park beyond just acknowledging that we were in bad shape! On October 2, the administration introduced a series of amendments to the Supplemental Appropriations Bill. One of those, under the category of State Aid to Local Government Entities, stated: "Payable out of the State General Fund (Direct) to the New Orleans City Park Improvement Association $2,500,000."

The next week, Commissioner Dardenne appeared before the House Appropriations Committee to explain that City Park, despite its name, was actually a state asset that required assistance because virus restrictions had shut down all of its revenue-generating capability. By Friday October 16, the Supplemental Appropriations Bill had been approved and sent to the governor! Here at last was the financial relief the park had been seeking for eight months. While we had to determine how the park would receive the $2.5 million, I was certain that these funds would provide stability to our finances and ensure that we could continue rebuilding our revenue base.

The governor finally signed the bill (which became Act #45 of the Second Special Session) in the middle of November, erasing any doubt that the appropriation would be subject to a line-item veto. We immediately began discussions with the state Department of the Treasury over how we would receive the funds.

The Treasury told us that they keep a record of each state agency's financial issues, which factors into how they distribute various funds appropriated by the legislature. For example, if the Legislative Auditor determined that an agency had not accounted for its petty cash properly or that some type of fraud had been perpetuated on an agency, then they might hold up paying appropriated funds until additional cash controls had been put in place. Who knew! Because we had no "black marks" on our record, Treasury allowed us to apply for all $2.5 million at one time—which, of course, we did. We informed our Finance and Executive committees that when the funds were received, we would put $1.5 million back into reserves to help balance the budget, and we would use $1 million until the end of the fiscal year to reduce our monthly loss.

The State Moves Backward

Across America, the rise in the COVID-19 infection rate was dramatic. A second and possible third wave of infections was reported in almost every state. By the middle of November, Louisiana had experienced over 225,000 reported cases, and more than 6,000 people had died. So on November 24, the governor moved the state back to Phase 2, which reduced indoor gatherings to 75 people and outdoor gatherings to 150 people. Restaurants were limited in capacities, and bars were closed indoors if the parish you were in had more than a 5 percent positivity rate.

The restrictions continued to devastate our event business. In October, we had originally booked forty-one catered events (mostly weddings). Of those, thirty-six were canceled or postponed. In November, thirty-one events were originally booked and only one took place. A similar scenario was playing out with December bookings.

We did begin our Celebration in the Oaks season as a drive-through experience (as opposed to a walk-through in the Botanical Garden and Amusement Park), and our early reservations looked promising.

Summing Up 2020

The Friends of City Park asked me to write a CEO letter to be included in their fall 2020 newsletter, which went out to their 5,000 members. What to say? The following is what I wrote.

Well—it has been quite a year! In February the Park was on track to have a very successful programmatic and financial year and was routinely ranked as one of the finest public parks in the nation. In March, Governor John Bel Edwards issued an order to stay at home as a result of the impacts of COVID-19. Over the next six months, the Park lost over $4.0 million in budgeted revenue and had laid off 1/3 of its full-time employees.

We went through Phase 0, one, two and then 3.1, 3.2 and 3.3! We all learned to wear a mask, social distance and other actions to "stop the spread." The Park was completely closed then allowed to open some of its facilities, albeit at a much-reduced capacity. We frantically went on a fundraising campaign and began to educate the State's legislators on how the Park is funded and why State support was urgently needed to help overcome the loss of revenue. The impacts of COVID were frequently compared to Katrina with some commenters opining that Katrina caused everyone to leave home while COVID caused everyone to stay home! The references to Katrina also hit home with a message that recovery from a historic disaster such as Katrina, or the Great Recession and such as COVID-19, take a long time. The impacts on public health and the economy will take years if not decades to overcome.

Hurricane season arrived and New Orleans was in the "Cone of Uncertainty" at least seven times eventually being significantly impacted by Hurricane Zeta in late October. More than 30 storms were named in the most active storm season on record. Our thoughts and prayers go out to those sections of the State that were heavily impacted by Hurricane Laura.

We had a historically contentious Presidential election and the murder of George Floyd reminded us of the long road ahead to be sure everyone in our country is afforded an equal opportunity to succeed.

But there have been bright spots. Late in October the Legislature with the leadership of Governor Edwards approved $2.5 million of supplemental relief which will allow the Park to avoid drastic steps which would otherwise have been necessary without those funds. Many thanks to the Governor and Legislature for recognizing what an asset City Park is and coming to our aid.

And the race for a vaccine appears to be successful with broad application in the new year.

And Celebration in the Oaks will be held this year despite all the restrictions with a driving tour starting on Thanksgiving night!

I want to thank everyone for the support they have shown for the Park and for understanding that recovery will take a long time. But with your help we can do this! Have a wonderful and safe holiday season and I will see you in the new year—THANK GOODNESS!!

Bob Becker

2021

The following year was full of highs and lows. The board finally chose a new CEO to lead the park. At the end of March, I was at last able to retire after twenty years of service to the park and fifty years of public service to the City of New Orleans. The board gave me the title of CEO emeritus.

On January 6, a mob believing the false statements of Donald Trump that the presidential election had been stolen stormed the U.S. Capitol and instigated an insurrection against the country. And the virus continued to mutate into numerous variants. A significant portion of the population resisted taking the vaccine that had been developed in 2020, which allowed more people to get sick and delayed the country being able to reach some sort of herd immunity. So the virus continued to require various restrictions and set infection records even into 2022.

The park's financial position stabilized with funds from the Supplemental Appropriations Bill and state assistance with our past insurance bill. This meant the new CEO was able to begin rehiring for jobs I had been forced to eliminate.

On August 29, exactly sixteen years after Hurricane Katrina, Hurricane Ida struck the city and the area directly west of New Orleans, leaving devastation to rural and small communities in its wake. The park was spared, except for the loss of trees and some minor building damage.

In the following chapter, I will recap our accomplishments and challenges that lie ahead for the park.

CHAPTER 16

What We Accomplished and Challenges Ahead

It is not the strongest of the species that survives, nor the most intelligent, but the one more responsive to change.
—Charles Darwin

Accomplishments

Our accomplishments can be divided into several categories including planning, management, finances, capital projects, and recovery from Hurricane Katrina and COVID-19. Let us start with planning achievements.

Planning Successes

As I have tried to demonstrate, the park has always been committed to planning. Our success in receiving money during the Great Depression was directly tied to the fact that the park had a written and adopted plan and could put the federal relief money to use quickly to address the unemployment situation. Even the various planning efforts that highlighted the ridiculous funding platform that the park was saddled with were very important, in that they helped raise the public's awareness and understanding of our circumstances.

However, without a doubt, the preparation, adoption, and implementation of the 2005

Master Plan was the most important planning achievement in seventy-five years. The plan created the opportunity for other uses in the park by first closing the South Golf Course and later limiting the golf footprint to the area north of Harrison Avenue. The releasing of over two hundred acres of land from golf made possible the Big Lake and Festival Grounds projects as well as construction of the Louisiana Children's Museum and the ongoing development of the Wisner Tract into a passive recreation resource. Additional achievements of the plan were reimagining the front of the park as more of an entertainment zone, with investments in the Amusement Park and construction of the miniature golf facility and the Great Lawn. Moving the tennis complex to Marconi not only provided land for those uses but gave the park a nationally recognized recreation facility. Consolidating our service uses along the railroad tracks adjacent to the interstate and reducing the golf complex from four courses to two were also significant accomplishments.

Perhaps the most important achievement of the plan was its timing. It was prepared during 2004 and 2005 and adopted only five months before Katrina hit. So, it was very recent and had already been vetted through an extensive public-engagement process. Funders who came to the park after the hurricane were therefore assured that the projects they were being asked to fund were approved and well planned. In addition, because the plan had initiatives across many areas such as sports, environmental upgrades, the Botanical Garden, and Amusement Park, there was literally something for every funder. If someone wanted to give money for tree replacement, we had a project; if someone wanted to give money for playgrounds, we had a project; if someone wanted to give money for tennis or stadium renovations, we had a project.

The Master Plan specifically listed the capital projects necessary for implementation, with the total cost estimated at $115 million. While many questioned how the park could raise this level of capital funding in the thirteen-year timeframe we projected, I was certain that if we were not aspirational and ambitious, the plan would carry little weight. Governments and private funders all appreciated that we were bold and that their contributions would completely revitalize the park. They were right. After Katrina, we combined the losses sustained with the investments outlined in the plan and created a new goal of $160.5 million in investments by the park. We have raised approximately $127 million toward that goal!

If you add to this total those investments made by others in the park, such as the Children's Museum, NOMA's sculpture garden expansion, Equest Farm, etc., the plan will have directly accounted for over $200 million in investments. Without the plan, we would not have raised nearly that amount of funding!

While the plan has been amended seven times in fifteen years, the amendments have been consistent with the original vision and have allowed the document a degree of flexibility.

Management Successes

1. We created a chief operating officer position to take responsibility for operating the line departments, freeing up the CEO to pursue overall agency goals. Department heads such as the director of the Botanical Garden, director of tennis, director of catering and sales, etc., now report to the COO.

2. We created a chief administrative officer position to take responsibility for such things as the safety program, property inventory, risk management, and the Police and Human Resources departments.

3. We established the first chief development officer position to centralize our fund-raising program and to provide a direct link to the fundraising efforts of the Friends of City Park.

4. We consolidated activities such as management of the stadiums and management of the sports fields under a director of athletic services.

5. We also merged our entertainment

and amusement activities under a director of amusement services, to bring under one director the Amusement Park and miniature golf.

6. We had no Information Technology Department, so we created one to take on our expansion into point-of-sales systems, website management, Internet monitoring, and supervision over our telephone and technology initiatives. This department reported to the CAO.

7. We were able to initiate regular salary increases alternating between 3 and 5 percent and a one-time salary supplement between years of those merit increases. Between 2010 and 2019, City Park gave more salary increases than virtually any other agency of state government.

8. The Human Resources Department began a quarterly employee newsletter, quarterly social gatherings, and periodic "all staff" meetings where we share important information with the entire staff. They also developed a comprehensive employee handbook, began an orientation program for new employees, and along with the Finance Department implemented a new payroll system that allows employees to see all their benefit information and request paid time off, among other personnel actions.

9. We implemented ethics and sexual harassment training along with periodic customer- service training. As of 2020, we have hired minorities as director of athletic services, director of amusement services, police supervisor, and HR director. More than half of the entire staff is composed of minority staff members.

10. We completely revised our website in 2012 to provide new information and act as a fundraising and community-support tool, and we continue to upgrade.

11. We separated the concessions function from the catering function, allowing our director of catering and sales to focus on the largest gross-revenue generator while creating a new concessions department. The COVID-19 crisis forced us to eliminate the concessions department, return that function to the catering department, and rethink the concessions effort to maximize efficiency and save costs.

12. Incredible as it may seem for a 1,300-acre park, we had no horticultural program for any areas outside the Botanical Garden. In 2013 we created a five-person horticultural team attached to our Grounds Department. They beautified many areas of the park and established our "wildflower" program, which has been a huge attraction over many years.

13. We moved golf management to a third party and eventually placed it with the Bayou District Foundation.

14. In September of 2022, the board of the City Park Improvement Association decided to shift the employees of the park out of State Civil Service into a new 501(c)(3) organization called the City Park Conservancy. This entity then entered into a contract with the CPIA to manage the park. This arrangement is similar

Visitors enjoying our wild-flower field (Courtesy Sonny Randon Photography)

to that of several other park systems, including Audubon Park and their various facilities. While CPIA remains the legal and financial entity responsible for the park, it has no staff and relies on the conservancy staff to operate the park. Thus in a strange turn of events, the staff that began as employees of the nonprofit CPIA transitioned into state employees, then had the golf staff move to a nonprofit entity, and have now returned to being employed by a nonprofit organization! Many of the park's management and financial challenges still remain with the conservancy, and time will tell how they will be addressed.

Finances

To say the park's finances were dismal in 2001 would be a dramatic understatement. We had been operating at a loss for four years, had no meaningful operating reserves for a park our size, had a very small endowment, and were overly dependent on just a few sources of revenue. It took me only a few months after my arrival to recognize what many park commissioners and general managers had understood for many years— there was no public support for the park's operations. We were 100 percent dependent on earned income and donations.

In early 2002, we held a retreat for the board in which I outlined our current status, and we developed a strategic plan going forward. It was not a new master plan but a short-term plan designed to improve park operations and finances. Using that plan as

our marching orders, we began a long-term effort to convince public officials that the park had to change its financial model if it was ever to reach its potential. Some of our financial accomplishments since that time include:

- With the help of our legislative delegation, board members, and the Friends lobbyist, we were able to secure a portion of the state tax on slot machines mainly at the Fair Grounds but also a small allocation from tracks around the state. We have received approximately $2 million annually in public support, which was initially used for recovery projects but eventually migrated into our operating budget.
- We persuaded the legislature to create a taxing district for public improvements, which allows us to capture the sales tax generated in the park from both the city and the state. While the state has not heretofore chosen to participate, we have received and expended over $2.7 million from the tax proceeds from the city on capital improvements since 2008.
- We began a campaign to grow the park's endowment. Beginning with just $46,000, we were able to grow it to a peak of $6.4 million by January 2020. We received challenge

gifts from a local foundation and as well as from foundations and corporations to support various park initiatives, such as tennis-complex maintenance and Botanical Garden programming. Of course, the strong bull stock market after 2009 was very helpful. Only in recent years has the park drawn on the endowment, for repairs to the tennis complex and various playgrounds, upgrades in the Botanical Garden, and most recently support for park operations during the COVID-19 emergency.

- In May 2019, New Orleans voters approved a redistribution of recreation tax dollars that will provide City Park with approximately $2 million for operations for twenty years. The approval by over 76 percent of the voters was the result of several aspects of the tax, mainly that it did not entail a tax increase and it was for a limited number of years. It was also due to the relentless campaign that the staff and board made through the years to inform the public that the park was not receiving any operating support from the city in spite of the fact that it was located in New Orleans and half the attendance came from there. We pledged to use the funds to increase security, improve trash collection, and invest in the park's infrastructure. When combined with the state funds,

the results of our efforts would be, in a normal year, approximately 20 percent of our operating budget, or $4 million a year. While this is still far removed from other parks that receive 65-75 percent of their operating budget through public tax sources, it is still a huge improvement from the situation we were in in 2001.

Capital Improvements

Since the adoption of the 2005 Master Plan, more than $200 million has been spent in the park on capital improvements: approximately $128 million by the park and approximately $74 million by other entities.

Examples of the projects built by or for the park with funding from various sources include:

1. A new Administration Building on Palm Drive.
2. Amusement Park improvements, such as new rides, bathrooms, and food and beverage facilities.
3. A new twenty-six-court tennis complex on Marconi Drive.
4. Botanical Garden improvements, such as a new entrance, outdoor kitchen, and the Enrique Alférez Sculpture Garden.
5. The Great Lawn.
6. The new miniature golf complex called City Putt.
7. A new maintenance building in our service corridor next to the railroad tracks.

8. Redevelopment of the Big Lake area and construction of a new Festival Grounds.

9. Comprehensive renovations to the two sports stadiums, such as new synthetic turf and scoreboards.

10. New playgrounds and park furniture.

11. A new dog park.

12. A new reception facility, the Arbor Room, at Popp Fountain.

13. Parking improvements at the Arbor

NOLA City Bark opened in 2010

Room and in Tri-Centennial Place between Dreyfous Drive and Victory Avenue.

14. Construction of a new championship golf course and clubhouse on Filmore Avenue.

15. Three miles of shared and dedicated bike and jogging paths.

16. Planting of more than 7,500 trees as well as a variety of lighting, drainage, and water-infrastructure improvements throughout the park.

Examples of the projects built by other institutions or organizations in the park include:

- The Louisiana Children's Museum.
- The expansion of Christian Brothers School.
- Construction of a new covered horse rink at Equest Farm.
- City construction at Gernon Brown Recreation Center and the police horse stables.
- Expansion of the Besthoff Sculpture Garden.
- Various road and bridge improvements by the city or state, such as the paving of Filmore Avenue, Wisner Boulevard, and Harrison Avenue and the construction of the Wisner overpass.

Funding for all the improvements has come from a variety of sources. As of January 2020, the breakdown of funding is as follows. All amounts have been rounded to the nearest million.

State funds	$49,000,000
City funds	$14,000,000
Private funds	$60,000,000
Park funds	$11,000,000
Federal funds	$34,000,000 (non-FEMA programs such as the submerged roads program)
FEMA	$33,000,000 (will rise somewhat when damage claims close out)
Total	$201,000,000

While the response to the damage rendered by Hurricane Katrina is certainly a major factor in the total funding, the park's ability to rally governments, foundations, corporations, and individuals behind the vision of the 2005 Master Plan also accounts, in a key way, for this success.

Recovery from Hurricane Katrina

No account of the park's success would be complete without mentioning the recovery from the devastation of Hurricane Katrina. Just as we were beginning to implement our plan and raise the profile of the park to governments and fundraisers, we were annihilated by the storm. Catastrophic damage, the forced layoff of virtually the entire staff, loss of all our equipment, and having minimal operating reserves almost seemed too much to overcome. However, step by step we began restoring parts of the

The Louisiana Children's Museum opened in City Park in 2019

park and implementing the plan. Unless you have experienced a major disaster and have the responsibility of coming back from that disaster, it is very hard to understand the fortitude and perseverance necessary to achieve success. In the early years, the few staff we had remaining had to pick up trash and take shifts on lawn-mowing equipment in addition to their regular duties. Our employees worked in trailers for more than five years before a new Administration Building could be built, and replacing our equipment took years. Board members picked up trash and showed up en masse when we had landscaping projects such as plantings at the Peristyle and Arbor Room. All the while we searched for money and battled with FEMA to get the damage funds the park deserved.

It was an incredible experience I hope never to repeat!

As a result of our recovery, the park and park staff have received numerous awards through the years. Those awards are listed in appendix C.

Challenges Ahead

Prior to the onset of the COVID-19 crisis, I would have said that City Park was in a very good place. We had built our operating reserves to over 10 percent of our annual operating budget, developed the endowment to over $6 million, and completed all of the goals of the 2005 Master Plan by 2018. The operating budget had doubled from the pre-Katrina days, and we increased our Grounds and Horticulture departments to the point that we often got compliments on how well we kept up the park. Our approval ratings were out of sight!

We were hosting more than three hundred special events a year in our various facilities, had just passed a city property tax redistribution that promised a much-needed shot in the arm of public funding, and were experiencing record attendance.

Our facilities were well maintained, we had received a national award for our tennis complex, and we had just seen the opening of the second phase of the Besthoff Sculpture Garden and the new Louisiana Children's Museum.

Of course, we still have challenges even with all of the accomplishments. A partial listing of those issues includes the following.

Board

We need to continue to diversify our board and prepare a new generation of leadership, as senior members rotate off and institutional memory is lost.

Management

There is limited opportunity for advancement in our small organization, which has led to the loss of important staff members. There is a serious need to recruit and hire a program manager and marketing director.

Up until this point in history, City Park has primarily been a provider and renter of facilities. There is a huge opportunity to better market those but also offer programs centered on all our facilities and open space.

The park will need to undertake continual salary analyses to be sure pay is competitive enough to attract the talented individuals needed in the future. The park will also have to ensure that the training and support it provides to employees invests in their future, addresses any of their concerns in the workplace, and promotes an environment in which everyone can achieve their potential.

Financial

First, although the endowment is in the $6 million range, it is terribly low compared to other great regional parks and not enough to provide significant annual support when there is a crisis. Growing the endowment is a fundamental challenge.

Second, our financial platform, even after the addition of the city property tax funds, is still far too dependent on earned income. This continues to put great pressure on the board and senior management to generate operating dollars using park land, which, after all, is the only real resource the park has to generate funds. This will continually put the park somewhat at odds with those in the community who believe it has been developed to a maximum extent.

Third, important revenue generators are experiencing competition from external attractions. Miniature golf and the Amusement Park face competition from other entertainment activities opening in the city, as well as from people choosing to stay at home to play videogames. Celebration in the Oaks is being challenged by holiday light shows in other parishes and even at our own Convention Center. There is a great need to invest in new amusement rides and exhibits at these facilities, to keep them at the front of the market.

Fourth, weather events over the last few years have clearly demonstrated the park's vulnerability to increased rainfall and colder temperatures. Since most of the revenue comes from outdoor events and activities, adverse weather has caused the park to end recent fiscal years with a loss. This trend may dictate investment in indoor facilities.

Master Plan and Land Use

The physical master plan should be comprehensively updated sometime in the next several years. It was adopted in 2005 and has been amended seven times, so it is due for a thorough review in the future. As previously mentioned, balancing various interests—offering different types of recreation and cultural facilities to meet community needs, raising the necessary revenue to deliver services, and preserving what makes City Park special (i.e., trees, landscaping, general open space, community access, and historical buildings)—will be a challenge as it has been almost from the park's founding.

Implementing the plan for the 100-acre Wisner Tract and finding a long-term solution for the problem of maintaining a 1930s high-school football stadium (Tad Gormley) are immediate issues. Finally, the park's three-year strategic plan was disrupted by the pandemic and will have to be reformulated, particularly in light of the new management organization.

Other Issues

Unique issues will always be surfacing from time to time that must be addressed and resolved. The final placement of the Beauregard monument is still uncertain, and implementation of the park's role in the urban water plan by improving its capability to store storm water must be finalized.

And then there is COVID-19. In the space of a few short months, between March and July 2020, the explosive advance of the contagious virus completely altered the status of "where we are"! The loss of budgeted revenue for March ($700,000), April ($975,000), May ($800,000), and June ($800,000) turned a financial year that was promising to end in the black into one that, despite every effort to trim expenses, wound up in the red.

The precipitous drop in income meant that we had to implement immediate cost-saving measures including salary reductions, hiring freezes, and even furloughs and layoffs. By the end of June 2020, we had reduced the full-time employee count from 112 to 96, or 15 percent. By the end of July, we had furloughed or laid off one-third of the full-time staff.

While we were finally able to secure state operating support in the October 2020 Second Special Session of the legislature, which stabilized our finances, until there is widespread adoption of the vaccine and an end to the virus producing variants, there will continue to be many challenges. Will facilities face capacity limits again? Will the public be willing to patronize our facilities in the "age of COVID"? Will the new "stay at home" economy mean that our dependence on earned income will become even more of a weakness? The uncertainty of the impact of the virus and the fact that government authorities essentially have not been able to project an end to the pandemic mean that one of the park's strongest assets—its ability to plan for its future—will be hampered.

While I would like to say that the "state of the park is strong," no one can make an assertion like that about anything. The advantage the park has in facing this enormous crisis is that we have done the heavy lifting caused by Katrina. This time, the challenge is not to rebuild but to continue to find ways to absorb the impact of the pandemic and avoid losing the gains we have made.

CHAPTER 17

Lessons Learned, Thoughts, and Other Ramblings

Not one thing stays the same during this life.
—The Buddha

My twenty years with City Park were both exhilarating and traumatic. They were filled with the proverbial highs and lows and went by so fast it hardly seems possible. Honestly, it seems like yesterday that I had only been on the job a month or so when the 9/11 tragedy struck, and look how that one incident changed everyone's lives. I think I have gained a deep understanding of my strengths and weaknesses. (I am clearly addicted to bullet points in my writing!) I also have come to reflect on certain work and life experiences, and now it is time to share these remembrances, the good and the bad and, as they say, the ugly.

Business District in the mid-1970s led to a great variety of improvements. These included the creation of the Downtown Development District, several historic districts, and a CBD zoning ordinance, all tangible achievements that altered the future in the CBD. Yet in all the time I spent at the City Planning Commission developing plans and designing how they would be implemented, the pre-Katrina one stands out to me as such a practical example of the worth of that process and of actually having a plan. Virtually everything we have accomplished at the park since Hurricane Katrina has used that plan as a foundation, and it continues to guide the park's progress.

The Importance of Having a Plan

I am a professional city planner, so this lesson shouldn't be such a revelation. The work that I and others did on the Growth Management Program for the Central

The Importance of Having a Plan *Before* Disaster Strikes

This seems obvious, but it's not. Planning is hard. Drafting a plan that is visionary and bold often goes directly against the desire to play it safe. To prepare a plan that is not controversial—one that does not arouse the citizenry and is easy to agree to—is not going to fundamentally alter the course of events.

In 2005, we needed a bold plan. The park was in such a deteriorated physical and financial condition, with such a bleak future in front of it, that simply "rearranging the deck chairs" was not going to set a progressive direction. We needed something visionary that would inspire and be aspirational. But this was not easy to achieve. For example, proposing the closure of one of the oldest golf courses in the South (the old South Course) was highly controversial and drew substantial criticism at our public-engagement events. Moving our tennis complex, which had been in the front of the park for more than one hundred years, was also a flashpoint. Yet we needed to make changes such as these to provide land for other activities. The board, staff, and constituents argued it out. We tried to make the public understand why these and other initiatives were essential. The board and staff took substantial criticism.

However, when Hurricane Katrina devastated the park, the major initiatives of the plan were already approved, and their implementation was more about securing financial resources. The argument of whether or not we should do them had already taken place.

It is always hard to be bold before the disaster. Citizens generally do not accept change very well, especially radical change, and after a disaster, the first impulse is to put things back the way they were as quickly as possible. That is one of the reasons why planning for the City of New Orleans after the hurricane was so traumatic. No one wanted to listen to bold ideas about holding water or what areas of the city perhaps should not be rebuilt. The time for forward-thinking planning was prior to the disaster, when there would have been adequate time to debate the issues and secure general agreement. We did the difficult work of planning before the disaster and thus were able to act immediately to use recovery money and donations to implement the plan without spending years trying to develop one under the most terrible conditions of a heavily damaged city. So while the city was developing the Unified New Orleans Plan and a variety of neighborhood plans as a basis to receive federal assistance, our planning was complete and we could get to work implementing our projects.

All Plans Must Have an Overarching Goal and Strategy

Our first goal was to complete implementation of our plan by 2018, the 300th anniversary of the founding of the city in 1718. This gave us immediate focus and a sense of urgency. Although we thought we had thirteen years to implement the plan, the hurricane suddenly accelerated the timeline to accomplish the goal. It is always good to have a date in mind for executing the plan.

Second, while our plan contained more than fifty capital projects, a set of strategies informed all of them: close the South Golf Course, move tennis out of the central area, reduce the number of golf courses to free up land for other uses, consolidate service uses along the railroad tracks, and secure additional sources of public funding. Everything else in the plan—the buildings, jogging trails, tree plantings, investments in existing facilities—fell in place in line with the strategies.

Expect and Plan for the Unexpected, and Have Cash on Hand

The unexpected will happen and continues to happen, as evidenced by the plague of COVID-19. In a disaster, no matter what kind, there is no substitute for cash! When Hurricane Katrina hit, the park had little cash on hand, no substantial reserves, and virtually no endowment. We could not pay most of our staff past August 29, 2005, and thus had to lay off over 90 percent of our team, which greatly inhibited our recovery. We could not take immediate action in the park to clear debris, replace our ruined equipment, or begin a reforestation program. We had to use very limited resources to refund deposits we had received for future events such as weddings, which further diminished our ability to recover.

Fifteen years later, when the COVID-19 crisis hit, we had over $2 million in our reserves and were able to retrieve funds we had sent the state for future capital projects. Like Hurricane Katrina, the virus crisis almost immediately wiped out all of our revenue. However, unlike the hurricane, having reserves allowed us to take a more measured approach to dealing with the loss of revenue without having to lay off 90 percent of the staff. While reductions in staff were necessary, they were not as numerous and not as urgent to implement.

Even if you are a traditional government park agency, you should find a way to fund cash reserves you might need in an emergency. Establish an endowment that can only be used for such purposes, research if your parent government would secure a line of credit you could immediately draw on, and be sure you understand the insurance coverage your parent agency has and how quickly you can access those proceeds. Trust me—when the going gets tough, cash is king!

It Is Very Difficult to Be Entrepreneurial as a Public Agency

Up to the 1980s, many government agencies, including parks, received 100 percent of their funding from a public tax source. Since then, the financial model has transformed to one where agencies of all sorts are expected to generate more and more of their budget through "earned" income. This usually begins by charging fees for service. If someone wants a building permit, then they pay a fee, which presumably pays for employees to review and issue the permit. Traffic tickets presumably pay for enforcement personnel.

However, over the years this concept has evolved to the point that public officials often look to "partner" with private enterprise in order to generate income for the general fund. Leasing of public land or providing tax breaks or capital funds often is the public's "ante" in this process.

For parks, generating income has taken the form of building shelters and renting them, operating a wide variety of food and beverage outlets or renting park land to private enterprises for those outlets, and providing land for wave pools and championship golf courses. The average formula for parks' total revenue today is about 45 percent coming from earned income and 55 percent from a public tax source.[1] City Park was the poster child for relying on earned income, having to account for 90 percent of our operating budget through the operation of various "businesses." Even after the city's dedicated tax dollars started flowing in 2021, the park still had to raise 70 to 80 percent of its operating income through entrepreneurial endeavors.

Why is this? I believe it is because our citizens do not wish or cannot afford to pay for the level of recreation services they desire. Perhaps they see the affluent purchase services such as swimming pools, private clubs with first-class facilities, camp programs, or fitness centers and want the same thing. But they do not want to or cannot pay for them through general tax dollars. So governments and park agencies provide those facilities and services by being entrepreneurial and supplementing their tax-supported budgets with earned income. Governments at all levels could simply say that they will deliver the level of services the citizens are willing to pay for and call it a day. However, the pressure to provide facilities and programs is overwhelming, hence the constant search for funding methods beyond taxation.

This is harder than it seems. Most public agencies are constrained by the civil service system governing their employment. That system, while doing an excellent (some would say) job of establishing fair and equitable standards for public employment, is not set up to promote entrepreneurial activities.

Entrepreneurial activities, at their most basic, are about taking and rewarding risk. However, the public does not want their officials taking risks with their money. That is foreign to the traditional role of government. Thus, you have this contradiction of the public agency and its employees urged to generate more and more of its income from sources other than taxes, yet the system they work under does not generally reward the risk taking that, in most circumstances, is essential to generating that income.

If the State Civil Service Commission had not been supportive of City Park's status and provided the park the freedom to establish qualifications for unusual or unique positions such as amusement ride mechanics and food and beverage managers, set compensation and work schedules, and set our own disciplinary policies and standards, the park could not function as an entrepreneurial agency. Many other parks throughout the country, understanding the pressure to generate income and seeing that it could not be accomplished in a traditional civil service structure, have set up management methods designed to bypass these issues. Increasingly, public agencies have elected to contract with nonprofit groups to operate America's park and recreation system. The City of New Orleans has adopted this approach, contracting the nonprofit Audubon Nature Institute to operate Audubon Park and various public facilities. Central Park in New York also hires a nonprofit for its management. It is interesting to note that the City Park Improvement Association, a nonprofit corporation, operated and managed City Park under authority granted to it by the State of Louisiana and the City of New Orleans much before, to my knowledge, any other nonprofit managed a park in the United States.

In 2022, the CPIA chose to move the employees out of civil service and contract with a nonprofit to manage the park. It is hoped that this new management approach will allow for more efficient fundraising and an ability to conduct entrepreneurial activities not possible in a government agency. The park has been extremely successful at development partnerships primarily because of the latitude provided by State Civil Service. The new City Park Conservancy will now have the opportunity to continue that success as a private entity. It is clear that as long as the public demands a level of service it is not willing to pay for through traditional tax sources, the park will have to carry on its tradition of entrepreneurship.

The Consequences of Being Entrepreneurial in a Time of Crisis

Being increasingly entrepreneurial leaves an agency vulnerable when a crisis cuts off its ability to generate earned revenue. Today, crisis comes in a variety of manifestations. During Katrina, rain, wind, and flooding caused City Park to lose all of its ability to generate revenue. During COVID-19, the restrictions put in place to reduce the spread of the virus decimated our revenue.

In both instances, we petitioned the government to provide the lost revenue through general tax dollars. The state, in the years following the hurricane, placed City Park in the general-fund budget until the park was able to repair its income-generating facilities. It was the key to our recovery. During the COVID-19 crisis, we appealed to the state to provide gap funding until the restrictions were lifted and the park could begin to generate its normal earned-income percentage.

It is said that those who "live by the sword, die by the sword," and there is certainly some truth to that proverb when applied to parks that derive a significant share of their operating income from self-generated revenue. When times are good, governments and citizens reap a huge advantage, because the park is able to offer more facilities and programs. However, in a crisis, when that earned income is dramatically reduced or eliminated entirely, then, unless governments can come in and financially support the park, reductions of programs, services, staffing, and pay will almost certainly occur. Catastrophes always magnify underlying weaknesses, and being overly dependent on earned revenue can certainly be considered a weakness.

Building an Endowment

All park agencies should have dedicated endowments to provide a cushion against crisis or general reductions in government operating support. This is doubly true for entrepreneurial park agencies, since income-earning park facilities such as golf courses, tennis courts, and even to a degree

sports fields must compete with the private recreation market for discretionary dollars. As an example, City Park's Celebration in the Oaks was the region's premier holiday light show for years. However, park agencies in adjacent parishes have developed their own versions in recent years, cutting into the revenue generated by our event.

How do you start building an endowment? This can be accomplished through a variety of ways. Sometimes individuals or companies will donate money to an endowment for facilities or programs that are in line with their philosophy of giving. We have endowments specifically for our tennis complex, buildings in our Botanical Garden, as well as program support for the garden. Sometimes, you may be able to generate a significant financial contribution as a result of a unique real-estate venture or circumstance. For example, the Audubon Nature Institute secured over $5 million for its endowment from a real-estate exchange on the city's riverfront. Many other organizations used the settlement they received from the BP Oil Spill litigation to create or supplement their endowment. Other organizations dedicate a specific percentage of their construction budget to go into an endowment to provide funds to maintain that facility.

While fundraising for capital facilities, City Park has received monies that have been applied to a specific endowments (Pepsi—tennis center, Azby Fund—Pavilion of the Two Sisters, etc.). We have also created a general park endowment, which allows broad use of the interest from private fundraising and a planned-giving program for almost all our needs.

The challenge we have found with endowments is trying to balance the donors' specific wishes with the need to have maximum flexibility to use the funds. Donors fear that if a fund is not established to support their particular interest, their gift could be used for other park needs that they may consider less important. To date, City Park has eleven funds, some of which do not have enough money to generate meaningful income for a specific project or facility. The park has tried to address this issue by designating future gifts from the planned-giving program to the general endowment. Hopefully, over the long run we will succeed in building up that endowment.

The Importance of Perseverance

Recovering from a manmade or natural disaster is more akin to a marathon than a sprint. It is easy to give up, and there is truth to the old saying that "when the going gets tough, the tough get going." Some people take their insurance money and move on, some relocate to a more normal environment for their family, some immediately retire, and others are simply not heard from or seen again. The twenty-two people who stayed with City Park to begin the rebuilding process after Katrina embody the value of perseverance. We can also reflect on the many years when park leaders made every effort to inform the public that it was necessary to provide tax support in order for the park to achieve success and a stable future. Almost from its founding, park leaders have emphasized the need for public support. It took 169 years from the time John McDonogh provided his vast estate to New Orleans and Baltimore, out of which the beginning of City Park was created, until our citizens voted to provide property-tax revenue to the park.

There is no substitute for dogged perseverance guided by a vision and plan. It is a key to not only recovery but building a better future.

The Lie of "We Are All in This Together"

In every crisis, a rallying cry goes out, trying to encourage the feeling that everyone is equally impacted, everyone is feeling the same pain, and everyone is making equal sacrifices. "We are all in this together"! Nothing could be further from the truth.

If you have lost your job, principal source of income, or some of your salary, you are not in the same boat as others who have. Large-scale disasters, whether manmade or natural (including disease), always lay bare the inequality that underlies most economies and social institutions.

After Katrina, if you did not have insurance

on your home or business and that home or business was destroyed, it was nearly impossible for you to recover and rebuild your life. If you were poor and lost your job, or your family was broken up and dispersed, you had almost insurmountable obstacles to overcome. On the other hand, if you could afford adequate insurance, did not lose your job or livelihood, and/or had substantial savings, you had an excellent chance at recovery.

During COVID-19, if you lived paycheck to paycheck, relied on your job for your health insurance, and then lost it when you were laid off, you were almost totally dependent on the federal government to support you, through moratoriums against evictions or through enhanced unemployment benefits. You were not "in it" with people who owned their home, had significant savings, or received substantial dividends from stock investments. If you were a blue-collar worker who couldn't work from home, you were impacted by the strangulation of the economy caused by the governmental restrictions enacted to "slow the spread."

City Park employees suffered layoffs, furloughs, salary reductions and other negative actions as a result of the park's unique financial structure, which more closely resembles a business than a public agency. Our employees were not "in it" with other state or city employees, many of whom continued to receive their full salaries while people employed in business experienced all of the above and more.

In a crisis, we are *not* "all in this together"!

Thoughts on the Role of Surveys

Reflecting upon my career as a planning director and being responsible for developing and implementing the City Park plan, it occurs to me that planners have become too dependent on surveying citizens about what they want. To be sure, it is important to understand the views of neighborhood and special-interest groups when developing planning recommendations. No one would deny that. But I have seen too many instances where planners and decision makers believe that that is the only meaningful input into the development of the plan. As professional planners, we suggest uses and programs that would be right for the community, but our training and experience are often assumed to be not important as long as we give citizens what they want. If all we do as professional planners is to survey to ascertain desires, and we don't put forth our ideas and argue for them, then we deprive communities of important information and alternatives that should be considered.

When we surveyed citizens for the 2005 plan, dog parks were not ranked highly. Now our dog park is one of the highlights of the plan, and almost every park plan in the country considers dog parks a potential use. Citizens did not think it necessary to relocate the tennis courts, but we insisted it was needed to improve the courts and implement the plan. Over five thousand citizens (many not from New Orleans) signed an online petition opposing the new golf course, yet in 2020 that sport was one of the few activities permitted by authorities. Our course produced a net profit to support other areas of the park, as well as maintaining nearly 30 percent of the entire park.

It is important to understand the wishes of the community, but those wishes should not be the only factor in deciding what goes into a plan. Planners have an obligation to put forth their own ideas, recommendations, and best practices, even if they don't match the survey results!

Acknowledgments

As I look back over the twenty years of my tenure, I recognize that our team achieved many successes. Who makes up our team? The list of contributors is long.

The Board of Commissioners of the City Park Improvement Association

I served with hundreds of board members and ten board presidents. During that entire time, I never had a single member ask me for anything that would bring him or her personal economic gain. In fact, this is true of all the elected officials I dealt with in my career! While some members did not attend many meetings or used their membership to pad their resume, overwhelmingly our board has been extremely generous with both their time and their money. They have opened doors to potential funders and have never hesitated to go on a fundraising call or meet with elected officials about public funds we were pursuing. Many members have served a full eight years on the board, and a few have served longer after leaving for one year as required by the board's articles.

While all the board members have contributed, I must single out the ten presidents I have served with. Unless you have held that position, you cannot estimate the amount of time that is required. Particularly after Hurricane Katrina, the period of the Beauregard monument controversy, and the effort involved in passing the redistribution of the city's millage, those presidents put in an unbelievable amount of time on park business.

The Park Staff

I have long told our entire team that the reason we have been so successful raising private funds and public support is because of their efforts. Everything from cutting the grass to picking up trash, operating the various park facilities, and accounting for all the funds we generate is a result of the work of our staff. There have been difficult times, such as following Katrina and the salary reductions associated with COVID-19. When I got to the park, they did not have the tools to do their job, from grass-cutting equipment to a decent website, and there had been no salary increases for years. Yet they persevered, and a great deal of our accomplishments owes directly to their efforts.

Volunteers

Many people do not understand the importance of volunteers in operating a large urban park. Volunteers do most of the planting in our Botanical Garden and raising of plants in our greenhouse. They routinely remove invasive species that have made the park home and maintain many of our bio-swales or wetlands. After Hurricane Katrina, volunteers picked up trash and cut grass in various places for more than a year and repainted several of our buildings. While volunteerism peaked following the storm, we currently average more than three thousand volunteers annually. Most come from our local community, but many come from visiting conventions and tour groups who want to perform community service. Often they bring their own tools and even pay for dumpsters and new plant materials. We love our volunteers!

Donors

In this work I have listed just a few of the park's donors. Sometimes they are responsible for large gifts for capital projects; sometimes they are thousands of individuals who give small amounts as part of a fundraising campaign or annual fund appeal. We have donors whom we only know about when their gift through our planned-giving campaign is realized years down the road. All told, private gifts have represented about 30 percent of the total of $200 million that have been spent in the park since Katrina! I have to give a shout-out to the park's development staff, who doggedly pursue all opportunities to contact old and new donors, present the park's needs, and try to find a way for individuals and groups to support us. They do a tremendous job.

Elected Officials

1. Louisiana Legislature. All public agencies depend on the support of various elected officials for their success. As a state agency, we particularly rely on our state representatives and senators for passing laws favorable to the park and appropriating funds. Just a few of the actions they have taken since 2001 that have benefitted the park include:

- Passing legislation allowing the park to receive a share of the state tax on slot machines at racetracks throughout the state.
- Passing enabling legislation allowing the park to create a Special Taxing District covering the area of City Park.
- Appropriating nearly $50 million for capital projects in the park (including state investments in roads and bridges and the Children's Museum).

Perhaps the most important support the state gave the park during my tenure was placing us in its operating budget for four years, which allowed us to rebuild our revenue base following Hurricane Katrina. Since the park was totally devastated and could not generate any operating income, that four-year period of direct state support in the general fund essentially saved us. The park will always be grateful to Gov. Kathleen Blanco and her administration for their support at that watershed event.

2. State and City Staff. I would also like to acknowledge the work of state and city staff in our recovery. At the end of the day, it is the rank and file of city and state civil servants who turn basic appropriations into bricks and mortar. We have had great support from all of those who have been involved in park projects.

3. State Civil Service Commission. Special thanks must go to the staff and members of the State Civil Service Commission, who have given the park the freedom to function as an entrepreneurial entity and raise 90 percent of our operating revenue through the "businesses" in the park. Their understanding of our special circumstance is in no small way responsible for our success.[1]

4. City Councilmembers and Mayors. The City Council and mayor have also provided tremendous support. They have participated in the Special Taxing District; passed laws incorporating park rules and regulations into the Code of Ordinances, which allows us to call on the New Orleans Police

Department for assistance; and appropriated over $14 million in capital funds during this period. The City Council was also 100 percent behind the tax election, which will mean over $2 million to the park annually until 2041.

5. Friends of City Park. This organization was founded in 1979 with a mission to support the park. Their first project was to hire a horticulturist (Paul Soniat, our current Botanical Garden director) and fund his salary for five years. They also used the first Lark in the Park to raise funds to erect a fence around the garden. Through the years, the Friends have added fundraising events such as Martini Madness and Ghost in the Oaks (for Halloween), raised their membership to over five thousand, and provided volunteers for countless events. In 1994, they hired their first employee and have continued to be aggressive in their fund-raising plans. Specific building projects they have supported include the renovation of the Peristyle and the construction of City Putt and the Arbor Room at Popp Fountain. They have also funded equipment purchases, such as police cars, tractors, a new train engine, as well as a scoreboard at Tad Gormley Stadium. The Friends have raised nearly $5 million for improvements in the park.

6. Botanical Garden Foundation. As the principal support organization for the garden, this group has raised funds for a variety of projects, the most recent being the Outdoor Kitchen. Their main fundraiser, Magic in the Moonlight, is a black-tie dinner held outside in the garden in the fall. They are spearheading the effort with Garden Director Paul Soniat to get the garden accredited by the American Association of Museums.

I want to personally acknowledge several people who were instrumental in my success as well as those who greatly contributed to this book.

- Dottie Ziegler and Denise Joubert, who were my assistants when I was CEO and were invaluable in helping me "learn the ropes" and manage the board's affairs.
- Casie Duplechain, who helped me decipher the mysteries of the park's photo library and corrected my original manuscript. Both as director of the Friends and later as my chief development officer, Casie was an integral part of the park's success.
- Kerry Guillory, the park's IT director, who helped me access the image library and generally assisted me in managing my computer files and records, all the while offering much needed encouragement.
- Natalie Weiss Brasset, whose computer skills and overall manuscript guidance were absolutely necessary to bring this publication to fruition. Natalie also prepared many of the materials I used to make presentations on all manner of park issues.
- Darrell Hunt, the Friends of City Park's lobbyist who first identified a source of state operating funding, managed our capital outlay requests, and shepherded all of our state legislation during my tenure. Though he was not a member of our staff, his work was crucial to the park's success.
- Scott Campbell, Nina Kooij, and the staff at Pelican Publishing, who enthusiastically supported publishing the park's story.

APPENDIX A

Presidents of the City Park Improvement Association

L. Tissot	1891-1896	Frank J. Stich, Jr.	1982-1983
Paul Capdeville	1896-1922	Robert A. Peyroux	1984-1985
E. W. Smith	1922-1924	William R. LeCorgne	1986-1987
C. F. Claiborne	1924-1934	Fred M. Smith	1988
Felix Dreyfous	1935-1946	Margaret R. Read	1989-1990
George Grandmann	1947	Milton F. Hilbert, Jr.	1991-1992
H. Dabezies	1948-1949	Thomas S. Davidson	1993
Frank Stich	1950	George D. Hopkins, Jr.	1994
Joseph Lallande	1951	Charles A. Snyder	1995
Allen H. Generes	1952	Peter M. Smith	1996
Fred D. Ketchum	1953	Gary N. Solomon	1997
Edward J. DeVerges	1954	C. Hearn Taylor	1998-1999
H. Edward Heiny	1955	Digges Morgan	2000-2001
Charles E. Whitmore	1956	Edward C. Mathes	2002-2003
R. M. Salvant	1957	Patrick J. Butler, Jr.	2004-2006
E. L. Zander	1958	Paul J. Masinter	2007-2008
Herbert Jahncke	1959	Mike Marsiglia	2009-2010
Albert F. Backer, Sr.	1960	Robert E. S. Lupo	2011-2012
Earl R. LeCorgne, Sr.	1961	William D. Hoffman	2013-2014
George J. Riehl	1962-1963	Susan Hess	2015-2016
Ernest A. Carrere	1964-1965	Steven L. Pettus	2017-2018
Percy H. Sitges	1966-1967	Larry Katz	2019-2020
James S. Janssen	1968-1969	Jay Batt	2021-2022
Richard A. Peneguy	1970-1971	David Waller	2023-2024
J. Garic Schoen	1972-1973		
Harold C. Mauney	1974-1975		
Paul. R. Kalman, Jr.	1976-1977		
Waldemar S. Nelson	1978-1979		
J. Barbee Winston	1980-1981		

APPENDIX B

City Park Leaders

Through the years, the person in charge of City Park has had a variety of titles: keeper, general manager, superintendent, and most recently chief executive officer. The following are those individuals who have led City Park since 1891.

Victor J. Anseman	1891	Ellis Laborde	1950-1978
George Marks	1891-1892	William Rapp	1979-1985
Charles Andler	1892	Joseph Buscher	1985-1991
Joseph Baum	1892-1904	Charles Spears	1991-1994
Joseph Bernard	1904-1926	Patrick Dayton	1994-2001
George Vinnedge	1926-1934	Dr. Robert Becker	2001-2021
Marcel G. Montreuil	1934-1950	Cara Lambright	2021-

APPENDIX C
Recent Awards

Following are awards and recognition the park, board, and staff have received since 2005.

Outstanding Planning Award from the Louisiana Chapter of the American Planning Association for the new park master plan, 2005

Outstanding Service Award from the City of New Orleans to the twenty-two staff members who were with the park following Hurricane Katrina, 2007

Bureau of Governmental Research Excellence in Government Award for the efforts of the staff in the recovery of the park, 2007

Role Model Award from the Young Leadership Council to Robert Becker, 2008

Allstate Sugar Bowl Distinguished American Award to Tony Biagas, director of Athletic Services, 2008

Special Recognition Award from the Denver Service Center of the National Park Service to Robert Becker, 2008

National Planning Award from the American Planning Association for the park's master plan and its implementation following Hurricane Katrina, 2010

Distinguished Alumnus Award from the College of Liberal Arts, University of New Orleans, to Robert Becker, 2013

Great Places in Louisiana from AARP

Family Service of New Orleans honor for volunteer, civic, and charitable contributions to the city to Robert Becker, 2013

Lifetime Achievement Award from Bureau of Governmental Research to Robert Becker, 2014

Louisiana Great Places Award from American Planning Association, Louisiana Chapter, 2014

Hero of the Recovery honor by *New Orleans Magazine* to Robert Becker on the tenth anniversary of Hurricane Katrina, 2015

Silver Linings Honoree award from the Louisiana Children's Museum to Robert Becker, 2015

One of sixteen parks worldwide that deserve a special effort to visit according to BuzzFeed, 2018

Editor's Pick for Best New Orleans Attraction from *AAA Southern Traveler,* 2018

Outstanding Facilities honor by the United States Tennis Association for tennis center (Patti Todd, director), 2019

Leadership Award from the Urban League of Louisiana to Robert Becker, 2019

One of the 15 Best City Parks in America from Thrillist, 2019

One of seven Gorgeous Green Spaces in some of the world's biggest cities—from Tripadvisor, 2019

Executive of the Year Award from *Biz New Orleans Magazine* to Robert Becker, 2019

Urban Hero Award from Urban Conservancy to Paul Soniat, director of the New Orleans Botanical Garden, 2019

Outstanding Organization Award from Girl Scouts of Louisiana, 2020

APPENDIX D

Chronology

The following is a listing of the major events/accomplishments beginning with the adoption of the park's master plan in March 2005. Many of these accomplishments focus on the rebuilding and opening of park facilities following Hurricane Karina.

March 2005: The first new master plan in more than twenty years is approved.

June 2005: Act 430 of the Louisiana Legislature provides the park, for the first time, with revenue from the state tax on slot machines at the Fair Grounds.

July 2005: The park closes the South Golf Course.

August 29, 2005: Hurricane Katrina virtually annihilates City Park.

September 2005: Twenty-two staff members return to the park and debris clearing begins.

October 2005: First volunteer events for debris cleanup are held.

November 2005: The equestrian center reopens.

December 2005: Train Garden in the Botanical Garden is restored.

December 2005: Celebration in the Oaks, the park's traditional holiday light display, opens for nineteen days.

February 2006: The Pavilion of the Two Sisters in the garden is renovated and opens.

February 2006: The golf driving range opens with makeshift facilities.

March 2006: The Botanical Garden restoration is completed, and garden opens.

March 2006: Storyland playground is repaired and opened.

May 2006: The new Robert B. Haspel Stage opens in the garden.

September 2006: Tad Gormley Stadium opens after basic repairs.

March 2007: The Amusement Park opens after extensive repairs.

April 2007: Rugby and lacrosse fields open.

May 2007: The park's lagoons are restocked with fish by the Louisiana Department of Wildlife and Fisheries.

June 2007: A new fitness trail opens.

June 2007: Damaged trees along Lelong Drive are removed and new live oaks and crepe myrtles are planted at the main entrance to the park.

June 2007: The new bike path on Robert E. Lee Boulevard opens.

August 2007: New picnic furniture is installed next to the Amusement Park.

August 2007: New Japanese Garden in the Botanical Garden opens.

September 2007: Picnic shelters open after repairs.

November 2007: The historic carousel in the Amusement Park opens after extensive renovations.

January 2008: A new playground opens next to the Amusement Park.

February 2008: The Stanley Ray Playground opens after repairs.

March 2008: The old antique car ride in the Amusement Park is repurposed into a birthday village and opened.

April 2008: The Dunbar Pavilion in Storyland opens.

August 2008: After extensive renovations including new bleachers, scoreboard, and field, Pan American Stadium opens.

August 2008: The Casino Building opens with new Parkview Café.

September 2008: The North Golf Course opens after repairs. Pro golfer Billy Casper dedicates the course.

October 2008: The new bike path along Wisner Boulevard opens from Robert E. Lee to the Wisner overpass.

November 2008: The new Ferris wheel opens in the Amusement Park.

November 2008: The park receives its first funding from the new Tax Increment Financing District.

February 2009: The new Cinderella's Castle opens in Storyland.

February 2009: The historic Anseman Bridge is renovated.

April 2009: A new artificial-turf field is installed at Tad Gormley Stadium along with restroom and locker-room renovations.

September 2009: New water-quality monitors are installed in park lagoons.

September 2009: New lights are added at the soccer fields.

October 2009: A new volunteer center opens in a relocated shotgun house on Harrison Avenue.

October 2009: The Big Lake walking trail opens in the area formerly occupied by the South Golf Course.

January 2010: Couturie Forest is restored, with 2,050 trees planted.

January 2010: Harrison Avenue is resurfaced and contains a new dedicated bike path.

March 2010: Historic Popp Fountain is restored.

March 2010: The new NOLA City Bark Dog Park opens.

March 2010: The Goldring/Woldenberg Great Lawn opens.

April 2010: The driving range building is repaired and opens.

May 2010: A new baseball field opens on Roosevelt Mall.

July 2010: The new Musik Express ride opens in the Amusement Park.

September 2010: The Disc Golf Course opens on Palm.

September 2010: A new fishing pier opens on Marconi Drive.

December 2010: The new Tri-Centennial Place parking lot and bio swale opens between the Botanical Garden and Stanley Ray Playground on the site of former tennis courts.

January 2011: The new Administration Building opens and park staff move out of trailers after five years.

March 2011: The new City Park/Pepsi Tennis Center opens on Marconi Drive with 26 courts and a new clubhouse.

March 2011: New fitness equipment is installed on Stadium Drive.

June 2011: A new observation deck is installed on Laborde Mountain in Couturie Forest.

August 2011: All road repairs in the park damaged by Hurricane Katrina are completed.

September 2011: The new Arbor Room event center opens in the Popp Fountain location.

November 2011: 100 new LED lampposts are installed.

March 2012: Renovations of the historic Peristyle are completed.

March 2012: The park's endowment reaches $2 million.

June 2012: Grow Dat Youth Farm opens on land provided by the park on Zachary Taylor Drive.

August 2012: The Softball Quadraplex partially reopens, with three fields restored.

November 2012: The Morning Call coffee stand opens in the Casino Building.

December 2012: The Matt Savoie Soccer Pavilion opens on Marconi Drive.

December 2012: The 5,000th tree is planted since Katrina.

December 2012: The new Festival Grounds opens on the site of the former South Golf Course.

December 2012: A new covered fitness center opens on the Festival Grounds.

December 2012: A newly planted wetland opens on the Festival Grounds.

February 2013: Additional renovations begin in the Amusement Park, with new restrooms, new rides, and a café.

May 2013: The new miniature-golf complex, City Putt, opens.

May 2013: A new boat and bicycle concession opens on Big Lake.

September 2013: Filmore Avenue is resurfaced and a bicycle path added.

September 2013: A new covered rink in the equestrian complex is completed.

October 2013: The park's endowment exceeds $3 million.

October 2013: The old maintenance buildings are reroofed.

May 2014: Parker's Café and new restrooms open in the Amusement Park.

October 2014: A new pedestrian bridge to Couturie Forest is completed.

December 2014: The state signs a construction contract for a new South Golf Course, and construction begins in February 2015.

February 2015: The new Ladybug Rollercoaster opens.

May 2015: Pan American Stadium's synthetic field is replaced.

July 2015: The Tri-Centennial Place improvement project begins with renovations to the Peristyle plaza, the Tolmas plaza, parking, and lighting on Dreyfous Drive.

August 2015: The park receives an oil-spill settlement check from BP and deposits it in the reserves.

October 2015: The Enrique Alférez Sculpture Garden opens to the public in the Botanical Garden.

November 2015: The Oscar J. Tolmas Visitor Center opens as the new entrance to the garden and Storyland.

September 2016: Parking improvements and a pedestrian path are completed at the Arbor Room.

October 2016: Extensive drainage improvements completed at Festival Grounds.

October 2016: The arrival garden is completed in the Botanical Garden.

December 2016: The new South Golf Course is substantially completed.

January 2017: Parking improvements are completed at the Pelican Greenhouse.

April 2017: The new golf clubhouse and South Golf Course open. The Bayou District Foundation assumes management of the golf complex.

June 2017: The park's endowment exceeds $5 million.

August 2017: The synthetic field at Tad Gormley Stadium is replaced.

August 2017: The new maintenance buildings at the golf complex are completed.

September 2017: The new Wisner overpass is completed and opened.

October 2017: The Marconi Bike Path is completed from Robert E. Lee to Harrison Avenue.

November 2017: Magnolia Playground opens.

February 2018: Exterior renovations to a small maintenance building are completed.

April 2018: The inaugural Hat Luncheon is held to create an endowment for the park's trees.

May 2019: The expansion of the Besthoff Sculpture Garden opens on land provided by the park.

May 4, 2019: City voters approve a recreation

tax millage proposal, which allocates .61 mills to City Park or approximately $2 million for twenty years beginning in 2021.

July 2019: Renovations are completed at the Casino Building and Café Du Monde opens.

July 2019: The park's endowment reaches $6 million.

August 2019: The Louisiana Children's Museum opens on land formerly occupied by the South Golf Course.

September 2019: The Outdoor Kitchen opens in the Botanical Garden.

September 2019: Storyland reopens after extensive renovations.

January 2020: Construction begins on a new maintenance complex.

March 2020: The governor issues an executive order closing all park facilities due to the COVID-19 pandemic. Golf courses are allowed to stay open.

May 2020: Some park facilities reopen as part of the state's Phase 1 reopening plan.

June 2020: The state enters Phase 2 of its reopening plan. The Amusement Park and stadiums remain closed and weddings are limited to 100 guests.

November 2020: Louisiana Legislature appropriates $2.5 million to the park for COVID relief.

September 2022: City Park Improvement Association signs agreement with newly created City Park Conservancy for management of the park.

(Courtesy Sonny Randon Photography)

Notes

Chapter 1

1. In subsequent years, the University of Buffalo became part of the larger State University of New York System and today is called the University at Buffalo.

2. When planning was beginning for a new bridge over the Mississippi River in New Orleans, the preferred location turned out to be parallel to the existing bridge. But the details of how that crossing would be designed seemed destined to be left up to the Louisiana Highway Department. Worried that they would produce a design detrimental to the city, Harold asked Bobbie if he could come up with a conceptual drawing of how the bridge would work, including on and off ramps, etc. In a few hours, Bobbie came up with a schematic that was later mostly followed by the state.

3. Ellis Laborde is the longest-serving manager of City Park, serving as its head for twenty-eight years.

4. I also had plenty of odd experiences in my time managing City Park. Here are just two examples of the kinds of things that go on in a large public park. In 2013, one of my police officers went to one of our shelters to close for the night. He inspected both the ladies' and men's rooms, including looking under the partitions, to be sure no one was still there. He locked the restrooms and left. A few minutes later, he received a 911 call from the police dispatcher relaying that a woman had called saying she was locked in the restroom. When the officer arrived and let her out, he asked why she did not respond when he called out for any occupants. She replied that she was standing on top of the toilet because she was afraid of catching a disease if she sat down, and she didn't say anything because she didn't want the officer seeing her standing on top of the toilet! In 2014, we responded to a police dispatch call about a battery that had occurred in the park. When our officers arrived, one suspect pushed another suspect toward the officers and told them that Mr. B had pinched his wife on the buttocks, he confronted Mr. B, and Mr. B then punched him in the eye!

5. While Pat Dayton had the title of general manager, Beau Bassich had the title of executive director. Pat was supposed to operate the park on a day-to-day basis, while Beau raised money. In practice, the employees never knew whom to approach to answer their questions or get direction.

Chapter 2

1. Much of the discussion of the history of City Park comes from *History of City Park New Orleans,* by Sally K. Evans Reeves and William D. Reeves, 2000; *New Orleans City Park: Its First Fifty Years,* by Workers of the Writers' Program

of the Work Projects Administration, 1941; and *New Orleans City Park,* by Catherine Campanella, 2011.

2. See C.O.B. #78, Folio 613 in the New Orleans Conveyance Office.

3. *New Orleans City Park: Its First Fifty Years,* 17.

4. Hurricane Katrina struck New Orleans 114 years later to the day.

5. Section 2. Council Ordinance #5547, August 29, 1891.

6. It is interesting to note that the delegation of authority to a private nonprofit organization to manage a public park makes City Park perhaps the first example in the country of what is now considered common practice. For example, Central Park was placed under nonprofit management in the 1980s. There are pros and cons to nonprofit management of public facilities, but in general, when a park agency is governed by the strict requirements of a civil service system, its ability to generate revenue to supplement or even supplant public tax dollars is extremely limited. That situation has led governments to put many of their operations in the hands of private or nonprofit entities, which have no such restrictions. If a public park agency is not burdened with the constraints of civil service, the case to turn it over to a private entity is not nearly as strong.

7. Section B. State Act #130, 1896.

8. Some of this discussion is taken from the Section 106 Consultation Report undertaken by the state to determine the park's eligibility for National Register designation in 2007.

9. In 1932, the park exchanged land with the Orleans Levee Board that gave the Levee Board the right of way for the former Robert E. Lee Boulevard and gave the park two narrow pieces of land along Beauregard Avenue and Marconi Drive. This was an effort to secure some park frontage on Lake Pontchartrain, which had been cut off with the construction of the roadway

and the Lake Vista subdivision. The CPIA's long hoped-for goal of creating a lakefront park has never been achieved.

10. Section 106 Consultation Report.

11. "City Park Master Plan," draft interim report, EDAW Inc., September 1981.

12. Another repercussion from the proposal to lease park land was that the board, under pressure from elected officials, expanded its membership to include appointees by the governor, mayor, City Council, and Louisiana Legislature.

13. *New Orleans Times-Picayune,* March 29, 1984.

14. Executive Summary, "Revenue Master Plan and Management Study," by the American Institute for Leisure Resources, Wheeling, West Virginia, 1990.

Chapter 3

1. Postlethwaite & Netterville conducted these independent audits when the park's fiscal year was October 1 through September 30. In 2004, the fiscal year was changed to correspond to the state's fiscal year of July 1 through June 30.

2. The state has a peculiar method of allocating funds from the capital outlay budget. It is a priority system going from Priority #1 funds to Priority #5 funds. In this system it is actually better to have funds in Priority #5 than in Priority #2, 3, or 4. Don't ask! Our tennis funding came in Priorities #1 and #5.

3. Other recipients include the New Orleans Sports Foundation and the New Orleans Urban Tourism Training Fund.

Chapter 4

1. For greater detail, see "New Orleans City Park Master Plan: Vision for the 21st Century—City Park 2018," adopted by the City Park Improvement Association, March 29, 2005.

2. "New Orleans City Park: Summary of Market Factors," by Economic Research Associates, 2004.

3. Laura Burnett of the Wallace staff drafted significant parts of the foundational statements and plan concepts, and Carlos Cashio translated them into renderings and drawings.

4. Positive comments included: "The work you are doing at City Park is a great blessing for all citizens of New Orleans. Your vision will have a transformative effect on City Park, which is one of the great, and often under-appreciated, treasures of our City." Of course, as with any public hearing, some comments were not as constructive: "However, I do not appreciate my issue (lack of an ice-skating facility) that I presented to be made a joke of. . . . Then you waited until I sat down to give the lame excuse that the rink lost money, which I already had figured out given the fact that you and your cronies have zero knowledge of running such an enterprise."

Chapter 5

1. Hurricanes, since 1971, have been categorized into five ascending classes of severity depending on several criteria. This system of classes, called the Saffir-Simpson Damage-Potential Scale, was based on the experience with Hurricane Camille, which struck the Gulf Coast. Category 1, with sustained winds between 74 and 95 miles per hour, represents the least lethal hurricane, while Category 5, with winds in excess of 156 miles per hour, produces catastrophic damage.

2. Pat O'Shaughnessy, memo to author, 2019.

3. Joey Scaffidi, memo to author, August 26, 2019.

4. Leslie Kramer, memo to author, 2019.

5. *Katrina Thoughts After 15 Years: Recollections of Jacqueline Sullivan* (2020).

6. *The Great Deluge: Hurricane Katrina, New Orleans, and the Mississippi Gulf Coast,* by Douglas Brinkley, 2006, 79-80.

7. The following were the initial twenty-two people tasked with rebuilding City Park: James Arthur, Beau Bassich, William Bayle, Robert Becker, Anthony Biagas, Minette Bruce, David Carpenter, Christine Casey, Carolyn Constance, Rob DeViney, Darlene Duffard, John Hopper, Joel Jones, Kathleen McNamara, Michael Mariani, Mark Meunier, Pat O'Shaughnessy, George Parker, Paul Soniat, Val Taylor, Don Watson, Patrick Youngblood.

8. Other park staff used more creative means to enter the city. Jacqueline Sullivan, the deputy director of the museum, made her way back to New Orleans from Gonzales, Louisiana with the State Police by telling them she had to meet armed guards at the museum to protect the art. Pat O'Shaughnessy crossed Lake Pontchartrain on the Causeway and was able to talk his way past a National Guard checkpoint on Metairie Road at the Seventeenth Street Canal. Paul Soniat, the Botanical Garden director, tried to get into the park two weeks after the storm but was stopped by the National Guard. He then snuck into the park through backroads, where he was promptly met at the garden by soldiers with machineguns on an ATV. He talked them into letting him walk through the garden to assess the damage.

Chapter 6

1. Eventually, we had to tear off about a third of our house that had flooded. That third contained the den, bathroom, and laundry room. I spent the next five years taking our laundry to a laundromat before we could install a washer and dryer in our bathroom. It was good to own a laundromat in the years after Katrina!

Chapter 7

1. In spite of the seemingly never ending rotation of FEMA team members, several were very helpful during our recovery, although they often expressed frustration with the process. Ben McVea, a PAC group leader; Jim Stark, director of the Louisiana Recovery Authority; and Katherine Zeringue and Helen Miller of the FEMA recovery office were especially helpful.

2. Another lesson we learned was that once you

release a damage estimate, you can never walk it back. When we were asked to estimate damage in late September or early October, we had little capability to make such an estimate. But we did the best we could using square footages, eyeballing damage, determining whether a building was a total loss or could be renovated, and then using the RSMeans database to come up with an estimate. However, once we said $43 million, that number stuck regardless of any future adjustments we might need to make to the estimate.

Chapter 8
1. "The State of Housing in New Orleans One Year After Katrina," by The Opportunity Agenda, 2006.

Chapter 9
1. The commissioner of administration is the highest-ranking nonelected public official in Louisiana. It is comparable to a town manager for the state.
2. Associated Press article, March 29, 2006.
3. "What If This Happened to Your Favorite Park?" *Land and People Magazine,* by Trust for Public Land, Spring 2007.

Chapter 11
1. Parker is the park's mascot. He is a raccoon, albeit a cute and cuddly one!
2. As a part of our fundraising efforts, park board members began hosting cocktail receptions at their homes where they invited friends to hear about the park's condition and its recovery. We made a short presentation and discussed how the guests could help. At one of these parties, we met Vincent Giardina, who, along with Lisa Romano, was the trustee of a recently activated trust from the late Oscar Tolmas. A short time later, Vincent called asking for more information, which resulted in a $500,000 gift for the new Botanical Garden entrance. The Tolmas Trust has been a consistent supporter of the park ever since.

3. The following are just a few of the events held in the park in the last third of 2016: Annual Zulu Picnic in August, Louisiana Seafood Festival and Martini Madness in September, and Fall Garden Show, Ghost in the Oaks Halloween celebration, and Voodoo Music + Arts Experience in October.

Chapter 12
1. Much of the golf history in this chapter is taken from chapter 14 of *History of City Park New Orleans,* by Sally K. Evans Reeves and William D. Reeves.
2. Independent Auditors Report for fiscal years ending in 2001 and 2002, by Postlethwaite & Netterville.
3. *New Orleans Times-Picayune,* June 11, 2006.
4. Interestingly, although Rees Jones is an internationally known golf-course architect, not everyone is a fan of his designs. In an article published in the *Times-Picayune* on August 17, 2011, the professional golfer Phil Mickelson questioned Jones' design philosophy. He felt that Jones designed challenging courses for golf professionals but not so much for the average public golfer. He suggested that making courses longer and more difficult and intimidating for the "regular Joe" was one of the reasons participation in the sport was on the decline. Jones countered that he and Greg Muirhead, the Jones professional who laid out most of the new South Course, had provided a range of golf tees to reduce the length of the course and that there were plenty of opportunities for the public golfer to enjoy the golfing experience. The success of the South Course has proved that Mickelson's concerns were unfounded.
5. At one of the board meetings, a particularly agitated protestor called me a "righteous man" who would do the right thing by stopping construction.

Chapter 13
1. Because there is current litigation involving

the Beauregard monument, this chapter about the statue and City Park will be general regarding the issues being contested.

2. Application for National Register status for the Beauregard monument, National Park Service, 1999.

3. Ibid.

4. Ibid.

5. Minutes of the City Park Improvement Association, June 21, 1905.

6. Application for National Register status.

Chapter 14

1. Report of the Bureau of Governmental Research on the New Orleans Parks and Recreation Tax Proposal, 2019.

2. I felt that this language was necessary, as I had experience with a previous recreation coordinating body established under the UPARR (Urban Park and Recreation Recovery) program. That group was set up to ensure cooperation and coordination among a myriad of park agencies, but the agency heads eventually delegated attendance at the meetings to subordinates who had no authority to make decisions or commit their agency to specific actions. It eventually was disbanded.

3. Report of the Bureau of Governmental Research, 2019.

Chapter 15

1. The name of this disease is coronavirus disease 2019, abbreviated as COVID-19. "CO" stands for corona, "VI" for virus, and "D" for disease.

2. Centers for Disease Control and Prevention website, "Frequently Asked Questions," June 2, 2020.

3. On January 22, Donald Trump said, "We have it totally under control. It's one person coming in from China." On March 10, he claimed, "We're doing a great job with it. . . . And it will go away. Just stay calm. It will go away."

4. State of Louisiana Proclamation Number 25 JBE 2020.

5. In July 2020, of the eight weddings we had scheduled, five relocated to neighboring Jefferson Parish, where the restrictions were more liberal than in New Orleans.

Chapter 17

1. *Parks & Recreation,* July 2020.

Acknowledgments

1. How park employees were moved into the State Civil Service is somewhat unclear. The idea is mentioned in letters and board minutes as far back as the early 1950s. In 1962, with Act 405 of the Louisiana Legislature, City Park is recognized as a state agency, although it is likely that the park gained that status before that date. In 1982, in Act 865, park employees are specifically mentioned as being in the classified state service. The State Civil Service recognized this date as the year park employees entered its system. However, the park's 1992 Annual Report refers to 1992 as the date that park employees were converted to the classified State Civil Service.

Index